THE SEVEN AGES OF
FRANK
LLOYD
WRIGHT

THE CREATIVE PROCESS
DONALD W. HOPPEN

DOVER PUBLICATIONS, INC.
Mineola, New York

This book is dedicated to Mijo.

Bibliographical Note

This Dover edition, first published in 1998, is an expanded and revised republication of the work first published by Capra Press, Santa Barbara, Calif., in 1993.

Acknowledgments

The author appreciates the superb work of Irene Kupferman, who set in type this new edition; the care and talent of Steffie Kaplan, book design director, in presenting the text and graphics; the skillful editing and proofreading of the original text done by editor Kathy Casey for this Dover edition; and the assistance of John Grafton, assistant to the president of Dover Publications. Ernst Anderegg, Collin Games, Pedro E. Guerrero, and Anthony Peres graciously permitted use of their photographs. Taliesin West, the Guggenheim Museum, Johnson Wax Company and Western Pennsylvania Conservancy furnished photographs and renderings from their archives. The author thanks, for their encouragement and assistance: Edgar Tafel, Bruce Pfeiffer and Oscar Muñoz of the Taliesin Archives, Indira Berndtson, Dick Carney, Eve Siegel Tettemer, Peter Hay, Georgia Lyons Anderegg, John Sergeant, Nezam Khazal, William Allin Storrer, Noel Young, Connor Everts, and Eric Lloyd Wright.

Library of Congress Cataloging-in-Publication Data

Hoppen, Donald W.
    The seven ages of Frank Lloyd Wright : the creative process / Donald W. Hoppen.
        p.   cm.
    "This Dover edition . . . is an expanded and revised republication of the work first published by Capra Press, Santa Barbara, Calif., 1993"—T.p. verso.
    Includes bibliographical references and index.
    ISBN 0-486-29420-X (pbk.)
    1. Wright, Frank Lloyd, 1867–1959—Criticism and interpretation.   I. Title.
NA737.W7H66   1998
720'.92—dc21   98-20467
                                                                                  CIP

Manufactured in the United States of America
Dover Publications, Inc., 31 East 2nd Street, Mineola, N.Y. 11501

TABLE OF CONTENTS

Author's Preface

THE ENGLISH VILLAGE where I lived as a boy had beautiful old houses from the Middle Ages. They embodied the richness of medieval England, the feeling for the land, the nature of organic materials, a human sense of scale and intimacy. From Stonehenge to the village church and the great cathedrals, the British have expressed a marvelous earthiness, boldness, and power in their architecture. It is imbued, as is a Rembrandt painting, with a sense of mystery and presence. Yet to me, as a student in the early Fifties, modern architecture seemed mechanical, sterile and boring. I was in a culture that had lost its roots and passion.

On a rainy day in Tiranti's old bookshop in London I idly picked up *An Autobiography* by Frank Lloyd Wright, and stood transfixed all afternoon reading this extraordinary journal of his life and philosophy. For the first time I saw illustrations of his work: buildings that came out of the earth, yet the roofs floated above with a magnificent sense of freedom and space. It was an architecture both old and new, with roots in the countryside, yet truly of the modern time.

LETTER

I rushed home and wrote a long letter to Wright, full of my ideas about architecture and life, and was astonished ten days later to receive a letter with the famous Taliesin red square on the envelope. It read:

Facsimile of letter from Frank Lloyd Wright

```
Mr. Donald Walter Hoppen
Blunham House
near Bedford Beds
England


Dear Donald Hoppen:    Thank you for your good lotter.
Enclosed are the Fellowship terms - we would like to help
you get here if you are able to meet them.

    Sincerely,
    Frank Lloyd Wright

                    September 27th, 1952
```

The fee for Taliesin was then $1,500 a year for tuition and living costs. I had barely $130 to my name. I sent off another long letter to Wright with some photographs of my work, explaining my embarrassing lack of funds. Characteristically, he replied: "My dear Donald Hoppen, If you can get here, we will fit you in. Come."

Visiting the U.S. Embassy in London for a student visa I discovered that Taliesin was not accredited and I would need a sponsor to provide a full financial statement, a requirement hardly calculated to appeal to Wright. I wrote to him again and there followed a long ominous silence. It took me over a year to find a sponsor and I had to settle for a visitor's visa. Then I sent a letter followed by a telegram, asking if I could still come. This time there was no reply. I sensed it was up to me to prove myself to him. I sold everything and bought a boat trip to America.

Little did I realize that the voyage across the cold Atlantic to a foreign land was the beginning of an odyssey, a journey with genius into architecture.

LAND

From New York I hitchhiked a thousand miles to Spring Green, Wisconsin, home of Taliesin East. It was nine in the evening when I arrived at the "Dutch Kitchen," Hotel Spring Green. From a phone booth I nervously dialed Taliesin. Ling Po (a Chinese apprentice, I learned later) answered. When I asked if someone could pick me up, he replied sleepily, "Everyone has gone to bed. Why don't you call again tomorrow." (Taliesin kept "farm time," two hours later than "town time," a way of getting the most daylight from the working day.) I fell asleep depressed, thinking what an idiot I was to pursue this crazy dream, with no letter of acknowledgment, traveling all this way, spending all my money—and now being marooned in this tiny town.

In the morning I called again and was told someone would come by for me later. During breakfast I met Giovanni Del Drago, a Taliesin apprentice and Italian aristocrat, just back from a party in New York, who was also waiting for a lift. We waited all morning, until at last we saw Wright—with his porkpie hat, cape and cane—walk past the coffee shop.

I wanted to dash out immediately and introduce myself but Giovanni explained we could hardly ask Mr. Wright for a ride. I quickly learned that all apprentices, and most clients, not only addressed him as Mr. Wright, but also referred to him as such in conversation. It was afternoon before someone drove us to Taliesin.

MEETING MR. WRIGHT

When I arrived at Taliesin East I found Mr. Wright directing his apprentices in an ambitious tree-planting scheme. We were introduced and shook hands, then he took off to supervise the planting. Some apprentices were digging holes and I was requisitioned to move the big water truck to irrigate the new planting. I asked someone about the tree planting and was told that Mr. Wright had designed a lot of houses for the neighbors when he was young, and some of them he could no longer tolerate. If they were beyond help he tried to buy them, whereupon the Fellowship would throw a party and burn them to the ground, much to the annoyance of the local fire department.

The farmer who lived just across the road from the entrance to Taliesin liked his house the way it was and had no intention of selling it. Every time Wright passed by he was pained at the sight of this early "mistake" and could only hide it from view behind the trees we were planting. "A doctor can always bury his mistakes," he said, "but an architect can only plant vines." Or trees.

Mr. Wright said, "Boys, always build your first projects far from home." It was my first lesson from the master and I couldn't be farther from home.

Taliesin—meaning "shining brow," after a sixth-century Welsh bard—was Wright's Wisconsin home and studio. When I first saw it I was reminded of the English Cotswolds and its soft, honey-colored stone, a landscape of rolling green with buildings tucked into the hillsides. Taliesin had a touch of Tibet, a serenity and sense of mystery, but it was a very human building as well, which gave me the feeling of being embraced and secure within its walls. Like an ancient cathedral there were layers of meaning appealing to the conscious and the unconscious. Oriental carvings adorned the entry doors, an enormous Buddha sat serenely in the garden opening upon an endless stone loggia, and Oriental rugs and Japanese prints were everywhere. I was amazed by the size and complexity of this building. Like an old oak tree, parts of the building had died and crumbled, giving way to new construction ideas.

Everyone was friendly, assuming that I was a new apprentice, though I still had no confirmation. The next day I consulted the secretary, Gene Masselink, who said I must have an interview with Mr. Wright. But every time we set up an appointment, it fell through because of some emergency. After three days I couldn't take the suspense any longer and decided to sit in front of Mr. Wright's office all day until I had a decision. Along the walls was a continuous angled shelf on which sat numerous Japanese prints from Wright's collection (at one time it was the finest in America, before the Depression forced him to sell many). The assortment was changed weekly.

Finally, two hours later, Mr. Wright appeared and I showed him my portfolio (very Scandinavian in style). I had designed furniture in London for a living in England. With a smile he said, "This is all an affectation."

The first thing I noticed on meeting Wright was an extraordinary sense of refinement: he seemed to express energy rather than mass. It seemed that everything heavy or coarse had been burned away in a lifetime of creation. He was then 86 years old.

He was cordial as we discussed Wales, England, and his Welsh ancestors. He told me that he had to make $50,000 a year (equivalent to $500,000 today) to run Taliesin and was not going to be able to give scholarships anymore. Suddenly, he looked at his watch and said he had an appointment, picked up his cloak and was gone. I walked out to Masselink and told him we had our meeting, but what did it mean? Oh, he told me, he's opened the door. You're in. Mr. Wright likes you and has given you a scholarship. Later I was told by Mrs. Wright that he was deeply touched I had come all that way. (I didn't realize it at the time, but I had retraced the journey of his immigrant ancestors.)

Wright was American in the tradition of Whitman and Thoreau, a mixture of aristocrat and Midwesterner. He was always immaculately dressed in good English tweeds, woolens, silk scarf, and cloak. He liked to wear French cuffs with elegant cufflinks terminating his sleeves. (In architecture terminals were important to him.) There were stories about his "arrogance and cantankerousness," but I never knew him to be so.

Sometimes Wright spoke so effortlessly in his soft Midwestern accent that I did not appreciate the depth of meaning behind his words until years later. I had not yet realized the lifetime of trial and suffering that had led him to the extraordinary secrets he had discovered in the deep springs of the unconscious.

What struck me was Wright's youthful energy, his boundless enthusiasm, his capacity for endless renewal. Unlike other architects who developed and established their particular style, his work was forever changing and renewing itself. One day I idly sketched a chart of his life (pp. 186–87) showing the cycles of his work, punctuated by the disasters of his personal life.

I was amazed by what I had discovered. Cycles of great creativity were followed by lean periods and even disaster; and from the ashes of each disaster, like the fabled phoenix, a new architecture was born.

As I researched further into his roots I saw that Wright's life followed many myths: the ancient Greek myth of the tragic hero; the Welsh-Celtic myth of Taliesin, the shape-shifter able to take all forms; and Merlin the alchemist, who transmuted the ordinary into the extraordinary.

Myth is woven into the fabric of our psyche, providing the foundation for Freud's and Jung's psychological discoveries. The great myths describe man's deepest experience, his relationship with life and creation. Mythology is an ancient language—using art to communicate ageless truths. Great architecture manifests the invisible.

Frank Lloyd Wright lived his myth, and the myth lived in him. The chronological biographies of Wright's complex life had failed to capture the essence and meaning of his genius. Only by going to the deepest level of human experience can the full meaning of his architecture be understood. This is the mythic story of his life.

I have always been fascinated by the creative process, the sources of his inspiration. I observed Wright's working methods, his empathy for nature, his feeling for natural materials: wood, brick and stone. His gifts transmuted dreams into reality, transforming his interior primal energy into a living architectural experience. I sought to understand what he was trying to accomplish in the architecture unfolding within him: his insights, creations, successes, and failures. I felt like the apprentice offered work in Michelangelo's atelier. Fortunately, I had already met genius and knew that it clothes a very human personality. One apprentice observed that I seemed to be recording every word.

Schopenhauer said that while we are living, our life seems to be a series of unrelated events. Only when we look back is a deeper life pattern revealed. With the advantage of time we can now distill the essence of Wright's art.

4

Wright at exhibition of his work

Roots

"Truth Against the World."

FRANK LLOYD WRIGHT'S mother, Anna Lloyd Jones, came from one of the most legendary regions of Wales, a landscape adorned with mysterious standing stones and sacred dolmen, and bordered by the Prescelly Mountains whose great bluestones created Stonehenge.

The Welsh people are descendants of the Celts, who 2,500 years ago migrated across Europe to Wales from a region near Persia. The Celts, an Indo-European mixture, a union of East and West, were renowned for the richness and diversity of the changing forms they used in artistic expression. They were imbued with an extraordinary passion for life and the world of the spirit. With a deep affinity for the earth's primal forces, the Celts were acutely sensitive to the *genius loci,* "spirit of place." They "knew" the sacred sites on which to build, and for their standing stones chose those special stones, imbued with presence, that express the arcane energy of the earth. A standing stone marks Frank Lloyd Wright's grave at the family cemetery at Taliesin East.

Sacred dolmen in Wales

Taliesin's legendary tomb

"He was in league with the stones of the field," Wright said of his grandfather Richard Lloyd Jones, a passionately religious man. His family motto was the Druidic "Truth Against the World." In the Druidic religion no word was permitted for "God the Immeasurable." Out of notches carved with an axe in wood or stone, they created a language. The symbolic form of the family motto is carved on the gatestone of the cemetery of Taliesin East.

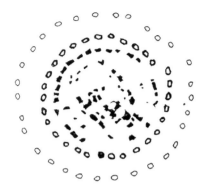

Stonehenge

Stone of *Devacci Fili Justus*

From the triangular three stones of a dolmen to the bluestone circle of Stonehenge, the Druids (Celtic priests) communed with the gods, the sun and the earth. They communicated the unknown through legend and myth. Their sixth-century myths and legends reflect their relationship with nature, creation and art.

The myth of Excalibur is emblematic of a people who, with a deep affinity to the earth, are able to tap its magical power. King Arthur is the chosen one who releases Excalibur, the energy imprisoned in matter. Merlin is the alchemist-wizard who draws his powers from a nature that timelessly renews herself.

"Taliesin," Wright said, "was the bard prophet who sang the glories of art at King Arthur's court." Taliesin told the mythic tale of the shape-shifter who can take all forms. His legendary cave tomb can be seen in Dyfed.

They each personify a quality: King Arthur, the enlightened consciousness of a Golden Age; Merlin, the alchemist who transforms the ordinary into the extraordinary; Taliesin, the artist who communicates, through form, the unknowable.

With their rich imagination and psychic second sight, the Celts are emblematic of the intuitive spirit and the language of the psyche: poetry, music, art, architecture, religion and myth. The myths describe humanity's deepest experiences. Wright's roots ran deep into this rich soil with its timeless archetypes, and the pattern of Wright's life followed its myths.

Richard Jones's house was situated in a green valley near the village of Llandyssul. He was a freeholding farmer, a lay Unitarian preacher, and a hatmaker of the conical "witches' hats" the Welsh wore. He claimed his hats were so strong you could stand on one. (Wright would later make a similar claim for his buildings.)

Richard married Mary (Mallie) Lloyd, daughter of a well-to-do Welsh family, and thereafter they used the family name Lloyd Jones. Frank Lloyd Wright's mother, Anna, was one of seven children.

Richard Lloyd Jones's house

Dyfed, a desperately poor area, was known as the "black spot" because of the rugged independence of its people. They were forbidden by the English to use their native Welsh language; in turn they refused to acknowledge the sovereignty of the English King and his Anglican Church. Even in Dyfed, Richard's new Unitarian religion was ahead of its time and unpopular, because it espoused the unity of all religions and a common god.

Inwardly rich and outwardly poor, Richard Lloyd Jones and his wife looked to America for a release from poverty, for freedom of religion and for the opportunity to realize their vision of a new Arcadia.

EMIGRATION

The mid-nineteenth century was the period of the mass migration of Europeans fleeing poverty and religious persecution, crossing the Atlantic, seeking the promised land.

Richard's brother Jenkin Jones, who had emigrated to America earlier, now urged his brother to join him in Wisconsin, where there was land for homesteading and tolerance for their religion. In 1844 the Lloyd Joneses and their seven children left Wales forever. They took a sailing ship from New Quay to America. At the beginning a storm forced them to turn back and take refuge in Liverpool. After a nightmarish journey they arrived in America.

In New York Richard was cheated out of money. The family, with seven children, the youngest only two years old, had traveled some 4,000 miles. Richard was tough. When their boat was locked in the ice for several weeks near Utica, he found work in the nearby mines. Later, on their trek to Wisconsin, the youngest daughter died and was buried by the roadside.

The Lloyd Joneses finally found land to homestead near the village of Spring Green. The green valley with its strange rock outcroppings reminded them of their Welsh homeland. They felt their vision had at last been fulfilled. Thomas, the eldest son, built a small house of wood and covered its stables with a traditional Welsh thatched roof. Over the years other members of the Jones family arrived, followed by Welsh craftsmen and stonemasons.

PATRIARCH OF THE EARTH

Developing the land, the Lloyd Jones family created the Arcadia of their dreams in the Wisconsin landscape. Intelligent and hardworking, the family prospered. Jenkin became a charismatic Unitarian minister. The sisters Mary and Margaret founded a coeducational progressive school, while James became a farmer and Anna a teacher.

The family was friendly with the Native Americans who still lived in the area. The Welsh family shared the Indians' empathy with the spirit of the earth, which resonated and permeated the land. Wright was to inherit this feeling for the American landscape.

FATHER

Frank Lloyd Wright's great grandfather left the north of England for America and became a wealthy landowner in Connecticut. Wright's father, William Cary Wright, born in 1825, studied at Amherst and Yale, receiving the classic education of a gentleman. William Wright, lacking the wealth to support that lifestyle, worked his way through a diverse range of occupations. He was a Renaissance man: lawyer, administrator, minister, teacher (of music, piano and rhetoric), musician and organist, constantly changing job and places. William Wright was a product of the restless dream of immigrant forebears who had crossed an ocean searching for a dream, an impossible perfection.

His son inherited this restless energy but harnessed it into a lifetime search for creation. Rather than seek a fantasy, he dreamed and built a reality and found the perfection that eluded his father.

William Wright married and moved to the obscure town of Lone Rock, not far from Spring Green, Wisconsin. His wife took in paying guests, among whom was Anna Lloyd Jones, a local teacher. When his wife died he became a most eligible man.

Anna chose him to pass on his talents to her children. Even though he was seventeen years older than she, he was the man of her destiny: college-educated, a musician and minister. In 1866, over the protests of her own family, they were married. Their son was to combine his father's sense of order and logic and his mother's Celtic insight and intuitive energy, a marriage of left and right brain. Architecture demands for its success a perfect marriage between practical order and timeless art.

MOTHER

With her Celtic gift of second sight, it is hardly surprising that when pregnant, Anna "knew" she would bear an architect son. She hung the walls of his future nursery with pictures of architecture to prepare him for his profession. "Believing in the power of mind . . . during the nine months she cut out every picture of a house that she could find and mounted them on the walls," wrote Pearlie Easterbrook, after a conversation with Anna. "Not a square inch of space was left uncovered. She left them there as the child grew . . . To her delight when he was three he would stand fascinated in front of a picture. He would say, 'This is my favorite today' . . . When he was six he would take a picture to her and say, 'This is a mistake. This should not be.'"

She fed him with pictures, filling his imagination with a brew of myth and legend. What excited him were the stories of the Arabian Nights, the Bible, myths that described worlds beyond worlds and the infinite adventures of the human spirit. Frank's imagination was fired by such tales as "Aladdin and his Magic Lamp," "Ali Baba's Treasure Cave," and the ancient Welsh legends "The Knights of the Round Table," "Camelot," "Merlin" and what Wright would later call, "Taliesin the bard that sang the glory of art at King Arthur's court." This was the myth that shaped the course of his life.

As Freud and Jung discovered, myths are metaphors that describe the processes of the psyche, the invisible realm beyond consciousness and reason, the uncharted world of the creative process. They portray the elusive world that appears in dreams, visions and insights.

"The lad was his mother's adoration. She lived much in him. After their son was born," Wright observed about his relationship with his mother, "something happened between mother and father . . . Anna's extraordinary devotion to her child disconcerted the father. His wife loved him no less but now loved something more, something created out of her own fervor of love and desire, a means to realize her vision." The boy, she said, "was to build beautiful buildings." Anna had a passion for education and beauty. As a teacher, she rode her horse through the landscape to the school.

His Welsh mother was a product of the soil, an earth mother, according to Wright, who "knew the ferns, the flowers, by name, the startled animals that ran along the road . . . every berry." This "league with the stones of the field" must have imparted power to her "imaginative vision."

She felt she had borne a chosen one. Guiding, teaching, nurturing, Anna inspired and protected her son. As matriarch and mentor, she helped him survive the vicissitudes of his tumultuous life: tragedy, destruction, persecution and trial. To the end of her days, if Frank became sick, she was there to nurse him back to health.

Frank was raised by his extended Lloyd Jones family, including grandfather, uncles and aunts, many of whom were patrons of his progress and work. In later years he received family support for the projects Romeo and Juliet, Unity Temple and Hillside School. The family fed a far-reaching network of clients and work that continued to the end of his life.

"In ancient Celtic fashion," wrote Emyr Humphreys of creative figures with a Welsh ancestry, "brought up by their mother's brothers . . . doted on by the women and cherished by the men, the elected repositories of age-old expectations. Through their families they had access to a magic more potent and more ancient than Merlin . . . There can be no doubt of their sense of destiny."

MODULAR GRID AND FROEBEL GEOMETRY

In 1874 the family moved to Weymouth, near Boston. Wright, at age seven, was given the use of a drawing board subdivided into four-inch squares. This established in his consciousness the grid system that he later used to establish order and rhythm in his architecture.

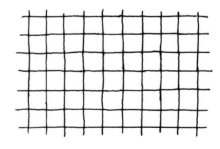

drawing-table grid

Anna introduced him at age nine to her discovery of the Froebel geometric building blocks, the archetypes of form. Froebel's philosophy that abstraction of form, not copying, is the prerequisite of education, helped develop Frank's understanding of three-dimensional form.

"I sat at the little kindergarten table and played upon these 'unit lines' with the square (cube), the circle (sphere), and the triangle (tetrahedron or tripod)," Wright explained. "Eventually I was to construct designs in other mediums. But the smooth cardboard triangles and maplewood blocks were most important. All are in my fingers to this day. In outline the square was

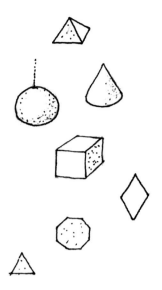

Froebel forms

significant of integrity; the circle—infinity; the triangle—aspiration; all of which to 'design' significant new forms."

As a child he had begun his journey through the geometric archetypes that later, as a man, he would realize in the forms of his architecture.

INVENTOR

As an adolescent, along with his crippled friend, Robie, Wright began to create his own inventions, including a water-velocipede, a catamaran and a water wheel. He formed a partnership to set up a printing press, to be known as Wright, Doyon and Lamp, Publishers and Printers. Wright was fascinated with the press's capacity for cheap replication of a design. He invented a scroll newspaper, based on the principle of the spiral. He designed kites of colored paper. He was fascinated by great building projects of dams and bridges. His multiple interests were converging into architecture and would have an influence on his later work.

NATURE, THE FARM

The first page of Wright's autobiography tells it in words as his design shows it in form. Nine years old, he is walking in the snow with his Uncle John. His uncle, with purposeful strides, proudly points to the straight line he has cut through the snow. "He ran first left," Wright elaborated, putting himself in the third person, "to gather beads on stems and the beads and tassels on more stems. Then right, to gather prettier ones. Again—left to some darker and more brilliant—and beyond to a low spreading kind. Eager, trembling, he ran to and fro behind Uncle John, his arms full of weeds . . . Uncle John points to the boy's wavering, searching line like a free vine running backward and forward across his own perfect path, with reproof. The boy was troubled. Uncle John had left out something—something that made all the difference to the boy." Wright rejected the straight path of the rational mind. What fascinated him was the diversity and richness of life, the uncharted journey into the unknown, the mysteries of nature's creations.

Working on his uncle's farm, he received a lifelong lesson on the cycle of life and death, seed and harvest, fallow earth and its power of regeneration. He was opened to the holistic interrelationship of life and what he called, "The rhythm of Life impelling itself to live."

Wright's approach to nature was not the sentimental view of a romantic poet. Working each summer at his Uncle James's farm, he experienced firsthand the processes of nature. At times the work became so exhausting that he ran away. But this education provided him with the resilience and endurance he would later call upon to survive.

THE SNAKE IN THE IDYLL

While working at harvest time, an exhausted Wright took a break. Out of the bundle on which he had been sitting, a rattlesnake slipped to the ground. Its tail began to rattle, its hostile eyes gleamed, Wright said. Some fascination

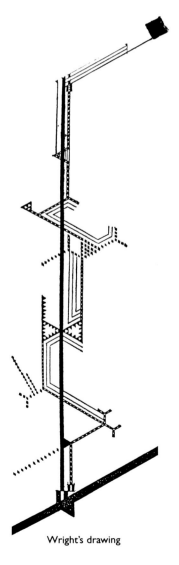

Wright's drawing

holds the lad, a sense of something predestined. To be lived again? Something in the far distant past comes near—as repetition? "Work—the plan," Wright perceived, "was interrupted by something ever a part of Life but ever a threat."

EDUCATION

Frank was surrounded by education. His parents were teachers, his aunts ran a progressive school and his uncle was a well-known minister. He had read most of the classics at home. Small wonder that he was indifferent to a classroom education. William Wright's income was now so small that his family depended on help from the Lloyd Jones family to survive.

When Frank was sixteen, his father walked away from his wife, their three children and most of his possessions, never to return. Was it a return of his restlessness or, jealous of his wife's preoccupation with Frank, had he finally given up an unequal competition? Even when his son became famous, years later, he made no attempt to make contact.

Wright was forced to drop out of high school and go to work to help support his mother. With the help of his uncle, he found work with Professor Alan Conover, Dean of the Engineering School of the University of Wisconsin, who was also responsible for the construction of several major buildings. Wright's work included supervising projects under construction. It proved to be a valuable experience. Wright was able to attend classes in engineering but left before the second year. His education had developed by learning and doing. It was a good beginning: his architecture would always grow from a sound engineering concept.

At age 18, Frank L. Wright, as he was then called, felt frustrated with his life in Madison. He felt he had reached an impasse—and for him growth would always be more important than security. One morning, without a word to anyone, even his mother, he walked out of his house, his job, and his studies, leaving behind his former world. The journey became his rite of passage: the end of childhood, adolescence and family. He was venturing into the unknown, where he would need to earn money and make a home.

CHICAGO

He knew his goal was to be an architect. He sold some books at a pawnshop, including Plutarch's *Lives,* his set of Gibbon's *Decline and Fall,* and a mink collar. By parting with the remnants of the past, he bankrolled his future and took off for the big city, Chicago.

He arrived at the office of Joseph Silsbee, an architect with an excellent reputation who was influenced by the English architect Norman Shaw. Silsbee's natural architecture used wood shingles and stone. He had designed the new Unitarian Church for Wright's uncle Jenkin Lloyd Jones. Jenkin was instrumental in bringing Silsbee, also a Unitarian, to Chicago. Silsbee was impressed by the young man and his sample drawings.

Wright served his apprenticeship, learning the basics of good building and eclectic design. After a year, now seeking new worlds to conquer, he heard that the famous firm of Adler and Sullivan was looking for a draftsman. He sensed it was to be himself. Wright gathered together a selection of his best work, took the day off and went to see Louis Sullivan.

THE MASTER

Destiny had already opened the door. Louis Sullivan was the acknowledged master of the Chicago resurgence, educated in Paris at the prestigious Ecole des Beaux Arts. His flowing art nouveau decoration was legendary. His phrase "form follows function" became the battle cry of the revolution in modern architecture. When young Wright entered his office, Sullivan "took me in at a glance. Everything I felt, even to my secret thoughts." Sullivan asked to see his drawings. "'You know what I want from you, do you? . . . Make some drawings of ornament and bring them back.' . . . He looked at me kindly and saw me. I was sure of that. The door to the drafting room was open . . . I was going to make one more." Elated, Wright returned to Silsbee's office. "The job's mine," he said to his friend, Cecil. "He saw, I tell you, that I can do what he wants done. Making drawings is just a formality." Friday morning, having worked late, night after night, on the presentation drawings, Wright showed Sullivan his work. Sullivan thought he had traced over Silsbee's drawings. When Wright responded, "They were not traced, too much trouble," Sullivan looked at him "with a glance that went clear through." He showed him his sketches done in the Sullivan style, and then some original work. "You've got the right kind of touch," Sullivan said. "You'll do."

Sullivan began drawing. When Wright saw his work he gasped and thought, "If Silsbee's touch was like standing corn waving in the fields, Sullivan's was like the passion vine in full bloom."

Wright was to begin work Monday morning, but when he informed Silsbee he was quitting, the architect was not pleased. "This doesn't seem quite up to your standard, does it?" Silsbee said. Wright felt guilty, though most draftsmen would have done the same, seizing upon opportunity when it came. After his painful split, Wright wrote: "Has every forward movement in human lives as it is realized, its own peculiar pang, I wonder . . . do the trees know pain when top branches . . . shut the sun from the branches below so those branches must die? . . . Life is this urge to grow."

WORLD ARCHITECTURE. CHICAGO FAIR, 1893

Working for Sullivan, Wright was a frequent visitor to the Chicago Fair of 1893, where Sullivan's Transport Pavilion was under construction. There, for the first time, he was exposed to a panoply of world architecture including the Japanese Ho-o-den wooden temple, a replica of one in Japan from the Fujiwara period, the Turkish Pavilion with its great overhanging roof, and pictures of Mayan temples. His imagination was ignited by the variety and power of ancient forms.

Wright stayed with Sullivan for more than six years. He was given his own room and soon promoted to the position of chief draftsman, entirely responsible for all of Adler and Sullivan's residential practice. As an architect, Sullivan paid Wright an unusual compliment: he asked Wright to design his new house in Ocean Springs, Mississippi, in 1890.

Sullivan came from Irish stock and shared with Wright a rich Celtic imagination. He sensed Wright's talents. "Sullivan, like Wright, was a latter-day Druid. He was also a mystic and a frustrated poet . . . Wright is likewise a romantic and a poet manqué, drawing inspiration from a Celtic background," wrote Grant Mansom. "We are dealing, in this relationship, with an association of two highly-charged and unconventional Celts . . . There are stories of conversations between Master and disciple that lasted throughout the night, discussions about Wagner, Herbert Spencer, Whitman, Richardson."

"I believe," Wright said, "the Master used to talk to me to express his own feelings and thoughts, regardless, forgetting me often. But I could follow him. And the radical sense of things I had already formed got great encouragement from him. In fact, the very things I had been feeling as rebellion was—in him—at work."

Sullivan saw Wright as the heir to his genius, who would carry the torch of architecture. For Wright, Sullivan was the father he had lost, a role model and teacher. In this fertile atelier of genius, something original began to germinate in Wright's being.

If Wright was influenced by Sullivan, so Sullivan could not but help being influenced by his protégé. Sullivan would criticize Wright's ornament as being too geometric. But if Sullivan had a more plastic sense of decoration, so Wright had a better sense of integral structure. As time progressed, the projects that Wright worked on began to exhibit original Wrightian forms: skyscrapers; the Schiller, Meyer and Stock Exchange Buildings; and the Charnley House.

"When in early years I looked south from the massive stone tower in the Auditorium Building, a pencil in hand," Wright said, "the red glare of the Bessemer steel converters to the south of Chicago would thrill me as pages of *The Arabian Nights* used to do with a sense of terror and romance."

Technology had discovered Merlin's alchemy: releasing the iron from the stone. In the caldrons of the furnace iron ore was transformed into the steel sinews that would make possible the new architecture.

Sullivan, like many a genius, knew he was the best. "Proud and arrogant he did not so much walk, as strut," said Wright. "If a luckless draftsman displeased him he was fired on the spot."

Wright, with his long hair and flowing tie, was already dressing in his own nonconformist way. Some of the draftsmen, jealous of his success, were provoked by his individualism and liked to tease him. On one occasion this got out of hand and developed into a fistfight during which Wright sensed he was winning; but suddenly, he said, "With a particularly animal scream—I've heard something like it since from a Japanese mad with sake, but never else—he jumped for a knife, the scratch-blade with a wooden handle lying on his board. Half-blinded, he came at me with it!" Wright exclaimed. "He was stabbing away at the back of my neck and shoulders. I could feel the blood running down my back . . . I grabbed the long, broad-bladed T-square on my board by the end of the long blade, swung it with all my might, catching Ottie with the end of the blade . . . He had intended to go to the Beaux Arts in Paris before long. He went without ever coming back to the office." It was the first time Wright had been attacked, but not the last.

MARRIAGE

At age 21 Wright married Catherine Tobin, who was three years younger than he. He would always be the man of her life and she was to remain forever loyal to him. After the wedding Wright asked Sullivan for help. Sullivan generously offered him a five-year contract with a large advance, sufficient for Wright to acquire a piece of land in Oak Park and build his own house.

In the following years, needing more money to support an expanding family, Wright began moonlighting, drawing plans late at night for clients and friends. When Sullivan found out, he was both angry and hurt by what he saw as a betrayal of their contract. When Sullivan refused to give Wright the deed to his now paid-for property, the two had a row. "When I learned this from the Master himself in none too kindly terms and with the haughty air now turned toward me too much," Wright commented, "I threw my pencil down and walked out of the Adler and Sullivan office never to return." He was not to see the man he called his "Lieber-Meister" for nearly twenty years.

"This bad end to a glorious relationship," Wright sadly reflected, "has been a dark shadow to stay with me the days of my life."

It was Wright's first experience of guilt. Perhaps it was his first glimpse of his own ambition that shocked him. He felt he had betrayed his Lieber-Meister, the man he loved and respected more than any other. In fact he had done no more than any other young architect ready for independence, following his own Muse.

The world Wright had painstakingly built during six years collapsed around him in as many minutes. Rejected by his Master, broke and without a job, a married man with a family to support, he was once more back on the street where, seven years ago, he had begun.

Frank Lloyd Wright at age twenty

The First Age
SQUARE & OCTAGON

WRIGHT'S EARLY PROJECTS were sometimes marked by their use of tall conical and steep roofs which at times echoed the Welsh forms of his grandfather's conical hats. In his first architectural projects he was like an embryo undergoing an eclectic evolution. Rapidly he proceeded through traditional styles of Rustic, Shingle, Classical and Tudor, though each successive project displayed an indefinable originality seeking to take form.

The first indisputable Wrightian presence appears in the **Charnley House, Chicago, 1891,** built while he was still with Sullivan. Wright proclaimed, "It is the first modern building." The decoration is Sullivanesque but the masses are his own. The roof plane with its geometric ornament and the subtle horizontal bands set in the wall indicate Wrightian elements that are later to emerge more strongly. The house is still a self-contained box with windows as pierced openings, reminiscent of an urban Florentine castello.

The **Harlan House, Chicago, 1892,** was considered by Wright to be the beginning of his own practice. Perhaps it was no accident that it caused the rift that broke him from Sullivan, for Sullivan must have seen that the apprentice had overtaken his Lieber-Meister. The projecting roof line, the

"I did not try anything radical because I could not follow up, I did not yet have the forms to express myself."
F. LL. W.

Unitarian Chapel

Charnley House

19

cantilevered balcony and the form of the dormer herald new Wrightian forms and the beginning of his own original architecture.

Wright opened his own office in Sullivan's Schiller Building. It was a good choice, for he had supervised its design. He felt optimistic for the future of his new independent practice. Wright shared the office with his friend Cecil Corwin, who sensed Wright's talent. "You are going to go far. You'll have a kind of success; I believe the kind you want. Not everybody would pay the price in concentrated hard work and human sacrifice you'll make for it though, my boy," said Cecil. "I'm afraid for what will be coming to you." Wright recalled, "I felt miserable. He was something of a prophet."

Now increasingly aware of his Celtic roots, Wright did as his grandfather Richard Jones had done before him and added Lloyd to his name: Young Frank L. Wright, draftsman, was metamorphosing into Frank Lloyd Wright, Architect.

OAK PARK, ILLINOIS

Before Wright's marriage, Anna, sometimes behaving more like a wife than a mother, followed her son to Chicago where she found a home to share with him on Forest Avenue in Oak Park, a rural suburb at the edge of the prairie. Another of her intuitive moves placed her son in the right place at the right time. Oak Park was a burgeoning suburb for the new entrepreneur who was ready to build an architecture as a measure of his success and taste. She had brought him to fertile territory.

The great fire in 1871 that destroyed much of Chicago fueled the careers of Sullivan and Wright and other architects in the rebuilding of the expanding city. Chicago, center of the Midwest, was experiencing a great building boom.

The move to Oak Park had placed Wright in the center of a rich vein of potential clients: a new breed of self-made businessman, open to the new, with a nouveau riche need for personal expression. His first clients included Winslow, owner of Ornamental Iron Works and the magazine *House Beautiful,* and W. E. Martin, who introduced Wright to his relatives who were owners of Larkin Soap, E. Z. Wax and other enterprises. These contacts led to a total of nine commissions. Wright's clients, respecting his genius and enjoying his personality, recommended him to their friends and colleagues as an excellent architect.

The **Winslow House, River Forest, Illinois, 1893,** was a jewel of perfection that could have fitted in with an academic style, except that already the essential Wrightian elements were present. His design elevates the great roof above the wall mass. The window wall plane of ornament becomes a band defining the roof from the brick mass below, and the break occurs not at the usual floor level but at the windowsill line. The front elevation and its entry are symmetrical and in perfect repose. The rear of the house with its diverse elements is less resolved, but it is a glimpse of a Wrightian repertoire yet to come. The freestanding bays with their interlaced brick corners anticipate future projects—like the Hanna House, four decades later. The octagonal brick stair tower with its stone cap presages his future architecture like a new shoot, thrusting out of the old.

Winslow House

THE TEST

Wright's friend and client, Edward C. Waller, lived across from the Winslow House. He was so enthusiastic about the burgeoning talent of young Wright that he was determined to help further his career. He invited Wright to meet his friend Daniel Burnham of the famous architectural office Burnham and Root, a powerful force in the Chicago world. Root, the partner, had recently died.

Burnham was deeply impressed by the Winslow House and made Wright an incredible offer: He would support him and his family and pay for Wright to attend the Ecole des Beaux Arts in Paris for four years with another two years of study in Rome.

It would have meant eventual partnership and heading a major firm—financial success beyond Wright's wildest dreams. If he had been a socially ambitious man Wright would have seized this once-in-a-lifetime opportunity for guaranteed security and success.

Wright perceptively saw it as a test of his integrity and confidence in his own vision. He didn't want or need a classical academic education. Nothing was going to divert his course.

He was embarrassed; to say no made him appear ungrateful to Waller. Desperately, "He looked at the door, the window, for some avenue of escape," Wright observed, but there was none. He gathered up his courage, and said, "No. Thank you, but I'm going on as I've started."

In the **Chauncey Williams House, River Forest, Illinois, 1895,** neighbor to the Winslow House, Wright and his clients chose and gathered boulders from the bed of the Des Plaines River, emblematic of the landscape's glaciation. Wright used them in a new style of stonework by the entry. He had now abandoned forever the old rustic stonework style for a new experiment in masonry. The dormer windows and steep roofs represent powerful Welsh forms not yet digested in his work.

NATURE

Wright could have been a great naturalist with his keen insight and understanding of nature, which provided a fertile source for his creations. He derived the abstract forms for his ornament from the surrounding plants, flowers and efflorescent foliage, transforming nature's ornament, the flower, into the abstract decoration for his colored glass doors and windows.

ROMEO AND JULIET, 1897

Wright's aunts asked him to design them a new windmill to pump water for their second **Hillside Home School, 1887,** on the site of his grandfather's homestead. Wright's uncanny sense of structure found expression in his design, based on the principle of the bamboo, whose strength depends on the combination of an outer stressed skin reinforced by internal horizontal membranes. The outer skin was wood siding while the floors provided the horizontal diaphragms. Ahead of its time, the principle is used for the design of the modern steel box girder for bridges.

The strength of the aerodynamic form that faces the prevailing wind is created, said Wright, by the embrace of Romeo, the masculine octagon, and Juliet, the feminine lozenge. Wright capped the tower with a conical roof, and thus echoed both his grandfather's design for his hats and his claim of their indestructibility. His uncles, however, were not impressed by his unorthodox design and predicted it would be blown down by the first storm. The young Wright, reassuring his aunts, said, "I am afraid all of my uncles themselves may be gone before Romeo and Juliet." Recently refurbished, the tower has withstood the storms for 101 years and still stands, outliving the uncles and even its creator.

In Wright's early projects the plan remained conventional and relatively untouched. With the **Husser House, Chicago, 1899,** the new energy begins to enter the plan itself, allowing the house to break out of the confined box to grow outward into the landscape in extended wings.

Romeo & Juliet

Romeo & Juliet plan

Hickox House

22

Japanese art had come to the West and in 1900 Wright wrote an article on Japanese prints and culture. As with Van Gogh and other artists, he was inspired by the Japanese prints, which confirmed his own discoveries. "They found the same source I did," said Wright.

In the **Warren Hickox House, Kankakee, Illinois, 1900,** Wright discovered the principle of simplicity. He saw, "The removal of the superfluous intensifies the essential."

The bold lines of the window elements, extending vertically and horizontally, and the defined roof, with its angular-gable soaring roof planes, are predominant and powerful elements contrasted against a light plaster background. With its powerful framed images, it is reminiscent of a Japanese Hiroshige print.

The **Ward Willits House, Highland Park, Illinois, 1901,** expresses the new concept of organic architecture. The cruciform plan is beginning its transformation into the pinwheel.

In the pinwheel plan for this house begins to emerge the truly Wrightian sense of movement and continuity. The spaces revolve like a galaxy around the pivotal mass of the masonry fireplace.

With Wright's uncanny sense of the site, he perceived that the horizontal line resonates with the prairie, the *genius loci,* spirit of place. In the prairie house the horizontal line is expressed by the raised plinth foundation, the low walls, the bands of windows, and leads up to the low eave balanced by the low-hovering hipped roofs.

The powerful simplicity of the exterior, both vertically and horizontally, creates a great sense of repose while the expansive spread of the house seems to effortlessly belong to the endless prairie.

The design introduces a new Wrightian element: in place of the usual center post to support the great roof above is glass. A continuous band of windows demonstrates the roof's new freedom to float above the structure of the building. The steep roof of his early houses has given way to the low hip

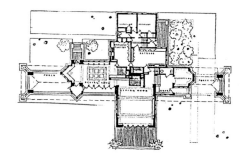

Willits plan

Willits House

23

roof. The upper wall corners are recessed, anticipating similar glass openings yet to come.

THE FIREPLACE

In Wright's plans the fireplace becomes the sun, the solar plexus—the fire in the belly—around which the life of the house revolves. Often, as in the Heurtley House, it is framed by an enormous arch; in Hillside School, by an enormous stone lintel above a mysterious cavern. In the Coonley House the fireplace becomes a great cubistic series of interlocking masses. Always it is high and vast, reminiscent of ancient palaces.

The fireplace represents an archetypal form celebrating mankind's discovery of fire (the pinwheel represents the archetypal sun wheel). For Wright the burning fire was an important metaphor for creation, "the alchemist's fire of transformation," the crucible where the architect takes matter—brick, wood, steel and glass—and transforms it into the forms of art.

When Wright was blocked and unable to see the solution to a design, he found the roaring fire a stimulus for creativity.

"Go make a blaze," Wright commanded, ". . . an aid to creative effort, the open fire." Relaxed, the changing flames of a fire awakened dreams, visions and new insights; invoked and illuminated images hidden in the darkness; opened doors to the imagination.

In his architecture the fireplace became the vertical core of the house. Its foundation and masonry come from the earth, its chimney reaches to the heavens. For Wright art and craft were inseparable: the vertical chimney that provides the aesthetic balance to the horizontal roof line also provides the engineering mass that anchors the roof's cantilever. And within its walls he hid the flues, vent pipes, central heating and other unsightly accessories that destroy the simple roof line.

Of the four elements—earth, water, air and fire—fire took a special place throughout Wright's life.

In the **Arthur Heurtley House, Oak Park, 1902,** Wright demonstrates his extraordinary range and use of materials. The great arched entry is balanced by the stepped horizontal courses of the brick, which in turn is balanced by the bands of plaster and windows above, and the whole is unified under the generous hip roof. The upper level permits extensive views across the prairie. On the outside the play of masses and voids gives a sense of mystery and excitement to a compact plan. Here also the fireplace is a cave: a great brick arch opening in a great masonry mass which seems to emerge from the very earth.

The entry is partly screened from the street by a low brick wall and introduces a new Wrightian element: the indirect approach in which one is led to make a detour to reach the entry.

At first Wright had accepted the traditional plans. Step by step he discarded the past to discover the present—first modifying, then changing, finally transforming his architecture into wholly new forms. This new energy first found expression in the exterior: the projecting balconies and receding wall planes; the forms of the alternately projecting and receding masses;

Sun wheel

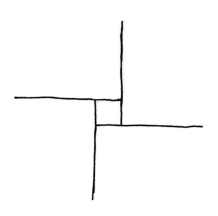

Pinwheel

24

the play of light and shade, of space and mass; the heavy elements of the earth balanced by the hovering elements of the roof. Only after the transformation of the exterior did his attention turn to revolutionizing the plan.

LARKIN BUILDING, BUFFALO, NEW YORK, 1903

A group of Wright's clients formed part of the Larkin mail order company and commissioned him to design a building embodying the well-being of its workers.

The site chosen was cheap, next to the railway tracks and smoke in an industrial slum. In this district without redeeming views Wright designed an introverted building, an inner world complete within itself around its own internal space.

Wright's discovery of vertical space began with his design for a house for the *Ladies' Home Journal* where the space of the living room ascends two stories. In **Hillside School, 1902,** he opened up the first and second floors into one vertical space, experienced from below and from the mezzanine above. Wright's projects sometimes took a slow journey from first discovery and concept to final opportunity and realization. Here Wright seized the moment to create a great vertical space, a core of space ringed by the mezzanine workspaces.

To the outer world Wright presented "a simple cliff of brick hermetically sealed." This great wall envelops a vast vertical interior space, illuminated by an enormous skylight above. The plan is a rectangular doughnut, ascending five stories high; its core is space itself, released through the vast skylight above. Bands of high windows are set between brick columns around the outer wall of each floor.

Just before construction began, something about the design seemed incomplete and troubled Wright: the correct relationship of the stairs and ventilation shafts to the central mass. He knew he was blocked. The contract to build had already been let. A sudden glance at the plaster model opened

"I saw that a little height on the prairie was enough to look like much more . . ."
F. LL. W.

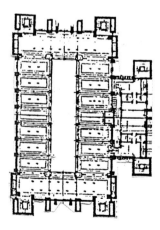

Larkin plan

25

the door. Wright exclaimed, "The solution that had hung fire came in a flash. The stair towers must be separate from the main block."

It would add $30,000 to the cost of the building. Taking the next train to Buffalo, and calling on all of his considerable charm, he persuaded Larkin of its necessity.

The great shafts of masonry soar upward as vertical towers. The elements are beautifully defined: combined stair and ventilation shafts at each corner and an entry wing servicing the mezzanine work areas around the great atrium space, with high bands of windows along the outer walls to balance the illumination.

The masses are skillfully articulated and separated from the central mass by insets or windows. It was a geometric and monumental building, but its scale is human, serving all of its workers in a naturally lit environment.

(This first celebration of vertical space presaged the evolution, half a century later, of one of his greatest buildings.)

Wright was frequently ahead of the existing building technology. If the things he needed did not exist he invented them: the first fully *air-conditioned* structure in America, the *wall-hung toilet* (cantilevered for easy cleaning beneath), architect-designed fireproof *steel furniture* (filing cabinets and desks). For the desks he designed cantilevered swing-out seats, and created custom *light fixtures* and *magnesite laundry sinks*.

Wright could have earned a lot of money on these inventions but told us, "I never patented and collected royalties for my designs since I felt that they should be available and free to all."

SUSAN LAWRENCE DANA HOUSE, 1902 & 1905

This demonstrates Wright's absolute mastery of materials, particularly brick and stone. Here he experienced the wealthy client of an architect's dreams and provided a setting for a social leader of the community. At first the existing house was preserved, but as Wright and his client progressed it was reduced to a vestigial element: the dynamic new supplanted the old architecture. The vaulted ceilings provide a soaring sense of space. Furniture, light fittings, leaded glass and fittings were designed and chosen by the architect to create a profound sense of harmony. The entry arch demonstrates Wright's mastery of the arch with its great Roman brick fan; it was Wright's most beautiful arch.

THE ARCHITECTURE OF MOVEMENT AND SPATIAL FLOW

When Wright took away interior walls to allow for more freedom and spatial flow he modulated both the flow of space and the flow of people—by a succession of architectural devices.

A favorite is the screen wall, which diverts traffic around it, creating a left turn, right turn, diversion in movement. The screen labyrinth contributes to the mystery of his spaces, making them seem endless.

As with Unity Temple, rarely is the entry to his buildings direct. One critic remarked that it seems as if you are being deliberately slowed down. You are diverted around a low wall, required to ascend several steps, must turn again, are compressed beneath a low entry ceiling and turning, yet again, are suddenly released and expanded into the luminous splendor of a high, extraordinary space.

Wright saw that architecture is an art in which movement is an essential element. He saw that the movement through its spaces is determined by the plan, which becomes a magical labyrinth in which one journeys and experiences the arcane delights and range of the architect's creative imagination. In his plans the architect becomes a choreographer. (Sullivan was the son of a dance instructor, Wright's father a musician: both understood movement.)

Movement enters a vertical dimension as stairs, ramps, mezzanines, galleries, balconies and vaulted ceilings open up new vistas of space and form. Space dissolves into space, rarely directly, but glimpsed through yet another offset turn in the plan. Wright's architecture expresses his own inner odyssey of discovery.

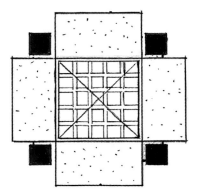

Unity Temple roof plan

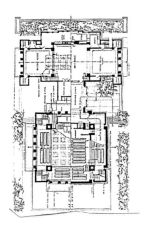

Unity Temple plan

UNITY TEMPLE, OAK PARK, 1906

With a minimal budget Wright chose the cheapest and lowliest material available—concrete. He chose the simplest plan—the square, symbol of integrity and the earth. The roof was a simple flat plane.

Wright, an earth sign, stood foursquare upon the earth. The building's relationship with the earth is expressed by its concrete foundation, which emerges from the ground to form a plinth. (He invariably placed his buildings on a plinth.) Rising from its plinth, Unity Temple displays the raw power of its simplicity. The four faces of the roof move outward beyond the square to create a cross and within its corners—in inspired fashion—the stair towers become special elements, in which form and function are one.

The leaded glass windows are continuous bands, set back behind the outer columns, which continue into the ceiling plane and become the matrix of the waffle grid of the amber skylights, so that both vertical and horizontal fenestration become one continuous element of light and space. The flat roof planes move out into the surrounding landscape.

Both light and space flow from the interior into the exterior. The division of the self-contained box is finally destroyed.

The various levels, the floating connecting bridges within, allow an interflow of space which moves throughout the building. Wright first inherited, then understood the secrets of the box, and now he transformed it, opening it to the outside, releasing its component planes, which now effortlessly move out and up as unique elements defining, but no longer confining, space. He raised and opened up the roof plane. Wright proclaimed "the destruction of the box." He had destroyed the box as a rigid container of space and opened it up to a rich continuity of space and light.

Halfway through the design Wright's vision was blocked. Already he had gone through thirty-three studies in an effort to overcome his biggest obstacle: to integrate Unity House, the social hall, into the main church.

He complained, "Always, some minor concordance takes more time, taxes concentration more than all besides . . . how many schemes I have thrown away." Wright needed to build up a powerful ambience to break through to a solution. "Night labor at the drafting board is best for intensive creation." He shouted, "Make a blaze in the work room fireplace! . . . Ask if it's too late

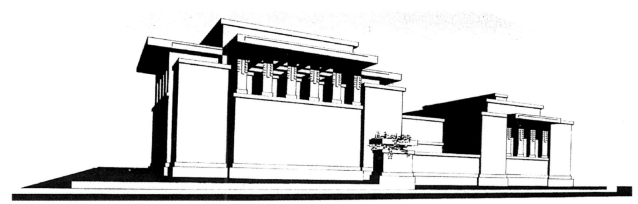

Unity Temple

to have Baked Bermudas for supper! . . . Ask Mother to play . . . Bach preferred, or Beethoven. To be an artist—to seize this essence . . . just behind aspect."

Wright found it easier to listen to the Muse than to present and sell her unconventional creations to his clients. Now he had the difficult task to present this unusual design to the building committee, one of whose members wanted a conventional church spire.

"The hardest of an architect's trials is to show his work for the first time to anyone not entirely competent or perhaps sympathetic. Already the architect begins to fear for the fate of his design," he rued. Wisely, Wright showed the plans first to the one member who was sympathetic and could understand what they meant. He was enthusiastic and able to swing the rest of the committee to approve the unorthodox design.

Wright's discovery of space made him euphoric, until he discovered Lao Tse's remark 2,400 years before: "The reality of a building lies not in its walls but in the space contained within." He consoled himself that he had discovered his own way to a universal truth, but his growing understanding of the philosophy of the East encouraged him to take his first trip to Japan.

In 1905 Wright and his client Ward Willits, together with their wives, visited Japan, and he began his collection of Japanese prints and other artifacts. He exhibited his Hiroshige prints at the Art Institute of Chicago the following year.

As usual, Wright was broke. He had to borrow $5,000 from his draftsman, Griffin, to pay for the trip. Wright spent all his money buying Japanese prints and when he returned was unable to pay back his draftsman. After an almighty row Griffin settled for a range of Japanese prints. Like many artists, Wright was hopeless about money. Not surprisingly, as an artist, his consuming interest was art, not the prosaic world of trade. What seized his imagination—and his checkbook—were works of art: Hiroshige prints, Oriental carpets, objets d'art, and sculpture. He was never enthusiastic about paying mundane grocery bills and ancient debts.

In 1895 Wright added a studio and playhouse to the house he had built six years before. He said, "At last my work was alongside my home, where it has been ever since. I could work late and tumble into bed. Unable to sleep because of some idea, I could get up, go downstairs to the 'studio' by way of the connecting corridor, and work."

The playhouse brought together three elements revealing Wright's relationship to the Muse, the realm of creation: the cave, the fire and the myth. The room with its barrel vault ceiling and warm red walls is a great cavern: Ali Baba's treasure cave. At the arched wall, like a shrine, is a fireplace surmounted by a large mural of *The Genie and the Fisherman* from *The Arabian Nights*. Wright's favorite stories show his love and understanding of myths that describe the creative process.

In Jungian terms the Fisherman represents the artist who casts his net into the sea (the collective unconscious). He catches a bottle sealed by King Solomon. Finding the way to open the seal, he releases the genie imprisoned within. The genie's energy is about to destroy the fisherman, who must rely

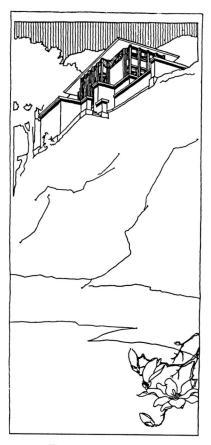

Thomas P. Hardy House

on his trickster wits to survive. He says, "How could such a great one as you be contained in such a small bottle?" (I had the same thought looking at Wright: how could all of Taliesin have come from this small man?) When the genie returns inside the bottle the fisherman closes the seal and the genie is under his control.

As the Druids long ago perceived, God and Creation come from a subtle, timeless dimension beyond the reach of rational words. Its arcane processes are communicated only through its own language: art, poetry, music and myth.

In Unity Temple Wright "had discovered space." But space itself is as mysterious as the Druidic god of creation: it is invisible, infinite, immeasurable and timeless. It cannot be measured, photographed or seen. Equally remarkable is the function of space in the architecture of the psyche. In the silent, timeless moment between two thoughts, space is the womb in which creation takes form. Lao Tse, Buddha, Christ, Krishnamurti, Zen masters and other teachers have pointed out that a cup is only useful when empty; a mind that is filled with the past is not open to the new. Unfettered by a classic academic education, Wright was open to the new. In Greek myths the Muse is the goddess who inspires man. Feminine and unpredictable, she eludes a direct approach. The artist seeks the Muse. Or is it that the Muse seeks the artist? Looking for an instrument receptive to her gifts, she seeks an imagination with the capacity to take her forms and the integrity not to change them. (Creation: In scientific terminology, a new impulse of energy causes a mutation in the brain cells.)

In the **Avery Coonley House, Riverside, Illinois, 1907,** Wright, with a fine client, was able to design a prairie house filled with the exuberance and rich-

Interior of Coonley House

ness associated with the great architecture of the past. He demonstrates that modern organic architecture is free of the constraints of the rationalist modernist tradition; that honesty does not have to mean an austere Calvinistic minimalism.

In 1907 Wright's life was showing the signs of success. In the Art Institute of Chicago the first show of his work received much acclaim. He was published in the magazines *House Beautiful,* 1906, and *Architectural Record,* 1908.

Word of Wright's original architecture had reached Europe. C. R. Ashbee of the English arts and crafts movement and Professor Kuno Francke from Germany visited Wright. Francke had recommended Wright's work to the German publisher Wasmuth and was eager to prepare a monograph of his work.

Besides all this, his work had attracted imitators. Most architects would take imitation as a compliment, but Wright saw it as against the very concept of original creation he preached. The truth repeated is a lie.

In 1904 Wright had designed the **Darwin D. Martin House, Buffalo, New York,** complex to extend over a large site. Extensive walkways covered by a pergola connect the various units: main house, garage, stables, conservatory and daughters' house. The "house" is no longer one entity; it has become a series of islands within the landscape. One travels through nature, which now becomes an integral part of the plan. The old divisions of inside and outside have dissolved. The completed project was one of Wright's largest. Along with the Dana, Coonley, and other projects, it brought Wright into the world of the rich.

The tide of fame was now lapping at Wright's feet. Even without Burnham's Beaux Arts help Wright was approaching social success and

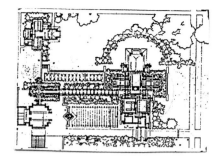

Martin plan

Exterior of Coonley House

31

recognition. He was in danger of becoming a fashionable society architect. Henry Ford visited Wright regarding a proposed new residence.

Harold McCormick, heir to the great tractor family fortune, admired Wright's work and asked him to submit a design for his new family seat on his property situated on the bluffs above Lake Forest, Illinois, in 1907.

The dramatic site was a match for Wright's own rich imagination. His drawings show an extraordinary scheme, bridging the bluffs and ravines: a prairie palace. Wright took the discoveries of the Martin House, with its interconnected structures, even farther, extending the complex laterally and vertically across the site. The wall between inside and outside has dissolved, and bridges, walks, pergolas become the links between the architectural elements. Extraordinary and as subtle as an Oriental design, the architecture becomes part of the landscape, appearing and disappearing within the trees, reflected in the waters of the lake below.

Mrs. McCormick, however, preferred a Renaissance fantasy to the Wrightian reality. By choosing a traditional architect to build a dead copy of an Italian villa, she helped bring to a close the Chicago naissance.

Robie plan 1st floor

The unique energy seeking expression in Wright reached its apotheosis with the **Frederick Robie House, Chicago, 1909,** appropriately the coda to his first golden age. Here everything came together into perfection—so that like some great ship from another world it floats serenely in the Chicago landscape.

The great hovering roof with its extraordinary cantilever was made possible through the client's new technique of welding the steel ridge beams into one continuous structure.

The dramatic roofs of the Robie House hover and penetrate the environment like no others. They represent the most perfect statement of the prairie house. It seems also to represent a Wrightian restatement of the ancient archetypal Greek temple transformed and realized in contemporary materials and technology.

The raised plinth—interfaced with the earth—is reached by ascending a series of monumental steps. The long rhythmic line of brick columns is reminiscent of Greek columns, and the great roof represents the Greek interface with heaven. In between is the sacred space for man, in the temple, totally secret and enclosed. But one thing the Greeks never experienced: the great interweaving space of the interior, flowing out into the landscape and expressing, as no other language can, the freedom of a new egalitarian age.

The stories of Wright's clients often matched the architect's own colorful life. Frederick Robie, inventor and maker of bicycles, seems to have existed for the sole purpose of siring the masterpiece. Within a few years of its completion his father, on his deathbed, extracted a promise from his son to pay all of his enormous debts. (In a vain attempt to fulfill his promise, his son had to sell the house and died a poor man.)

Wright had traveled from apprentice to Master in less than fifteen years, designing some 150 revolutionary projects. His energy broke the mold of nineteenth-century eclecticism to create a new architecture for the twentieth

Robie House

century. Master of continuous space and the horizontal plane, he created the new prairie school of architecture. Using the new, emerging technologies he transformed the rules of structure to achieve results never seen before in the history of architecture. He had given birth to his first golden age: the first meeting between architecture and technology. (It was as if the gods had given the architect of the Parthenon the gifts of space, structure, transparency and luminosity.)

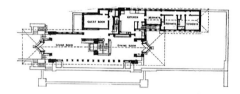

Robie plan 2nd floor

With a wife and six children to support, Wright's days and nights were filled with creation, work and battle: battle with conservative builders who resisted his unconventional building techniques and battle to persuade his conservative clients and their wives that his new architecture was better than the old way.

Wright was not always successful. He would sometimes supervise construction on his horse. It is said that when he visited the **A. P. Johnson House, Lake Delavan, Wisconsin, 1905,** and discovered that the client had painted the wood exterior white, Wright rode away, never to return. In 1970 the building was restored and the siding given a darker stain.

A new impulse of energy was transforming old rigid styles for living into a new sense of freedom and openness: transforming both architecture's form and its social infrastructure from the conventional parameters of the Victorian age. Wright was opening the world of a repressed, closed society with its accent on propriety, morality, secrecy, privacy, and zones of social conduct: parlor, library, formal dining room. Wright, removing the basement and attic, dissolving the old class divisions, freed the servants from working in a dark basement kitchen and sleeping in a cold attic. He transformed the old work place and servants' quarters into the new architecture.

He was attempting to move a society into accepting a new way of living, working and building. Wright took away not only the walls and doors, he liberated the lifestyle also. In the residence for Mr. and Mrs. Cheney, 1903, he omitted the interior walls between library and dining room to create one large open space.

In his own life he took down the moral barriers of Victorian society. After twenty-one years his own marriage had drawn to its end and he fell in love with Mamah Borthwick Cheney, a married woman who, because of her love for him, also sought divorce and freedom.

An independent woman, she was a free spirit who had outgrown her husband. Both Wright and Mamah were rebels, part of the new movement that demanded freedom from outmoded puritanical rules. (For challenging the old puritan order she would ultimately pay with her life.)

At the age of 42, Wright, after the birth of a score of seminal buildings, was exhausted. With the culmination of his masterpiece, the Robie House, the cycle of the first age was completed and his credentials as a modern master established. For sixteen years he had ridden euphorically on the crest of a great wave of discovery and creation, fueled by an energy seemingly endless, but now exhausted. The cycle of the first age was entering its negative phase. The imagination that had held and borne so many creations now sought renewal. Wright's confused state was demonstrated by his appointment of Holst, an unknown architect, to head the completion of Wright's last projects.

Depleted and exhausted, Wright was in the empty, painful void that follows a long period of creativity.

"This absorbing, consuming phase of my experience as an architect ended about 1909," he wrote. "I had almost reached my fortieth (42nd) year. Weary, I was losing grip on my work and even my interest in it. Every day of every week and far into the night of nearly every day, Monday included, I had added 'tired unto tired . . .' continuously thrilled by the effort but now it seemed to leave me up against a dead wall." Wright said, "I could see no way out. Because I did not know what I wanted, I wanted to go away. Why not go to Germany and prepare the material for the Wasmuth Monograph? I looked longingly in that direction."

Wright saw that his twenty-one years of marriage had reached the end. By leaving his wife and family Wright committed an unpardonable social sin. By leaving Oak Park with Mamah he irrevocably severed his connection with the old order. The resulting scandal would strike a mortal blow to his future practice. He would never regain his former preeminence as the Oak Park architect. He was walking away from a highly successful practice, the work he loved; sacrificing the secure domain of Oak Park, family and clients. In every way the cycle was finished: marriage, studio, the world of Oak Park. He had severed his connections with the past.

Middle-aged, on the outside once again, he was voyaging into the unknown, crossing an ocean to a foreign shore to become a stranger in a strange land.

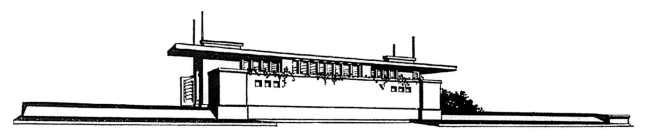

Yahara Boat House

Banff Pavilion

Frank Lloyd Wright at Taliesin East

The Second Age
MONUMENTAL ARCHITECTURE

THE JOURNEY TO THE WEST

ON THE BLANK WALL of Frank Lloyd Wright's frustration appeared a message from destiny: an invitation from the Wasmuth publishing house of Berlin to come to Europe to prepare a comprehensive book on his work. He was not fleeing, as the gossips claimed, but beginning a new odyssey. Retracing the ocean voyage of his Welsh immigrant grandfather 60 years earlier, Wright was approaching both his own roots and the roots of architecture.

Arriving in Berlin, he was hailed as the new master of modern architecture. Ludwig Mies van der Rohe said, "He was the personification of all we were seeking, a veritable fountainhead of the new architecture." H.T.H. Wijdeveld affirmed: "He is the chosen one."

The Wright publication was to influence the whole modern movement. If Wright was reinvigorating European architecture, he was equally, with his extraordinary insight, absorbing everything around him. Acutely sensitive to the *genius loci* in Italy he wrote: "No really Italian building seems ill-at-ease in Italy. All are happily content with what ornament and color they carry naturally."

At Mamah Borthwick's suggestion (she had traveled in Italy before), they settled in Fiesole, a village in the hills above Florence. Freed from the pressure of work, Wright began his work for Wasmuth, preparing the drawings and writings on his fifteen years of architecture.

He lay fallow, letting the rich energy of sun and landscape wash over him, recharging his body and spirit. Like countless architects before him, he was reborn in the rich culture of Italy. Here in the cradle of the Renaissance, he was synchronistically in the place where earlier architects had discovered and been inspired by the ancient forms. But Wright, as Victor Hugo had, saw ". . . the Renaissance as that setting sun all Europe mistook for dawn . . ." He regarded eclectic architecture as an imitation of a dead past.

What inspired him was not the old forms but the seminal energy that engendered and shaped them: it resonated with the forces that sired his work. He was enthralled by the sense of presence, the extraordinary timeless energy that permeated the ancient architecture. In France what held his attention was the Gothic cathedral. He marveled at the power and mystery of the Gothic and called it ". . . the most truly organic architecture—where

"Architecture is life itself taking form." F.LL.W.

37

form, structure and integral ornament are as one." Form, structure and ornament were all of one piece, made from the basic stone. He envied the master builder's power over an army of skilled craftsmen.

The pictures of temples and cathedrals that inspired him as a child had laid a seed, now germinating in his mind. He began to understand the arcane processes of creation and culture that gave birth to monumental architecture. Wright felt a new impulse of energy. He saw the beginnings of a new monumental architecture that would define the modern age. Flashes of revelation illuminated images not yet mature, and slowly these took form within his imagination.

"We do not yet understand pattern—for one thing because it is an attribute of a very high and older civilization," he said. "I had to break ground and make the forms I needed . . . The old architecture, always dead for me so far as its grammar went, began literally to disappear. As if by magic, new effects came to life as though by themselves and I could draw inspiration from nature herself . . . No longer a wanderer among the objects and traditions of the past . . . the world lost an eclectic and gained an interpreter. If I did not like the gods now I could make better ones."

Quoting the French statesman Georges Clemenceau, Wright remarked that "America may be the first society to go from barbarism to decadence without ever achieving a culture." However, Wright saw America not in shallow nationalistic terms but as a metaphor for a universal new age, a democratic way of life, with freedom, openness and honesty, a culture free of tyranny, elitism and secrecy. He saw the energy that is released in an open society. Was he not himself a product of this society, both child and prophet of the age?

The mind that was once exhausted was now recharged. The new direction was clear: not a return to Chicago but to Spring Green, Wisconsin, to build a house on the land of his forefathers. Why did he choose this particular place? There were virtually no clients in this rural region. Wright sensed the difficult times ahead. To ensure his independence he needed to be rooted in the land and the farm. (To us he said, "Boys, first find yourself a piece of land, that way you will always have food.")

It was to be a base from which the new architecture would spread, through his buildings and his philosophy. "My back against the wall," he wrote, "I turned to this hill in the Valley as my Grandfather before me had turned to America—as a hope and haven . . ."

TALIESIN

As a child Wright had heard the legend of Taliesin from his family. His journey to the Old World had awakened him to his heritage, and when he built his house on the brow of the hill, he named it Taliesin, the ancient Welsh name for "shining brow."

He was still not fully aware of the deepest implications of the legend that was to give the name to his house and transform and shape his life. The essence of the long Welsh poem that embodies the legend is as follows.

THE MYTH OF TALIESIN: THE SHAPE-SHIFTER
(SIXTH-CENTURY WALES)

An ugly witch, Caridwen, wishes to bestow upon her ugly son the treasures of all wisdom, beauty and alchemy. She fills a caldron with the magic ingredients of inspiration, prophecy and knowledge, places it over a fire and instructs her son to stir and guard the stew until it is ready to drink.

The son falls asleep. Then a boy, Gwion Bach, discovers the stew and stirs the magic broth. Three drops splash onto his brow and give him all knowledge, beauty and the ability to transform himself into any form.

The witch discovers and pursues the trickster boy. Just as she is about to catch him, he turns into a rabbit. She turns into a fox. He turns into a bird. She turns into a hawk. (They go on playing the game of shape-shifters.) Finally he turns into a seed of wheat and she eats him.

He arrives in her womb. When the baby is born she cannot persuade herself to kill him and she covers him with a blanket, places him in a tiny boat and sets him adrift on the sea (a symbol for the collective unconscious). The boat is washed up on a beach and discovered by a fisherman. The fisherman pulls aside the blanket and sees, shining in the darkness, the child's magic radiant brow. He exclaims, "Taliesin," and the boy replies, "So be it." Taliesin grows into a man and becomes the Druid bard-prophet who sings the glory of art at King Arthur's court, Camelot.

According to Robert Graves, in *The White Goddess,* Taliesin was a sixth-century historical figure who took the ancient myth and name for himself. The myth goes beyond the Druids, back to the Greeks (Medea with her caldron of rebirth becomes the witch Caridwen) and the Egyptians (Moses in the bulrushes becomes Taliesin). The Celts are thought to have come from a

Entry doors at Taliesin

39

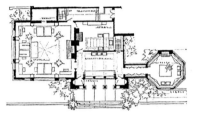

Studio, Oak Park

region near Persia. Gwion Bach represents the mortal who is transformed into the immortal Taliesin. It is the myth of life forever changing its form. Taliesin slowly takes form, stone by stone, beam by beam, on the brow of the Wisconsin hill.

Taliesin is both ancient and modern, containing the primal elements of East and West, in harmony, a timeless architecture of life itself, springing out of the earth. The walls were made of the limestone taken out of the hill quarry and laid by the masons from the local Welsh community.

Where he had played as a boy, absorbing the spirit of the site, he now returned as a man, master of his art, to make his stand, proclaiming his ancient family motto: "Truth against the world." Taliesin was to be his Camelot against the trials and tribulations that were to come. In Taliesin he was now lord of all he surveyed. This was the land of his Welsh forefathers, the world of his first projects—the windmill tower Romeo and Juliet and the **Hillside Home School, Spring Green, Wisconsin, 1902,** he had designed for his aunts.

Perhaps the softness of his recent Tuscany experience contributed to the mellowness of Taliesin, which seems to flow out of the hills of the Wisconsin

Wright's office at Taliesin

Living room at Taliesin

landscape. He used the Italian technique of mixing earth colors with the plaster, giving a tawny gold color to the walls that allowed light to penetrate. Taliesin is like no other building of Frank Lloyd Wright. Most of Wright's buildings represent an architectural statement, but Taliesin, rich as the earth itself, stands unique with its sense of tranquillity and repose. Wisdom is implicit, not explicit, and there are no eclectic details. The ancient spirit of Tibet and the East mysteriously pervades the place, in harmony with the spirit of the New World. Like an ancient cathedral, Taliesin has layers of meaning. The mystery of Taliesin defies analysis.

Chinese pottery and sculpture as well as Japanese prints and screens soon filled the rooms. "Hovering over these messengers to Taliesin from other civilizations . . . must have been spirits of peace and good will." (The only photograph Wright ever displayed by his desk was that of the Potola, the monumental architecture which defines the culture of Tibet, taken by George Ivanovitch Gurdjieff.)

Taliesin plan

Taliesin court

41

Coonley Playhouse

Because of his absence in Europe of nearly two years, and echoes of the former scandal, it was not easy to pick up the threads of his practice. Wright's old clients were loyal and saw the genius and generosity beneath his "honest arrogance." They lent him money when he needed it and provided a network to link him to new clients. The **Coonley Playhouse,**

Midway Gardens

Riverside, Illinois, 1911, and the **San Francisco Press Building, 1912,** demonstrate a new direction in his work. Wright was seeking a project in order to express his new concept for a monumental architecture. It was to materialize when a former client, Edward Waller, recommended Wright to his son, Ed.

MIDWAY GARDENS, FALL 1913

Ed Waller came to see Wright. Young and inexperienced, Waller was excited by his concept for a great indoor-outdoor garden restaurant that would celebrate the arts: music, dance, painting, sculpture. It was to be something akin to what Wright had experienced in Germany. Waller, with the impatience of youth, was convinced that Wright had the power to create immediately the magical design he wished for. Wright said: ". . . come back Monday."

ALADDIN AND THE ARABIAN NIGHTS

Wright was surprisingly open about his connection with the worlds of magic, myth and muse. He had commissioned the mural, *The Genie and the Fisherman,* for his own studio, as well as the statue, *The Muse,* for the Dana House.

In his autobiography, Wright wrote: "As a boy Aladdin and his wonderful lamp had fascinated me. But by now I knew the enchanting young Arabian was really just a symbol for creative desire, his lamp intended for another symbol—imagination. As I sat listening I became Aladdin. Well, this might all be necromancy but I believed in magic. Had I not rubbed my lamp with what seemed wonderful effect before? I didn't hesitate. The thing had simply shaken itself out of my sleeve."

In Aladdin's treasure cave of the imagination—the collective unconscious—Wright discovered the archetypal forms that fueled the great architecture of mankind, the world of abundance and exuberance, mass and ornament, form and complexity. In Midway Gardens and the Imperial Hotel he was moving in a magical world of rich encrustation, ornament and the decorative arts. Wright, like Picasso, had the gift to enter primitive and mythic worlds and transform them into modern form.

Midway Gardens was his first opportunity to experiment with the rich textures of his new monumental architecture. This was to be a garden beyond anything ever created in Germany. His imagination was inspired for a "garden of rare delights," an architecture to celebrate all the arts. He created a Babylonia of brick, block and concrete, a symphony of texture, ornament and art to match his full, exuberant imagination.

Wright, like the cubists, was exploring and celebrating the discovery of the geometric world. At Taliesin he had designed the limestone walls with alternating layers of projecting and receding stones, inspired, like Cézanne, by the cubistic geometry of a natural stone outcropping. For Midway Gardens he conceived the cubistic statues, including the marvelous "Goddess of Cubism" as it might be called; out of her outstretched hands spring endless cubes. He created the superb wall mural of circular and geo-

"Goddess of Cubism"

metric design. It was a style that the painter Wassily Kandinsky would later make his trademark, but Wright characteristically proclaimed, "I made Kandinsky before Kandinsky was invented."

Like Prometheus, who stole the sacred fire from the gods, so the artist brings back the fire of art to illuminate the human vision. The artist travels in the realm of the imagination. His odyssey moves into the psyche, a realm outside of time, beyond forms, boundaries and restraints, a world where everything is possible.

Wright had a profound feeling for the energy of creation. He knew that within every great culture lies the sacred, the still center of energy from which creation takes form. He said: "In nature there is a continuous, ceaseless becoming . . . the great in-between of which Lao Tse speaks, which is alive, which never ceases to be . . . all rhythmical according to innate principles. And if you can tune in on those principles your hand will have direction and your mind will succeed in tracing something from within yourself that is there and alive and ready to become something when you call upon it properly . . . when you become the pencil in the hand of the infinite, when you are truly creative . . . design begins and never has an end. Once you are aware of the spirit living in nature, you will never have to copy nature. If you want to do a tree, you'll do your tree . . . you could make a squash that might end all squashes . . . because living in you is a higher form of feeling than can exist in the vegetable kingdom . . . By way of it your own individuality will find its own fruition."

At Christmas we apprentices had the opportunity of presenting our work to Mr. Wright for his criticism. It soon became a dialogue on the creative process. Wright told us that his inspiration might come at about two in the morning when he would have a "dream" about the building and walk through it, inside and out, observing details and spaces until he knew it intimately. Only when he knew this archetypal building entirely would he begin to draw. He would bang on the door of his head draftsman at 5 A.M. shouting, "Jack, wake up, I have a new idea I want you to draw up."

The physicist C. P. Snow maintained that in the evolution of humanity only rare genius has the capacity for true three-dimensional imagination; most people can only project two-dimensional images. Wright was able to think in three, which accords with what he called "dreaming" a building.

I had the opportunity to pursue this line of thought with the educator J. Krishnamurti, who said that "in sleep for the first hour or so the brain is active making order and resolving the day's residue through dreams. When that is completed the brain is open to another kind of creative experience while the body is sleeping."

Wright advocated: "Conceive the buildings in imagination not first on paper but in the mind, thoroughly, before touching paper. Let the building, living in imagination, develop gradually, taking more and more definite form before committing it to the drafting board. When the thing sufficiently lives for you then start to plan it with instruments, not before. To draw during the conception or "sketch," as we say, experimenting with practical adjustments to scale is well enough if the concept is clear enough to be firmly held meantime. But it is best always to thus cultivate the imagination from within."

Wright's odyssey had brought him to that powerful and dangerous vortex of energy that fuels the forces of creation and destruction. The Hindu God Shiva represents both forces, mirroring Picasso's affirmation that "destruction precedes creation." The artist moves in a world of forces that, if uncontrolled, can overwhelm the mind, in the most extreme cases resulting in madness (Van Gogh, Nietzsche, or Schumann). Those who were close to Wright saw those forces inspire the best and awaken the worst. He would experience extraordinary insights into life, reaching the heights of creation, then plunge to the depths of despair, swept along by powerful and arcane forces.

In 1914 Wright's turbulent life seemed finally to have settled down to a perfect idyll. His love for Mamah was complete. She radiated forth the joy of life. It was said that when she entered a room she filled it with laughter.

She was a cultivated, cosmopolitan woman who, more than any other woman in Wright's life, understood him at every level. She furnished the house, entertained his clients and created an ambience in harmony with his architecture. Wright had enjoyed five wonderful years with Mamah. His practice was growing again to its former preeminence. He now had the perfect house and the perfect woman. Later, he would recall the ancient Japanese proverb: "It is said that perfection invites disaster."

The only flaw in their idyllic relationship (the flaw in which tragedy would take root) was that Wright was unable to marry Mamah. Catherine, his wife, refusing to let him go, denied him the divorce he wanted. In the puritan society of 1914, Wright and Mamah were flouting the tribal taboo, openly living in sin. But this lifestyle, encouraged by his motto, "Truth Against the World," was threatening to their secret enemies. In a corrupt world, the rebel is often persecuted and sacrificed for holding revolutionary views. Contradicting Wright's creative energy was the dark side of Midwest society, its sexual repression, righteous judgment and demand for retribution. These were the dark, destructive forces that would fuel the sick mind of a superstitious psychopath into justifying an act of punishment.

When Wright left Taliesin to supervise the construction of Midway Gardens, he was never to see Mamah again. At lunchtime on August 14, 1914, Wright's idyllic life was totally shattered, forever swept away.

The psychopath was the newly hired Barbadian servant, already living in Taliesin. Significantly, it was when Wright was away from Taliesin that the servant exploded. The thin-lipped cook, inflamed by a fundamentalist sect's condemnation that he was working in "a house of sin," went mad. Possessed by demonic ferocity, he poured kerosene on the floor outside the dining room, locked all the exit doors except one and set the torch to Taliesin. At the door with an axe, he ambushed Mamah, her two children and four others as they tried to escape. He destroyed everyone and everything in his path in an orgy of destruction, which ended only with his own suicide by poison. With righteous judgment, the tabloid press implied that the tragedy was Wright's own fault, a punishment for the sin of leading a "free" life.

Wright was seized by "black despair . . . she was buried next to Grandfather's grave . . . I wanted to fill that grave myself . . . I felt coming far-off shadows of the ages, struggling escape from consciousness . . . The struggle for freedom that swept my former life away, had now been swept away . . . I saw the black hole in the hillside, the black night over all as I moved about in sinister shadows . . . Totally she was gone."

As in a Greek tragedy, the power of destruction was terrifying. The structure of his world was demolished. Only his life was spared.

In Greek myth jealous gods strike down the hero's overweaning ego and destroy Prometheus's vision. For the first time in his life, Wright's powerful ego, with its fearless self-confidence and its mastery of all challenges, was shattered. Even to his mother he could not speak. Physically and emotionally exhausted, he had to use glasses for the first time. He wrote: ". . . for a while it seemed that I might be going blind."

He knew (like Orpheus) he must never look back. He said, "There is no past, there is no future . . . unless we realize that the Now is Eternity . . . time will desolate our hearts."

Wright's son John was to say, "Something in him died with her, something lovable and gentle . . . that Mamah had nurtured."

Wright must have asked himself the universal question: what is the meaning of such senseless tragedy? Is there utter perversity in the fabric of life that defies logic or justice? In every myth the hero needs to overcome the monster that blocks his progress, his growth. Only by understanding this, by going deeper, beyond the personal, can he transcend the challenge. The tragedy had broken his spirit, destroyed the mantle of his invulnerability. Traumatized, he was filled "with a deep sense of impending disaster."

Frank Lloyd Wright knew he might be destroyed, but the shock wave that destroyed his ego's mantle opened new fissures, revealing deep springs of primal energy. His despair took him to the deepest parts of his being, to the discovery of the doors that open to other worlds. In the depth of his psyche he found the alchemy that transmutes personal tragedy into objective art.

"Perhaps a new consciousness had to grow as a green shoot will grow from a charred and blackened stump," he wrote. Like the phoenix, slowly, out of the ashes of destruction, a new Taliesin took form.

THE JOURNEY TO THE EAST: REBIRTH

At the nadir of his despair Fate sent Wright a letter, an invitation to the East, transforming his life and work into a new and magical direction. He was sent across the ocean to another world, a radically different and ancient culture with the simplicity and tranquillity of Shinto and Buddha.

The letter from the commission of the Imperial Emperor of Japan awarded him the opportunity to design the new **Imperial Hotel, 1914, 1916,** in Tokyo. This was to represent Japan's new openness, a portal to the West.

The Baron Okura, emissary of the Emperor, had traveled throughout the West looking for the best architect to design the hotel. What drew him to Wright was their affinity to nature. In the pantheistic tradition of Japan, the love of nature is fundamental. Every stone, every tree has its spirit, and architecture is the art of being at one with nature. When they saw Wright's buildings, their extraordinary resonance with the landscape, they knew they had found the Western architect who could create a building in keeping with the *genius loci.* Writer D. H. Lawrence was known to absorb "the spirit of place" as well as any other writer. Wright too had this uncanny ability to sense the unique quality of place and design an appropriate architecture.

He had long admired and been influenced by Oriental cultures and had first visited Japan in 1906 to collect Japanese prints. He described a Japanese print in which "the elimination of the insignificant intensifies its power" as almost "autobiographical." What excited him was the principle behind Japanese architecture: simplicity, open plan, direct structural expression, non-load-bearing screens, as well as the inner and outer relationship with nature.

Imperial Hotel

At the entry of the Oriental Temple sit two stone Temple Dogs. One breathes in, one breathes out. They symbolize the cycle of creation, Yin and Yang, the Feminine and Masculine principle. Wright had used Lao Tse's remark, "The reality of a building lies in the space contained within its walls to be lived in," to create the space in his Unity Temple building. The feminine principle is invisible, the understanding of the negative; the space between the walls, notes, words, contains an energy more significant than the positive. The feminine principle is to be flexible, to yield, to survive.

Wright's personal tragedy opened him to foresee an even greater tragedy on the horizon and alerted him to a "deep sense of impending doom." He prepared a design that could withstand an earthquake. Alchemy is one of the gifts of genius; its power can transfigure personal tragedy into art. Wright wove his art into a structure that could survive doomsday. He used the feminine principle of flexibility to outwit the force of the temblor. He knew that a rigid building would break apart under the impact of a massive earthquake.

The site was an old marsh. He conceived a structure that, like a great ship, would float on segmented, massive concrete slabs supported on deep concrete pilings tied by flexible joints. Symmetrical and balanced, like a waiter's tray, it was to return to equilibrium after the shock wave.

In Europe Wright had envied the power of the master builders of the Middle Ages. Here, in the last years of feudal Japan, the gods granted him his dream. Day after day some 600 workers were under his command, cutting and carving the materials that would build his great edifice. Outside the city, a quarry supplied the large slabs of volcanic tuff stone, lightweight and rejected by the Japanese builders as an unworthy material. Kilns fired the Western-style bricks he had specially designed, while carpenters studied and copied the furniture he had shipped from Taliesin. Not only did he create the architecture, he had to design and build its Western-style structure, while training and controlling an army of artisans. He traveled to Beijing to oversee the weaving of carpets of his own design. Watching the weavers at work was to lay the seed of an idea that would later germinate on his return to America in the "textile" concrete block structures.

For relaxation he visited galleries and spent almost his entire fee collecting Oriental art treasures. Two freight cars were needed to ship them to Taliesin. His critics complained he was extravagant, more interested in buying art than paying his grocery bill. But to Wright these treasures were the vital food for his spirit. They contained the ageless secrets and discoveries of ancient artists that would provide him with an endless source of inspiration. He brought back ancient Chinese screens that became front doors for Taliesin. Henceforth, the entry to Taliesin was through the East, "the lands of my dreams—old Japan and old Germany."

Wright was one of the men, like Gurdjieff, who provided an interface between East and West. Living in Taliesin, midway between Orient and Occident, he was well situated to cross-pollinate three cultures. He had always admired the Gothic and its use of stone, "stretched to the limit." Chartres Cathedral transcends beauty by expressing in all its aspects the complex landscape of the mind. Wright's grief and search through the labyrinth of tragedy is exemplified in the dark cavernous spaces of the Imperial Hotel, an architecture of an almost gothic underworld. With its completion, his ghosts exorcised, came redemption. His later works in Japan took a wholly different and original turn, becoming lighter, more delicate and joyful—the **Odawara Hotel, 1917,** and the **Jiyu Gakuen School, 1921** (School of the Free Spirit).

After five years of continuous production, the gestation and building of the Imperial Hotel had left Wright exhausted and critically sick with pneumonia. His mother came to Tokyo to nurse him back to health. (Wright arranged for her invitation to the Emperor's garden party.) It was to be the last of many a journey in which she arrived to rescue her son.

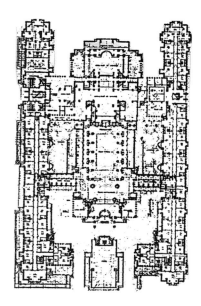

Imperial Hotel plan

1923: DOOMSDAY ARRIVES

Two years after Wright left Japan, Tokyo was demolished by the biggest earthquake of its history, 8.1 on the Richter scale. He was awakened by a telephone call in the middle of the night and was taunted by a tabloid press editor, who said: "The Imperial Hotel has been destroyed. A massive earthquake has destroyed all of Tokyo; 100,000 people are dead." (Actually, 180,000.)

Wright asked, "Are you sure? Read me the list." The editor read out his list, "The Imperial Bank, The Imperial Offices . . ." Wright responded, "You still haven't found the Imperial Hotel." Had it survived? Three days later the telegram came: "Congratulations! The Imperial Hotel is the only building to survive earthquake." Wright had won.

The Imperial was finally destroyed in 1968, not by nature but by man's greed and indifference, replaced by a bland modern tower. When Wright was asked to support the movement fighting for preservation, he refused and said, "No, the Japan I knew and loved no longer exists." Perhaps, because the hotel was U.S. headquarters during the occupation of Japan after World War II, it symbolized something the Japanese wished to forget.

ECLIPSE

Wright returned to California, after being away from America for more than five years. He was a forgotten man, his career in eclipse. He picked up one new project when a former client, Mrs. Millard, now living in Los Angeles, commissioned him to build her new house. He was looking for a project in which to realize the idea germinating in his mind. He knew that with the rising cost of skilled craftsmen in America, if he was to create a new monumental architecture, he must first invent the technology to build it cheaply.

THE "TEXTILE BLOCK" HOUSES

The alchemist of the Middle Ages sought to transform lead into gold, the ordinary into the extraordinary. Wright, the alchemist, turned his full attention to transforming the gray, utilitarian concrete block into an extraordinary magical, textured jewel. Taking small stones bound together with cement, he created a modern version of the Gothic stone he had admired. Here integral ornament was cast into the form of every block. One basic block could do everything, perform multiple roles: structure, wall, integral ornament and even roof. Cast in a mold charged with granite dust with embossed design and glass inlay, each block was designed as a piece of intrinsic architecture. It expressed perfectly his definition of "organic architecture: where the part is to the whole as the whole is to the part." His designs were cast into a mold from which an endless array of blocks could be cheaply mass produced by unskilled labor. The imprint of his inspiration was manifest in every block.

He had brought two distant worlds together. In Europe he had been inspired by the Gothic, in which the same stone provided wall, structure and ornament. In China, overseeing the weaving of the carpets for the Imperial

Millard House wall texture

50

Millard House

Hotel, he saw how the weft and warp provided the matrix upon which the rich texture of the carpet took form. These observations inspired him to use a matrix of horizontal and vertical steel reinforcing rods to support the texture of the blocks.

This technique produced a richness of texture and ornament unsurpassed since the Gothic. He called it the "Textile Block System." With it he could build a monumental architecture undreamed of in ancient times: the **Millard House, Los Angeles, 1923,** the **Storer House, Los Angeles, 1923,** and the **Ennis House, Los Angeles, 1923.** Freed from the constraints of stone, his architecture now had endless possibilities.

He could strip away the keystones and make glass corners, as in the **Freeman House, Los Angeles, 1923,** or span large spaces and create great cantilevers. Of the architects of the twentieth century, only Wright could provide the rich geometric design of the ornament—a true language for the Modern Age. He continued this work for the rest of his life. One of his last projects was for the **Arizona State Capitol, 1957,** which would have given Phoenix the cultural identity it so sadly lacks.

The **Barnsdall House, Los Angeles, 1917,** called "Hollyhock," was built for an individualistic, liberal heiress and used local structural techniques. Based on the cubistic abstraction of the hollyhock, the decorations were cast in concrete. The fireplace brings together Wright's favorite elements: fire and water, cosmos and art. In this romantic California extravaganza the opening in the roof reveals the stars and moon, which are reflected along with flames in the semicircular moat that rings the hearth. A beautiful geometric design by the architect is carved on the stone chimney breast. This extensive project contains several buildings. While Wright was away in Japan, supervision was accomplished by the Austrian architects Richard Neutra and Rudolf Schindler.

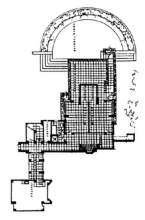

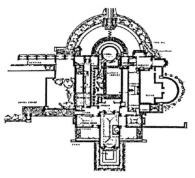

Barnsdall plan

The three masters of decoration shared common Celtic roots: Wright (Welsh), Louis Sullivan (Irish) and Charles Rennie Mackintosh (Scottish). The latter two created unique and beautiful designs using the sensuous flowing line of the art nouveau and the Celtic tradition. But all three were going against the tide. Modern architecture, with a puritan zeal, was stripping away ornament, reducing architecture to a bare functionalism. Mackintosh and Sullivan died broken men, bypassed by the changing whims of fashion. Sullivan died in a dirty hotel room in Chicago. Only Wright had the physical and mental toughness to survive. He had finally reconciled with Sullivan and helped support his Lieber-Meister with both friendship and money. Sullivan was elated with the evolution of Wright's work and saw him as a natural successor, the keeper of the sacred flame of architecture.

MIRIAM NOEL

In the Greek myth of the twins, Castor and Pollux, Castor is mortal and Pollux is a god. Like every man, Wright shared these dual roles. In the world of architecture Wright moved like a god but in the domain of woman he was all too mortal. He entered an alien world where the siren's call

Author's Note: Some years ago, I visited the Freeman House in Los Angeles. The building was being restored by its curator and USC. I sat with friends in the living room around the fireplace on furniture designed by Schindler. The best way to experience a building is to sit in it and absorb the spirit of the place. My eye was drawn to one of the concrete blocks cast for the restoration. I tried to understand the meaning behind Wright's matrix design, but reason failed. The forms were in a nonverbal language as incomprehensible to me as an ancient hieroglyph. That night I had a vivid dream of sitting in an ancient Babylonian room. I could feel the life of the city around me. My unconscious mind had understood the forms imprinted on the block. As if seeing light from a long-dead star, I was experiencing the energy from an architecture no longer in existence, resonating with archetypal energy. Wright's discovery of the source had transported me to another culture, for the psyche moves outside of time. The artist opens up new trails to unknown worlds, like the explorer Burton who discovered the source of the Nile and blazed the trail that others could follow. So too can we follow Wright's journey to the source of architecture.

would lead him astray into a maelstrom of destructive forces and conflicting desires.

While living in Europe and Japan, the boy from the Midwest had developed into a cosmopolitan gentleman. If Wright had a weakness for women, they, particularly as clients, had a weakness for him. For Wright was an attractive, handsome man, with the powerful ego fueled by charismatic energy and genius. He was at once visionary and practical; he built his dreams.

Wright could be quite earthy. An apprentice friend, Edgar Tafel, about to get married, was vainly attempting to start a bonfire against the wind. Wright came up to him and said, "Son, if you don't know the right place to start a fire you will never succeed with a woman!" On the other hand, at times he was on the verge of being prudish. At my first Taliesin dance, I was told that Mr. Wright was against dancing, which he called "vertical intercourse." Perhaps, as in his architecture, he preferred the horizontal line.

It is not surprising that, as the son of a minister, whenever he strayed from the puritan path he was predestined to be discovered. He only had to check into a Berlin hotel with a lady and it became a headline in Chicago. He wrote, ". . . but I was forgetful, for the time being, of grandfather's Isaiah.

Ennis House interior

Ennis plan

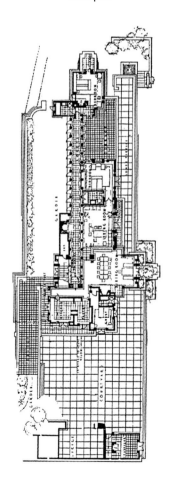

His smiting and his punishment." And later: "God might have been testing my character, but he knew that in architecture I always gave my best."

The dark wave of tragedy continued to stain his life. It had thrown him off balance, clouded his vision. Without Mamah, he was desperately lonely. He prayed for a companion. He should have been wary of "answered prayers." His life had just been destroyed. In the darkness of despair, he answered the call of another. He was to describe his relationship with Noel as "the blind leading the blind."

It began with a letter of condolence from "someone who has also suffered," signed, Miriam Noel. Wright recalled, "She wore a bejeweled cross and carried a book on Christian Science . . . Her health had been broken . . . A trace of some illness seemed to cling to her in the continuous, slight but perceptible shaking of her head . . . She was sensitive and clairvoyant, strange and violent things would occur around her . . ." She was a middle-aged femme fatale, a witch who would cast him under her spell.

They lived together, on and off, for several tumultuous years. In 1923 his mother died at age 81. He cried, "But she was so young." She had guided him throughout his life and supported him through every phase, every disaster. He was shattered by her death. He had lost the one person he could unquestionably trust. In desperation he married Noel. His wife, Catherine (with bad timing), finally granted him the divorce he had once sought to marry Mamah. He now thought that marriage would solve Noel's growing instability. Within the year, they had split forever. Freed of her spell, Wright was alone and at peace again in Taliesin. Visiting the ballet in Chicago, he became fascinated with the young woman in the next box. Her name was Olgivanna Lazovich. They soon became lovers.

Jealous of Olgivanna and rejected by Wright, Noel reenacted the tale of the revengeful witch Caridwen, who pursued the legendary Gwion Bach. Chased by the wrathful Noel, Wright and Olgivanna fled from city to city, from state to state, across the country to the West Coast. They took refuge in the house of a friend, where they were betrayed by the son to the police and press and thrown in jail. Noel had pressed charges against him for "illegally crossing state borders for immoral purposes." In San Diego Noel broke into his house and smashed the furniture. She transported her rage to Chicago, where she threw Olgivanna and her baby out of a hospital and into the street.

Frank Lloyd Wright had now become a favorite whipping boy of the tabloid press, which constantly harassed him and pilloried his character. (It was the tabloid press that paid Noel to instigate the harassment.)[1]

Noel overreacted, becoming a caricature of herself. Her spell was thus broken and the case against Wright was dismissed. Commenting on Noel, Wright said: "We came together under an evil star."

THE SEVEN LEAN YEARS

With the deaths of Mamah, his mother, and now Sullivan in 1924, the three most important people in his life were gone. He was alone in an increasingly hostile world. The Twenties were to be the most difficult period of his life.

The tragedy and turbulence of his private life had blown him off course. He was lost in a world of ghosts, separated in some strange way by an invisible barrier from the normal flow of wealthy clients and the tangible successes of Oak Park. His new clients were "phantoms who would finance schemes for skyscrapers, and then fade back into the shadows from which they came." His voyage was under a dark star.

When Frederick Guthreim visited Wright he found him without work and studying large books of photos of plants and cells. Frank Lloyd Wright was preparing for the future. While his fortunes ran low, his imagination soared. He designed a pyramidal cathedral for a million people, a unique cantilevered tower for New York, and a spiral observatory. (In time all these projects came to fulfillment.) This was the period for research and inner discovery: as with Leonardo da Vinci, his days were filled with sketches for

[1]The press had developed an appetite for scandal related to famous architects during the Stanford White love-triangle murder case in 1906.

Arizona State Capitol

visionary projects. There was little money, but this fallow time provided the gestation for his greatest works.

The fact that he would survive was due to his tough upbringing by his mother, aunts and uncles as well as his childhood experience on the farm, where he received his lifelong lesson: the cycle of life and death, seed and harvest, of patience and timing. He had developed an extraordinary resilience, a profound faith in life, the ability to regenerate after each disaster.

OLGIVANNA

In 1928 Wright finally got his divorce from Noel and married Olgivanna. (Their daughter was born in 1925; Wright was not built to be a puritan.) He had chosen a Western wife with an Eastern philosophy. Olgivanna was born in Montenegro, Yugoslavia, and educated in Moscow and Fontainebleau, France, by George Gurdjieff, a Sufi master (Muslim mystic) from Armenia. Wright's marriage represented a fusion of cultures and a new direction in his life. The ten lost years after the death of Mamah were over.

TALIESIN AND ISAIAH. THE SECOND FIRE, 1925

A year after Noel had left and Olgivanna had moved in, Taliesin returned to a tranquil state of being. One evening Wright was walking down from the hilltop when he saw the flames pouring out from Taliesin below. The fire, which was caused by an electrical fault by his bed, was fanned by an approaching storm.[2] He wrote: "For the second time Taliesin was in flames, the living quarters gone, and now the workspace was threatened! Suddenly, a tremendous pealing roll of thunder . . . The clouds of smoke and sparks were swept the opposite way. It was as though some gigantic unseen hand had done it and that awed the spectators. Super-human Providence perhaps . . ."

All that remained was the work space and the clothes on his back. He stood defeated. The treasures he had brought back from Japan—everything was gone. He refused the offers to save the things inside the house, shouting, "No, fight the fire. Fight! Fight, I tell you! Save Taliesin or let it all go! . . . I stood up there—and fought. Isaiah?" Wright rejected Isaiah, the prophet of the moral god Jehovah with his puritan sense of sin, guilt and righteous punishment. "Taliesin the gentler prophet of the Celts and of a more merciful god was tempted to lift an arm, to strike back in self-defense but suffered in silence and waited. But Taliesin lived wherever I stood! A figure crept forward to me from out of the shadows to say this . . ."

Wright lived his myth, and the myth lived in him. Taliesin was the myth that shaped Wright's life, powered the forms of his work and gave the names Taliesin East and Taliesin West to his house and Arizona work place.

He saw that the second destruction of Taliesin was not an end. For as Taliesin, generator of forces and unlimited forms, he could create endlessly, a Taliesin III, and a Taliesin West, for the power of the shape-shifter is his ability to transform, to create the shape for every site, the form for every function. His more than 1,000 different designs demonstrate his uncanny mastery in the art of form and transformation with the most diverse and extraordinary array of inspired solutions. The prairie house follows the horizontal line of the prairie, St. Mark's in the Bowery is a vertical tower for New York, Taliesin West adapts to the arid desert, Fallingwater matches the cascade in the forest, while Marin County Civic Center echoes the rolling green hills of Marin County.

Frank Lloyd Wright became the most prolific architectural shape-shifter of all time.

---

[2]Lloyd Wright (his son) claimed that at least one fire was caused by his father's habit of smoking, and falling asleep, in bed.

Frank Lloyd Wright and family
driving off to New York City

Taliesin West

58

The Third Age
TRIANGLE IN THE DESERT

THE AUCTION OF TALIESIN

WRIGHT WAS HEAVILY in debt. With no work coming in, the cost of rebuilding Taliesin and his legal battles with Noel left him broke, forced by the bank to sell his livestock and farm machinery to pay on his debt. He fought to save Taliesin, sacrificing one prized possession after another, including his collection of Oriental objets d'art. Finally, he was forced to sacrifice his greatest possession, his lifelong collection of Japanese prints. Considered the best collection in America, it raised only half its value.

In spite of all his desperate efforts, Taliesin, the land of his grandfather, Richard Lloyd Jones, was threatened by the bank with foreclosure. Two years before the 1929 crash, Wright's personal economic depression had reached its climax.

The Bank of Wisconsin took possession of Taliesin and expelled Wright. But ironically, in the spirit of Mammon, the bank officers, having no idea what to do with the most extraordinary house in America, used it only to store files. (As Joseph Campbell remarked, "The dragon guards the maiden, but is unable to use her gifts.")

Taliesin was faced with the ultimate disaster, to be auctioned off to the highest bidder. At the eleventh hour, Wright's friend and former client Darwin Martin came up with a way to save Taliesin. Calling on his acumen as a businessman, he devised a scheme to outwit Mammon. Forming a corporation called "Frank Lloyd Wright Incorporated," he issued stock on Wright's future earnings—no mean trick, considering the fact that Wright had no current work. Appropriately, the stockholders included the writers Alexander Woollcott and Charles MacArthur, art patron and client Mrs. Coonley, Martin, and Wright's sister and his attorney. The friends of the Muse raised $70,000.

Put up for auction, Taliesin was successfully bid by "Frank Lloyd Wright Incorporated," for $40,000. With poetic symmetry the earnings of the Muse saved Taliesin. The investors must have suspected that they might never get paid for their investment. It didn't matter. By affirming their faith in the arts, they saved Taliesin.

EXILE. WINTER, 1927–28

While this financial drama was unfolding, Wright was in exile in La Jolla, California, awaiting a solution to his monetary and legal problems.

A letter from Albert McArthur inviting Wright to help him with his Arizona Biltmore Hotel project in Phoenix signaled a change in the direction of Wright's life. Albert had worked for Wright at the old Oak Park studio and his father was a former client. They and Albert's brother had formed a business; they needed Wright's help and expertise in using his textile block system for their Arizona Biltmore Hotel project. Wary of Wright taking control of their project, they insisted he remain in the background, without credit for his work. Wright would be working under a man who had once been his draftsman. Fate thus presented him with an ironic challenge to his ego. The choice was work without name, or name without work. Certainly Wright needed money, but more than anything, he was desperate with the need to create again. What proved irresistible to him was the opportunity to use his textile block system in the largest block project yet to be built, and to bring monumental architecture to a desert environment. For the first time Wright's angular form appeared as the design on his textile block. Wright got his credit after all.

The McArthur brothers, admiring his work but lacking his artistry, changed ceiling heights and floor levels "for practical reasons," and thus destroyed Wright's subtle contrasts between low and high ceilings, intimate and expansive space. But Wright was never an easy man to work with, and to their credit, they brought to completion this amazing and complex project. Although scholars argue about authorship, Wright's signature is everywhere apparent, but the Hotel lacks the cohesion of his most personal and finest work.

This first encounter with the desert presaged Wright's lifetime involvement. Destiny had always presented a jagged path to Wright's life. In Phoenix he was introduced to a Dr. Chandler, who wished to build a resort to be called San Marcos in the Desert. When Chandler took him out to see the site, Wright responded: "There could be nothing more inspiring to an architect on this earth than that spot of pure Arizona desert he took me out to see." Wright made preliminary sketches for San Marcos on his return to La Jolla and delivered them to Dr. Chandler while en route to Taliesin III.

In the winter of 1928 Wright was able to return to Taliesin. He was still without funds, and the bank had been threatening to foreclose.

FREEDOM AND RENEWAL

The temperature outside Taliesin was 22 degrees below zero when the telegram arrived from Dr. Chandler, asking Wright to come and begin work on San Marcos. The future fee of $40,000 represented an end to Wright's financial problems.

To escape from the rigors of the Wisconsin winter, Wright and his men had to first battle their way through a blizzard, a howling vortex of snow, ice and wind, on their journey to the hot Arizona desert. It was a seminal journey, emblematic of his escape from a decade of darkness beginning with the tragedy at Taliesin that plunged him into a labyrinth of death, suffering, fire, persecution, jail and bankruptcy.

During this time his architecture reflected his own inner voyage through the labyrinth: the great cavern of the Imperial Hotel, the Arizona Biltmore banquet room, the dark ancient interiors of the textile block houses. The labyrinth became a decorative form on his blocks.

THE DESERT ARCHITECTURE

When Wright first saw the desert he had what was virtually a religious experience, a revelation that opened him to a totally new morphology of architecture. He said of his moment of insight, "Imagination of the mind is an awesome thing. Sight comes and goes in it as from an original source, illuminating life with involuntary light, as a flash of lightning brightens the landscape. So the desert seems vast but the seeming is nothing compared to the iridescent-effervescent reality."

It was no accident that mystics and artists found the desert landscape a place for inspiration, healing and regeneration. The Arizona desert is a landscape newly emerging from the chaos of cataclysmic upheavals. The primal forces of nature are expressed in the uneven and asymmetrical shapes of the mountains.

"The desert is where God is and man is not."
Victor Hugo, quoted by Wright

San Marcos in the Desert perspective *(above)* and plan *(below)*

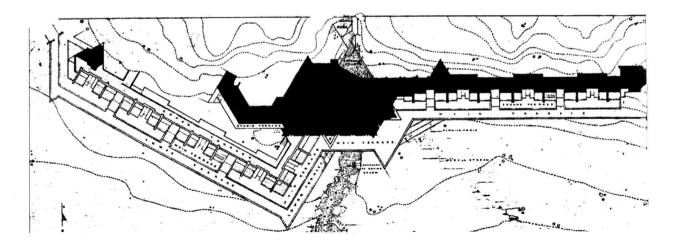

61

The desert represents a world of untamed, primal energy, yet to be softened by the elements or tamed by order. The energy of the sun, the clear air and the magical light are all-pervasive: recharging the body, renewing the spirit.

The heat, the high blue sky and the ever-present sun combine with the primitive terrain to shock the visitor coming from the rich green world of the north. The Swiss painter Paul Klee exclaimed, "For the first time I understood color—color has me."

THE TRIANGLE

"The first thing I noticed was the angle of the mountains; everywhere the 30- and 60-degree angle, broken only by the occasional equilateral triangle."—F.LL.W.

The angular desert mountains awakened latent images in his unconscious. In Wright's mind, new shapes began to germinate and take form. (As with the psychologist's Rorschach test, where the conscious mind "sees" in the abstract pattern of an inkblot the image hidden in the unconscious, so the exterior image resonates and invokes unconscious form.)

SAN MARCOS IN THE DESERT, CHANDLER, ARIZONA, 1927

Situated on several thousand acres of pure mountain desert, San Marcos was envisioned by Chandler as a desert resort for wintering millionaires from the East Coast.

"Everywhere the jagged line, the primal mountains, the savage sun world, sun death," wrote Wright. "The desert abhors sun-defiance . . . sun acceptance as a way of pattern is a condition of survival . . . integral ornament in everything . . . in building means dotted outlines and wall surfaces that eagerly take the light and play with it, break it up and render it harmless or drink it until sunlight blends the building into place with the creation around it."

The principle manifest in the desert inspired Wright's design. He echoed the angular-profile ribs of the saguaro in his design for the concrete blocks. The sunlight moving across the vertical ribbed surface was refracted and broken into a dotted line. The walls of San Marcos emerge from the desert floor as crystalline shafts thrusting out from the earth. The new emphasis is on the vertical rather than the horizontal line. The floor plan has undergone a profound mutation; shaped like a jagged, angular flash of lightning, its fundamental element is the triangle module. The dining room is a vast trapezoidal form. Here the monumental architecture was transformed into a new experience of light, space and openness.

saguaro

The materials of the desert provided the structural elements. The sand and gravel from the desert were mixed with cement and cast into molds to provide the basic, textile block system. He had created a passive solar system whereby the heat of the day was stored and released to warm the interior at night. During the hot day the walls provided a cool shelter without the need for air conditioning. A Czech architect (who had worked with Le Corbusier) recalled nearly fainting—along with others—in the 100-degree heat, while Wright drew away unperturbed.

The saguaro cactus (the organ pipe) was the primary vegetation that adorned the landscape. The structural systems of nature were an important source for Wright's inspiration. Wright could have been a great naturalist with his extraordinary insight into the workings of nature and organic structure. The inner secrets of growth and structure in nature provided him with the fertile ground for his creations.

Some years later I was at Taliesin West. One Sunday morning someone had placed a piece of saguaro cactus on the table in front of Wright, knowing how inspiring he found the nature around the camp. Wright said to us, "Nature builds in the desert, working with the minimum of materials in the most economical way: there is little water and hard, rocky soil. Building with the bare minimum is a good discipline for architects. With such scarce resources, plants have to develop a structural system that is very efficient; and in this, the tallest of the desert cacti, the plant uses a complex matrix of hollow fibers, with the outside of the column being a corrugated skin."

Saguaro plan

The folded skin of the saguaro both provides shade from the hot sun and supports its great height for centuries, behaving as a structural folded plane column. He adopted this principle of the folded plane for his projects such as Fallingwater, and used it in the integral self-support structure for the zigzag fence of Ocotilla and the walls of the Hanna House.

The rendering of San Marcos suggests one of the great Italian hill towns sitting perfectly at ease on its site at the base of the mountains. The entry road is skillfully set between two hills, like the entry to Ali Baba's cave. Here, we can glimpse what a Wrightian town might look like with its timeless sense of wholeness and tranquillity. Wright and his workers had completed the drawings, block molds and model. He was ready to begin construction.

But it was not to be. The stock market crash in 1929 killed the project. Only later did Wright realize the severity of the crash. Plaster models of the block system were left, sitting proudly in the center of the desert camp, never to be returned to. Over time the local Indians would slowly take away the camp and it disappeared into the sand. Dr. Chandler could pay only $2,500 of the promised fee and left Wright $19,000 in debt.

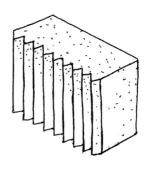

San Marcos concrete block

Wright said, "I have found that when a scheme develops beyond a normal pitch of excellence, the hand of fate strikes it down. The Japanese made a superstition of the circumstance. Purposefully they leave some imperfection somewhere to appease the jealousy of the gods. I neglected this precaution and San Marcos was never built." A lesser man might have been irrevocably crushed by this, the latest of a long string of disasters over many years. But Wright's capacity for patience and regeneration would save him once again. He wrote, "Never mind. Something had started that was not stopping thus."

Characteristically, his response was to purchase a magnificent, if used, Packard Phaeton convertible to take his new family back to Taliesin in, via a new client, St. Mark's Church in the Bowery, New York.

With his marriage to Olgivanna, the birth of Iovanna and the adoption of Svetlana, Olgivanna's daughter from her previous marriage, the circle of Wright's life was once again complete. He was back in the world of the family. For his ventures into the unknown, Wright needed a secure base, a ground to nourish his strength. Olgivanna supported him in every way: as a man, an architect and a prophet. His marriage to Olgivanna had exorcised, at last, the ghosts of the past. The taint of scandal that had dogged him for so long was finally erased. Potential clients who had avoided him because of the stigma attached to his life were now replaced by a new breed of clients who sought him for his independent philosophy. Reborn in the desert, redeemed by marriage, he was back on the course of his destiny, his life moving powerfully in a new direction.

LIGHT. OCOTILLA, 1929

"I found the white luminous canvas . . . such agreeable diffusion of light within . . . I now felt oppressed by the thought of the opaque solid overhead of the much too heavy midwestern houses."
F.LL.W.

The extraordinary light of the desert was reflected from the vast dome of the sky. The quality of the soft light, filtered through canvas, awakened Wright to a new experience, and the dark, cavelike interiors of the past were transformed into a new sense of openness to the world.

Ocotilla was Wright's desert encampment where he would develop and experiment with the design for San Marcos. He called the camp "Ephemera," for it sat on the desert floor like a butterfly and its physical life was brief. Its image, however, was published in the international magazines and achieved immortality. It was a spinoff from the San Marcos project, yet it represented the beginning of a whole new world. The floor plan for San Marcos was triangular. Wright easily crossed from one dimension to another, and moved the triangle from the plan into the elevation and section of Ocotilla.

ASYMMETRY

"Out here in the great spaces obvious symmetry . . . wearies the eye . . . closes the episode before it begins."
F.LL.W.

The asymmetrical form of the roof matched the surrounding mountains; 30 degrees on one side matched by 60 on the other, with a 90-degree ridge. Ocotilla was the seed that was to flower nine years later into Taliesin West in 1937.

Wright saw the world through the eye of a maker of forms. The asymmetrical mountains that emerge from the desert floor opened him to a new sense of freedom and introduced him to the dynamic power of asymmetry. The architecture of Ocotilla and Taliesin West reflected this new approach; gone was the symmetry and rigidity of the old classic order. Asymmetry expressed the freedom of the desert growth following its own "random" pattern. Perceiving the asymmetrical mountains of Arizona, he was inspired to build Taliesin West in their image.

TALIESIN WEST

In subsequent years, Wright would continue his migration to the desert to escape the cold winter of Wisconsin. Asked, by a client, where was the location of his office, Wright replied, "My office is wherever I am." Wright might well have called himself Taliesin after his Muse, but he chose to use it for his house, wherever that might be. After the two fires Taliesin had been rebuilt as Taliesin II and III. In 1937 he decided to create a new Taliesin in the desert and called his new camp Taliesin West. Built in a form and grammar totally different from Taliesin East, it well embodied his statement to us, "A great building is a cosmos unto itself, to be judged only by its own laws."

Ocotilla tent

64

Living room, original version

He bought 400 acres of federal land and began building Taliesin West, this time in a form to complement and express the desert *genius loci*. With no money for masons and relying on unskilled labor, he had to invent a simple system of construction. The alchemist sought a cheap material in which to hold his forms. He chose the materials of the desert itself. The hard, unworkable basalt stone was tied inside wood forms and a 12:1 mixture of desert sand and gravel was mixed with cement to create the concrete rubble walls.

Once again he showed in the imagery of his forms that a cheap material could achieve new heights of architectural expression. The angular, battered walls, rhythmically defined by "pour line" battens inserted in the forms, created a powerful expression not seen since ancient architecture. The delicate canvas roofs held in wood frames were in perfect harmony with the massive masonry elements. With time and experience, the walls became more sophisticated. Enormous rocks, chosen for their magnificent orange, blue and purple coloration, were framed by smaller stones whose projection was allowed to penetrate through the form.

Wright discovered, like Antonio Gaudí, that "light releases the energy trapped in matter" and designed skylights above the masonry fireplaces. Taliesin West was built by the apprentices in a surprisingly short time. In 1987 about 200 former apprentices returned to celebrate the fiftieth anniversary of Taliesin West. On a drafting table by the entry of the drafting room, someone had pinned a large sheet of drafting paper. At the top was written:

Living room fireplace

signpost

"Everything around you was built by us . . . Please sign your name." Soon the entire page was filled with signatures. For the first time, I was aware that this entire marvelous complex had been made by the apprentices. Unlike most university projects, there had been no support from government funding and no outside contractors.

I arrived at Taliesin in 1954. When winter started to hit hard in Wisconsin, the Fellowship moved to Taliesin West. Two big trucks were packed with all the models and plans. The huge rounds of cheese made on the farm, as well as the farm-cured hams, were loaded up too; we took all our farm supplies to the desert. Groups of three or four apprentices shared the available cars and we were allowed one or two weeks to make the trip.

We left Taliesin East and first headed north to visit some Wright houses. As apprentices, we had easy access to most of Wright's buildings. We then turned south, covering about 400 miles a day. We were following Mr. Wright's original journey from Taliesin East to Taliesin West, visiting many of his buildings along the way.

We now headed for Taliesin West. Abstract signs (Wright's logo, the square spiral) led us along dirt roads, passing through forests of saguaro and cholla cactus and ironwood trees; and then suddenly we glimpsed the canvas roofs and outer walls of the camp. We left our auto in the large parking lot outside. Above loomed a large stone tower draped with red bougainvillea. On the wall was fastened a large metal disc, acquired by Wright during a visit to an aircraft factory, brimming and spilling water over its edge. We crossed the gravel "moat," a barrier to discourage rattlesnakes, and ascended large steps to pass under a seemingly endless pergola of low beams (we six footers cocked our heads sideways) which ties the vast drafting room to the outer desert wall. Then you turn 90 degrees to the right, then 90 degrees

drafting room

to the left, down a dark, mysterious narrow corridor, like a labyrinth, and then turn yet again, finally emerging into a blaze of light and color, with brilliant bougainvillea growing in secret inner courtyards.

You are led down narrow galleries, up steps barely wide enough to pass; you are restricted, pulled, pressed, and taken through every kind of experience: light/dark, narrow/wide, low/high, beneath/above, mystery/revelation. Surprises everywhere! Low beams and low ceilings, where one almost grazes one's head, opening out suddenly into vast magical spaces with vistas of long stretches of desert reaching out toward the high mountains. Set in the wall of a long gallery, a shallow horizontal window at eye level frames an exquisite view of a camelback mountain.

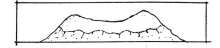

Arizona mountain

Years later in Knossos I recognized the same qualities of the palace in the desert embodying primary human experiences, a synthesis of king, priest, soldier, artist and worker: the summation of a culture. Here in another desert at another time is another palace, a celebration of architecture and democracy. In Knossos there was the sunken throne room; in Taliesin, the sunken fireplace and hearth by the drafting room: the hearth that can become a pool and the fire that can become water. (Wright, feeling that a fireplace should not be wasted in the summer, converted the flue into a waterfall and the sunken hearth into a pool.) Both Knossos and Taliesin West share a sense of mystery and primal energy. At Taliesin West, the soft organic light is filtered through the canvas above. Interior gutters run alongside the beams to catch the rain and return it outside.

The massive walls of enormous basalt rock fragments, colored by the elements of brilliant oranges, reds, blacks and blues, are set in battered concrete, and ancient Indian petroglyphs figured on the boulders by the triangular pool. A tranquil Buddha sits in the theater entry where ancient Japanese and Chinese sculptures are embedded in the walls.

Knossos celebrated the autocracy of a king over his people. Taliesin West celebrates the democracy of the individual and the birth of a new culture, drawing its power from the primal desert. Taliesin West is one of Wright's major and seminal buildings. In Arizona apprentices noted that Wright had a desert face. He wrote: "Olgivanna said the whole opus looked like something we had not been building but excavating."

sculpture with plant holder

belltower with Chinese pottery

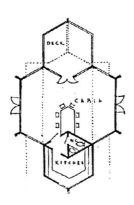

Lake Tahoe plan

According to Jung, the conquerors of America inherited the collective unconscious of those they destroyed. Wright was a sorcerer who could conjure up and evoke forms from the earth. Wright had discovered and tapped the source, the ancient forces of the earth that had fueled the ancient architecture, the Mayan, Aztec and Pueblo. Wright was well placed, himself a product of the American melting pot. In the crucible of his alchemy he fused the diverse cultures of the past into new cultural forms.

Wright incorporated the Native American spiral into his logo during the construction of Taliesin West and celebrated the tepee form in projects like the **Lake Tahoe Summer Colony, Lake Tahoe, 1922,** the **Nakoma Country Club and Winnebago Camping Ground Indian Memorial, Madison,**

68

Wisconsin, 1924, the **H. Johnson House, Windpoint, Wisconsin, 1938, "Wingspread,"** and the **A. Friedman House, Pecos, New Mexico, 1945.**

Wright never used a modern drafting machine. He had a special reverence for his triangles, as if some ancient memory recalled the moment when the secrets of the triangle were first unlocked in the desert cultures of Babylon, Egypt and Greece. The Egyptians celebrated their discovery of the triangle by constructing the pyramids, the biggest triangle of mass ever built by man. Characteristically, Wright was challenged by this to design an even larger pyramid of space, light and glass, "a steel cathedral for a million people," in New York, 1926, to celebrate the technological wonder of the twentieth century.

In the past he had used the triangle in the decorative design of his murals, stained-glass windows and light fixtures. He had used a diamond form in the plan of Romeo and Juliet. Wright could play with a form for years until a new challenge ignited in him a creative transformation.

Wright discovered the full power and potential of the triangle as an archetypal form, generating a whole new world of architecture. Beginning as the design of the textile block for the Arizona Biltmore, it moved to the floor plan of San Marcos and the diamond grid of the Cudney House. The triangle took a leap into the section of Ocotilla, the crystalline facet forms of the San Marcos Water Gardens and the Cathedral for a Million People, which was finally consummated as the Beth Sholom Synagogue in 1954. The **Rhododendron Chapel, 1953, Trinity Chapel Project, Norman, Oklahoma, 1958,** and the **Second Unitarian Church, Madison, Wisconsin, 1947,** represented other variations.

In the **Owen D. Young House, Chandler, Arizona, 1927,** the angle moved into the elevation, and the blocks, windows and profile are tilted at an angle of 45 degrees. Wright asked a lot, both from his clients and builders.

Wright could be critical of his own work. When his very angular **Boomer House, Phoenix, Arizona, 1953,** was finished he said, "It lacks a sense of repose." The house evokes the collision of two delta-wing jet planes; one is left in awe of the spatial imagination that could hold such complex forms.

In the desert he had discovered the angular world: of the mineral and crystal, the vector forces of molecular structures, the geometry of the space

"My tools: triangles and T-square—30, 60, 45 degrees: the three angles."
F.LL.W.

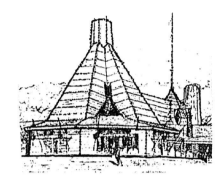

Nakoma Country Club

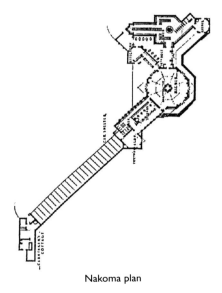

Nakoma plan

Young House

69

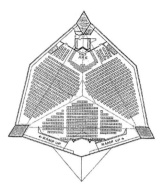

Beth Sholom
Synagogue plan

frame and truss. The triangle is a primal archetypal form of the psyche, Wright's symbol of aspiration, the Celtic form of the triad, the trinity of Christianity, a recurring form in the sand paintings and ornament of the Native American.

When Wright first used the equilateral triangle plan, he had trouble selling it to a client. The **Sundt House, Madison, Wisconsin, 1941,** with its triangular form and hexagon grid was considered too different, difficult and expensive to build. It was later built as the **Richardson House, New Jersey, 1951.**

Wright had more success with the diamond form and used it for the **McCartney House** and the **Anthony House,** both built in Michigan, 1949. The most successful form was the hexagon.

MOVEMENT

In the first age Wright had "destroyed the box," releasing its trapped space by opening out its corners. Now he went farther, replacing the old 90-degree angle of the plan with an angular module. He had broken the last vestige of the right-angle system and opened the plan to a new sense of plastic flow and movement. He saw that it was easier to turn 120 degrees than 90 degrees. (A diagonal shortcut avoids the long right-angle turn.) Wright had moved a step closer in his lifelong quest for a free-flowing plasticity of space. In the hexagon grid of the **Hanna House, Palo Alto, California, 1936,** he was able to put his discovery into action. Once he had built several buildings the way was opened for others to follow. The **Bazett House, Hillsborough, California, 1940,** and "Snowflake," the **Wall House, Michigan, 1941,** which combined diamond grid with hexagon form, were other superb examples built.

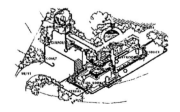

Hanna plan

REVELATION AND EPIPHANY

From the desert Wright received its secrets: Light, Triangle, Movement, Texture, Structure, Asymmetry, Economy, Simplicity and Taproot. They transformed his future work.

He transmuted ancient archetypes into a new language for the age and raised the simple forms of the desert to a breathtaking morphology of form. As with every great culture that discovers the timeless and universal archetypes to generate its forms, Wright traveled to the deepest levels of human experience to discover the archetypal forms providing the profound resonances of his work.

THE TAPROOT

One of Wright's favorite metaphors was the taproot of a desert plant that provides stability and plunges deep into the earth to find a spring untouched by the arid years of the desert above. Wright was equally describing himself; his roots ran deep, into the very archetypal sources of architecture. He survived the lean years by tapping this prolific source endlessly when there was little work. It provided him with the energy to create his most audacious projects during the arid Depression.

In the Twenties a truly modern architecture barely existed; no bank would provide financing since most architecture was conventional and eclectic. This was the greatest period of gestation and development of Wright's ideas. It was as if the gods had granted him a decade to play with new concepts and techniques. These were the "dreaming years" in which he discovered the seminal concepts that would later blossom into a magnificent reality.

His career had come perilously close, like Sullivan's, to a premature conclusion. The world might have written him off as a failure, but in these fallow years his consciousness was undergoing a profound transformation: his spatial perception was developing a four-dimensional awareness reaching out to new vistas. His imagination gained the capacity to divine, hold and express complex images and new concepts.

All of the previous experiences of his life, the worlds of Oak Park, Europe, the Orient, were converging into a new synthesis. In the caldron of

inspiration a new architecture was taking form. Taliesin, the sleeping giant, was undergoing profound changes that would transform him into a protean giant that would emerge to astonish his critics and the world.

As Wright grew older, Taliesin grew younger, crossing the old conceptual frontiers of architecture. His forms became ever more audacious, outpacing rival architects, going beyond the limitations of twentieth-century culture and technology. It was to lead to Wright's final Golden Age.

Wright's move to Arizona presaged the population shift to the West in the decades to follow. He did not so much follow a trend as initiate it.

Wright at Taliesin East

The Fourth Age
HORIZONTAL PLANES

IN 1929 THE DARK CLOUD of the Depression was moving across America. The postwar "good time" era was drawing to a close. The desert years had taught Wright how to achieve the maximum utilization from the minimum of materials. In the economic desert of the Depression, it was necessary to invent new techniques for architectural survival. Wright had said that with the removal of the superfluous, "the Japanese print was almost biographical in its influence on me." He brought the lesson of simplicity to the age of economy.

That same year Wright designed a house for his cousin, Richard Lloyd Jones, in Tulsa, Oklahoma. The first project, using a triangular plan, was not built. The second version was stark in its simplicity. A concrete block house, it is significant by the absence of any ornamental design on the face of the block. If the third age of monumental architecture had celebrated richness and complexity, the fourth age represented its opposite: economy and simplicity.

Wright was always aware of the forces of change occurring in society around him, and equally he was a creator of changes. His anticipation of changes in American lifestyle to the servantless society led to the open kitchen, reflecting a new sense of family, in which the wife needed to see and talk to her husband and children, and sped the debut of the carport, which made the automobile speedily accessible.

The **Malcolm Willey Project, Minneapolis, 1932,** introduced a flat roof, an open kitchen plan and the beginning of the carport.

The **Second Willey House, 1934,** shows the breakthrough in space that Wright was seeking. For the first time the kitchen opens directly into the dining-living room space. The kitchen-dining space is itself a classic of the new architecture, with its high asymmetrical window reflecting the roof-ceiling plane above. The kitchen, with its superb cabinetwork and fine detailing, no longer a homely utilitarian room, is transformed into an architecture equal in quality to the adjoining living spaces. With its pitched roof, the Willey house expresses the richness of the prairie house transformed into a new modernity.

All this was to lead to a new architecture following the needs of a new society: the creation of the Usonian house, an open plan of continuous space.

Impressed by Samuel Butler's visionary book on a new America, titled *Usonia,* Wright borrowed the name for his Usonian house. It was designed

"When everything is removed, that which remains is all powerful."
Lao Tse, 600 B.C.

Willey plan

for an ideal democratic society in which everyone could own or build a new house. Taking up this challenge, Wright completely rethought the structure of the American house. Stripping away everything superfluous, he reduced the house to its bare essentials, using basic plywood for the walls and roof structure. Beginning at the ground, he used the cheapest floor, a concrete slab on grade, omitting both basement and wood flooring. Aware that a concrete slab would be cold in the Wisconsin winter, he invented a new heating system. In the East he had admired the warm floors provided by Korean hot-air flues built under the floor. In his version, heating was supplied by hot-water pipes embedded in the concrete slab. It was a first: Wright had invented the radiant heating system.

The surface of the concrete floor slab was colored brick red and scored with the lines of the grid upon which the house was planned. It was sealed, waxed and polished. In place of the conventional 2" × 4" hollow stud wall the solid walls were laminated with a plywood inner structural core, covered with insulation board and finished with horizontal cypress or redwood boards held in place by an inset batten detail.

The walls became a series of planes, locked to the floor with splines, used like Japanese screens to define spaces. The garage was replaced by his new invention, the carport, which provided both a handsome porte-cochere for the entry and a third roof plane in the rhythm of interrelated horizontal planes. The complex of multilevel planes continues into the interior space with a low soffit, which sets a measure for the internal scale and serves as a conduit for the utility services and integral lighting provided by simple porcelain lamp sockets set in wood boxes.

The kitchen-workspace flows into the dining area, which in turn becomes part of the living room, creating one continuous flowing space. Corridors become well-lit galleries, connecting the major spaces with rooms. The continuity of the interior spaces enhances an awareness of the totality of the whole.

Jacobs House

Exterior of Jacobs House

Like a conjurer building a house of cards, Wright demonstrates the incredible power of the plane. Used horizontally it becomes roof, ceiling, soffit, and earth floor. Used as a vertical plane it becomes a series of screens defining and connecting interior spaces. Continuing into the landscape it creates a symbiotic relationship between inner and outer spaces. The screen walls stop at a band of clerestory glass, which allows for the ceiling-roof plane to effortlessly float above. The roof planes enhance and resonate with the flat plane of the earth.

The horizontal line is further developed by the raked horizontal courses of the brick with flush vertical joints and by the recessed battens of the

Interior of Jacobs House

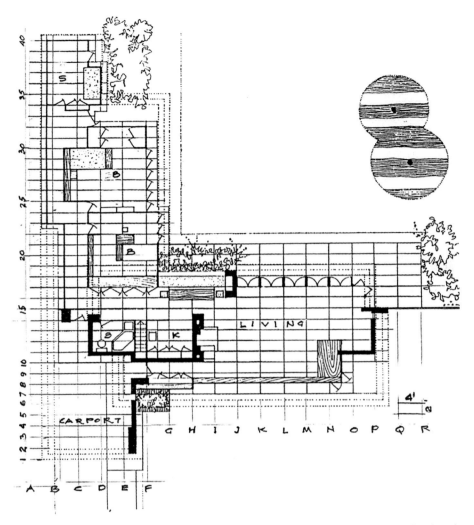

wood siding. The balancing, vertical elements are provided by the brick chimney mass and the rhythmic succession of French doors and bands of casement windows.

The brick fireplace utility core, with its central plumbing for kitchen, bathroom and boiler, allows for an economical basic plumbing unit which can be factory made.

The roof, no longer pitched, becomes a series of flat planes; made of plywood, it is covered with an asphalt composition roof. The flat roof is the cheapest, simplest and most problematic of all roofs, and has become almost a cliché—and a cross—for modern architecture. Its tendency to leak was to forever bedevil the architect's career.

Wright discovered that by elevating and separating this "lid from the box," he had transformed it into a free-floating horizontal plane. The interrelationship of three or more planes generates an extraordinary sense of tension and energy.

In the Usonian houses the hovering roof planes seem to float above the wall screens. With their successive rhythms they share an extraordinary

78

affinity with the surrounding space. The overlapping planes with their subtle difference in heights combine into a magical order, like the pattern of three musical bars—or the vibrant brush strokes of a Zen Sumi-e painting.

The roofs effortlessly cantilever out to interpenetrate the surrounding space. The roof system is constructed cheaply with three layers of 2" × 4" rafters. The layers progressively cantilever out in steps, each layer cantilevered from the one below, expressed as two steps terminating at a slender fascia. There are no gutters, only small leader pipes set into the roof. The 2" × 4" grid system allows the use of standard sheets of plywood and 16-inch spacing of roof joists.

Ornament has dissolved and become integral with the very structure of the building: the pattern of the wood siding, the texture of the horizontal bricks, the stepped fascia of the roof, the rhythm of the fenestration.

Throughout the house every detail becomes integral, economical ornament. The vertical grid that establishes the precise height of the wood siding makes for the integral arrangement of bookshelves and built-in furniture. It defines organic architecture where "the whole is to the part as the part is to the whole."

The Usonian house was planned for small, economical lots. Unlike the tract house, which spends much of its budget on the street facade to impress the neighbors, the Usonian house "turns its back to the street" and the neighbors. To achieve the maximum use of the land the house (with its fenestration) is oriented to the garden area. The high clerestory windows provide both light and privacy for the occupants.

Wright eschewed expensive materials like marble, terrazzo and exotic woods, preferring to put the money where the architecture is. The ultimate test of an architect lies in his arrangement of the basic materials; the way the parts and spaces are put together demonstrates the depth and range of his imagination.

The stunning simplicity of the Usonian roof lines was in startling contrast to the ugly roofscape of a typical builder's house with its proliferation of pipes, vents, air conditioners, and other appendages.

The bill for the materials for the Jacobs house was no more than the cost for the conventional house across the street. Wright demonstrates the mastery of his craft by making a work of art out of the simplest of building materials.

As so often happened, the first project for a Usonian house, for Hoult in 1934, fell through for lack of funds. Nevertheless the basic research had been done and Wright now had to wait for a suitable client to take his concept into full realization. A first design was invariably a model, a precursor of what was to come. Whereas some architects make a house to order, as a tailor does, Wright looked for a suitable client to build his design discoveries.

In 1936, Herb Jacobs, a young journalist, nervously wrote a letter to Wright asking if he would consider accepting a commission to design a small house to cost not more than $5,000. The architect seized the opportunity and in 1936 the first Usonian house was built.

RULES

Years later, Jacobs told me that when one critic complained about Wright's not matching a particular wall to the grid line, Wright responded: "If I can make the rules, then I can break the rules!" He saw the rules as something to work with, play against, and when necessary, go beyond.

Jacobs recalled that, for years, scholars had pondered over why there was a reduced roof cantilever on one side of his house. "It was simple: I didn't have the $15 to pay for the longer rafters."

The Usonian house, in spite of its apparent simplicity, conveys a deep richness, a powerful sense of presence, warmth and humanity; the ineffable sense of life itself. Wright had released the energy contained in the space between walls and planes, between the inner and outer worlds. Although the Jacobs house was an aesthetic success, it netted Wright a fee of only $500.

Along with the Usonian Automatic, a concrete block version for which the client could make his own blocks, more than a hundred Usonian houses were built during the next decades. The **Pauson House, Phoenix, Arizona, 1940,** was a magnificent solution for a desert environment.

Mies van der Rohe, whom Wright respected, and who understood Wright's use of the plane better than anyone, came to visit and admired both Taliesin and the Jacobs house, then under construction.

THE INTERNATIONAL STYLE

Although Wright and the modernists had certain elements in common—the flat roof, modern materials, and absence of eclectic details—the modernist approach to architecture was generally sterile and mechanical to Wright.

The conflict was highlighted by Le Corbusier's phrase, "The house is a machine for living." When he wrote to Wright requesting an interview, he was rejected. Wright said, "At least with him I know who my enemy is."

Le Corbusier responded by calling Wright "the blue-eyed prairie dog."

Wright saw Le Corbusier as the prophet of the rationalist and puritan movements which had found expression in a rigid, intellectual ideology for modern architecture. Le Corbusier was a dry, austere, intellectual Swiss architect whose theories, appealing to other intellectual architects, entered the mainstream of modern architecture to replace human insight with formula, dogma and rules.

Le Corbusier was a prophet who achieved fame by preaching the formula the new mechanistic world was seeking. His City of the Future, with its rows of identical high-rise apartments, resembles a computer circuit board, with its mechanical array of repetitive patterns. In one scheme he used the roofs of a series of apartments as a freeway.

As a dry intellectual, he was poorly equipped to understand human needs. Nevertheless his concept was taken up by his followers to become the blueprint for urban renewal in London, Paris, New York and other major cities. Its mechanical, dehumanizing effect is reflected by these projects' slow degeneration into urban ghettos, a festering world of hopelessness and crime. Many of these buildings have had to be destroyed.

BROADACRE CITY, 1932

Wright's family had been members of Chicago's Hull House, abiding by its emphasis on social reform. Wright was attuned to "the spirit of the age" and in sympathy with Roosevelt's New Deal, with its emphasis on public works and cheap housing through the Federal Housing Authority.

Broadacre City was Wright's reply to Le Corbusier's plan and was his own version of the English Garden City. The Usonian house became the basic residential unit for Broadacre, where every person would have an acre of land and enjoy freedom and space, in a decentralized, human environment, combining the best of urban and rural worlds.

In ancient cities, like Siena, the city plan was as instinctive and organic as the arteries of a living organism. Man's internal shift from his instinctive center to the left brain was expressed by the nineteenth-century engineer-surveyor's invention of the modern gridiron plan, with its mechanical, repetitive city blocks—itself a negation of traffic flow. The modern city is a product of man's mind, a concrete example of greed, commerce and soulless efficiency. It is overcrowded, with its traffic reduced to gridlock, its air polluted, its ghettos breeding crime and the homeless.

Wright saw that Japan and China, as with all great cultures, drew their marvelous art from a profound rapport with nature. Now, divorced from their roots, they have lost it. When asked to help save his Imperial Hotel from being destroyed to make way for a bland International-style hotel, he said, "No, the Japan I knew and loved no longer exists."

Perhaps because people in modern cities are isolated from nature—their center moved from the intuitive to the rational—their ancient sensitivities for nature have atrophied. They have become alienated from the landscape and its gods.

"God made the country, man made the city."
Spanish proverb

As people are products of nature, their health and vision depend on their roots in the earth. Without nature people lose their balance.

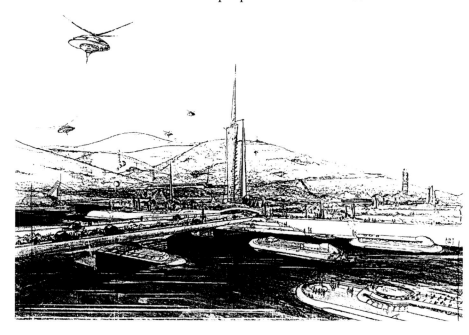

Broadacre City

81

Broadacre would restore the balance: living in the country and working in a human-scale natural environment. Now, at a time when there is a massive migration from the country to the city, Broadacre would restore the balance and provide a healthy alternative. As it was designed to utilize the mobility of the automobile, today it would be even more possible. With modern communications, computer, fax, and the advent of small high-tech industries, the decentralized city is possible and desirable. Already decentralized communities built around Silicon Valley and the San Francisco Bay successfully exist. In England, Finland and throughout the world, decentralized communities combining housing and light industry in a country setting are being built. Broadacre City is eminently possible today.

Broadacre City featured one-acre lots on a grid, but this was only a starting point. The model was designed as modular, both for convenience in its transportation and for flexibility for future developments.

Wright saw that the unimaginative surveyor's gridiron plan was oriented to the north, not because of human needs, but to suit only the surveyor's convenience—his compass pointed north. Wright, perceiving that this denied the sun to everyone on a north-facing block, tilted the axis of Broadacre 30 degrees to admit sunlight to more rooms. In later years, as Wright continued his journey through the geometric archetypes, his site plans changed to reflect their angular and circular forms. In the following years, the **Usonia 1 Project, Lansing, Michigan,** which included the **Goetsch-Winckler House,** was representative of several projected Usonian communities: **Usonia Homes, Pleasantville, New York; Galesburg Country Homes,** and **Parkwyn Village,** near Kalamazoo, Michigan, were among other built or projected communities. The first task of the newly formed

Left: plan for Broadacre City;
Right: Usonia I

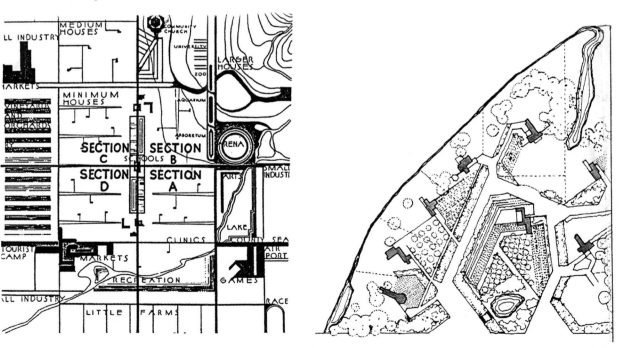

Goetsch-Winckler House

Fellowship was to build a giant model of Broadacre City which would be exhibited in Pittsburgh and in Rockefeller Center, New York City.

Over his lifetime, Wright's prodigious output of some 1,300 designs created all the vital elements to build Broadacre City, ranging from a simple gas station to a mile-high tower. As with Rodin's *Gates of Hell,* Broadacre became emblematic of his *oeuvre.* Tafel says that Wright would ask him "to make a couple of prairie houses" to add to the model.

The Usonian houses continued to evolve, becoming ever more perfect: the roofs hovered without visible support while the cantilevers extended even farther, challenging the limits of economical wood construction. Supervising one such house, Tafel secretly added a steel beam to the plans to stiffen the structure, but the preppy apprentice refused Tafel's advice and the wood beam collapsed. Wright responded, "It's not possible; it worked on the other house!" Whereupon, Edgar Tafel confessed. Wright was so irate he said "You're fired!" Taking Tafel to the train station, Olgivanna exclaimed to him, "Oh, Edgar, how could you!" Tafel explained the situation, adding, "Better it collapse far away than locally." When Mr. Wright returned, Olgivanna said, "Frank, I don't want to hear any more about it, the matter is closed."

THE ESTABLISHMENT AND THE REBEL

In the Great Depression of 1929 Wright's name was rarely heard; his career was considered in eclipse. He was surviving through writing and lecturing.

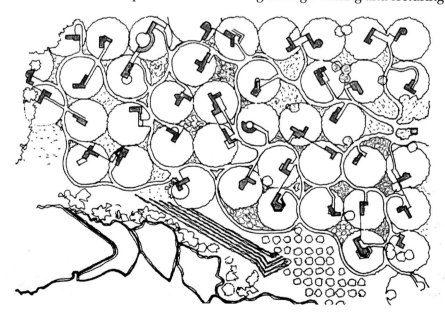

Galesburg Country Homes proposed site plan

In 1930, Wright gave the Khan Lectures at Princeton. At age 62 he could have accepted his place as an icon in the pantheon of architecture, rested on his laurels and retired as a grand old man. Always the revolutionary, Wright refused to join the Establishment (academia or the American Institute of Architects), nor would he worship its gods. He paid the penalty and was ostracized. (When an A.I.A. fact-finding committee visited the aftermath of the Tokyo earthquake, its report omitted any mention of the survival of Wright's quakeproof Imperial Hotel.) As with Orestes in Sartre's *The Flies,* who refused to worship the god Zeus and paid the penalty of persecution by the Furies, so Wright was denigrated by the media Furies with character assassination. The Establishment and the media would invariably describe and dismiss Wright as a good architect in his youth, but now an arrogant, cantankerous old man.

But instead of retreating from the media, Wright had now discovered how to turn the tables on them, how to use the media to his own advantage as a ready-made megaphone, in order to reach the public. In the manner of another Celt, George Bernard Shaw, he could be counted on to make witty and outrageous statements that appealed to their hearers. Asked what he thought could be done to improve Boston, he replied, "Bury it!" The public enjoyed his candor.

Under Olgivanna's influence, 1932 saw the creation of Wright's *An Autobiography.* She was a good psychologist. She knew the best way for him to exorcise the ghosts of the past was to write it all down. For the first time the world had the opportunity to read Wright's own version of the complex life he experienced from within. It is a remarkable book, filled with deep, almost unfathomable insights into the creativity, complexity and tragedy of his life. In place of the worm's-eye view of the gossip press, this story of his life, thoughts and philosophy revealed his character and strength in a new light and attracted the attention of a new breed of individualistic clients who would choose him for his independent thought and integrity.

Some of these personal insights can be found in his letter to Jens Jensen, 1928: "The only difference between Olgivanna and myself is that she believes that the creative instinct is the original birthright of mankind and in most of them it lies dead . . . by proper treatment it may be revived. I too believe . . . but that owing to his betrayal of himself, he has sterilized himself . . . this creative instinct dead in most . . . three-fifths of humanity lacks any power of that kind. Now I believe the creative instinct in Man is that quality . . . of getting himself reborn into everything he does, everything he really works with. By means of it he has got the gods if not God. It is his imagination that is chiefly the tool with which this force or faculty in him works.

"By putting a false premium upon will and intellect he has done this injury upon himself . . . Now how to get it back—this quality of Man—back again to men . . . That, Jens, is why I am interested in this proposed school. I should like to be one to initiate steps that would put a little experimental station at work where this thing might be wooed and won, if only to a small extent. I know it cannot be taught."

At the age of 64, then considered retirement age, with only three projects built in the last seven years, Wright was resigned to the fact that his career was over. He would start his own school.

THE TALIESIN FELLOWSHIP, 1932

Out of the influence of Olgivanna came the birth of the Taliesin Fellowship in 1932, which used the old Hillside School for its first apprentice students. Although some of the new apprentices, like Edgar Tafel, could pay only part of their tuition fee, Wright accepted them.

Wright wanted to develop architects who would understand, continue and expand the work of organic architecture. He sought a way to transmit his own discovery of the creative process to a new apprentice, so that in the daily relationship with genius some invisible spark might ignite the sleeping potential of youth into a new creative individuality.

Before he had married, Wright's organization had been rather like when he was working on Midway Gardens, with his son John, his draftsmen and others, who would all sleep in the construction shack, maintaining very much of a masculine architectural group.

Wright's primary concern was architecture, and he was too busy to handle the day-to-day activities of the Fellowship. The structure of the Fellowship was in many ways the responsibility of Olgivanna. A confluence of two streams of energy, two different concepts of Taliesin, led sometimes to certain contradictions in its operations.

Olgivanna had been a member of Gurdjieff's School for the Harmonious Development of Man, and her idea of the Fellowship was modeled on her own experience at Gurdjieff's Institute at the Prieure, outside Paris, in the early 1920s. Other members there included Peter Ivan Ouspenski, well known for his book *Tertium Organum*, and writer Katherine Mansfield.

Gurdjieff, an Armenian, was a remarkable teacher with an extraordinary insight into the human condition. The Zen teacher Alan Watts called him "the rogue saint." He was a shaman, a trickster—a magician with a lust for life. One of the first Westerners to visit the Potola monastery in Tibet, he had been deeply involved in Sufi and Oriental teachings on the development of human consciousness. He said that most people were mechanical, asleep, but in this dream state thought themselves awake. His teaching was to awaken the seven primary centers in the student into a heightened consciousness, to develop a true individuality. Gurdjieff differentiated between personality and essence: the former was a product of social and cultural conditioning, which prevented the development of essence or true individuality.

At his school the students lived as a community, doing all the necessary work as a part of their education. An overdeveloped intellectual or aristocrat might find himself cleaning out the pigsties, or scrubbing the old floors with steel wool. (Or on the garbage detail, as happened to me at Taliesin.) In many ways the structure of the Taliesin Fellowship followed similar lines.

Wright experienced firsthand Gurdjieff's methods at their first meeting in New York. Olgivanna arranged a meeting between the two most important

Wright at the drawing board

men in her life, her teacher (Gurdjieff) and her husband. Arriving at Gurdjieff's apartment at the appointed hour, the Wrights were told by a secretary to wait, that Mr. Gurdjieff would be ready in a moment. Time passed and the secretary returned with yet another apology for the delay. Finally, Wright, not used to waiting, his patience exhausted, flew into a rage. At this moment Gurdjieff appeared. "I'm sorry," he said. "I had no idea you were here!" Wright looked at him and burst into laughter: "Thank you, I needed that!"

Both Wright and Gurdjieff had been deeply influenced by the East and their philosophies were merged into the very structure of the Taliesin Fellowship. Wright called Gurdjieff "a truly organic man." When Wright suffered from kidney stones, Gurdjieff prepared him a meal composed of such hot spices that Wright told Olgivanna that this might be the last time she would see him. Next morning, however, he awakened cured. Later, when the doctor told Wright to give up coffee, Gurdjieff claimed it was safe if taken with lemon. Fellow architect Bruce Pfeiffer and I ordered coffee with lemon in a Scottsdale cafe. We discovered the lemon precipitated the caffeine to the bottom, but alas, it also destroyed the flavor.

APPRENTICE LIFE AT TALIESIN

Mrs. Wright was responsible for the day-to-day organization, the formation of work groups. Around her were the people interested in her philosophy as well as personal friends. Around Wright were Gene Masselink, secretary; Wes Peters, Wright's son-in-law, who was an architect, engineer and crew chief; Jack Howe, who was Wright's head draftsman for more than twenty years; and about a dozen "senior apprentices." They had the authority to be in charge of work groups but it was all very informal. No one had an official title.

Wright's idea of the apprentice was supposedly based on the Renaissance concept of master/apprentice, where learning is by doing (and perhaps also by osmosis). I suspect, though, that it was closer to the Zen master/disciple relationship, where individual creativity is awakened through the interaction with a remarkable presence. Certainly those apprentices who chose a literal copying of Wright's forms achieved little, while those whose creational genius was sparked off by Taliesin were the ones who achieved their own individual expression of architecture. Wright's holistic approach to education was that to be a good architect you must become a complete person. As with Jung's "integrated personality," intellect, emotion, intuition and sensation must all be activated.

"Great architecture contains the masculine and feminine, all the aspects of man. A great building, like a great cathedral, expresses the full range of the human being," Wright said. (Although he would describe the Larkin Building as masculine, it sired the feminine Johnson Wax Building.) He saw the modern architect as fragmented. In many architects the intellect was overdeveloped, creating only ingenious systems and ideologies, which lacked human scale and needs. In no way was Taliesin similar to the contemporary, technocratic, systems-based architectural school. Humans' centers include thinking, feeling, instinct, intuition, sex, rhythm and movement.

What Wright was trying to convey to us—and to nurture—was his own insight and experience of nature that he had learned working on the farm: his sensibility for nature, for the site and for the nature of materials.

In one book on Wright, the writer dismisses the ancient Japanese affinity with nature as pantheism, thereby denying half the cultures of the world, including the Native American Indian, whose sacred regard for the earth preserved the American landscape. For every artist and architect, a sensitivity to the spirit of place, the site, the stone, the tree, is essential.

During one Sunday talk, an apprentice asked Wright about his Welsh roots. Wright replied: "That old Welsh Mabinogion, the triad . . . King Arthur's Round Table . . . Genius means the inner nature of the thing. A genius is a man who has an eye to see nature . . . A genius is a man with the heart to feel nature . . . A genius is a man with the courage to follow nature."

Ultimately the architect's expression depends on the depth of his sensibility and Taliesin was established to develop a fully balanced man in which working with the actual materials and processes of architecture was an essential part. Wright wanted us, by working with our hands, to experience the unique quality of materials: wood, brick and stone. Ed, the old Welsh mason, taught us to feel the grain of the stone, and how to lay it.

Entering the famous drafting room at Taliesin East at night was quite dramatic. A dark forest of oak truss beams loomed above our heads. Suspended beneath the beams hovered some Taliesin red (a terra cotta color) light tracks, which Wright had acquired from the Museum of Modern Art when they had an exhibition of his work. There were just these spots in the darkness directed down onto the forty drawing boards. At the end of the room was a big fire of oak logs burning, and on the stone lintel were inscriptions. There were maxims inscribed on the beams in the Hillside School also, and one of Wright's favorites was "As a man does, a man is." This was the cozy end of the room, where Wright liked to work. In the mornings we would know he was approaching, because around 10 o'clock we would hear him as he came down the corridor, clearing his throat. It was the cue that the master was appearing.

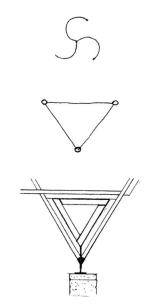

(top to bottom)
Celtic form, Celtic triad and truss frame

THE SORCERER'S APPRENTICE

One day I discovered a tiny secret staircase leading up to a mezzanine above the drafting room. One could look down through the forest of trusses. This became my private space, where I could leaf through the yellow tracing-paper sketches by Wright. I had always taken for granted Wright's clean, sweeping architectural roofs but became increasingly curious about what happened to the vent pipes, the furnace flues, gutters, and downspouts that clutter ordinary buildings. Here were the archives containing the techniques, craft and magic of a lifetime: groupings of pipes, chimneys incorporating heating flues and ducts, steel "flitch" plates to stiffen timber beams and cantilevers. The apprentice was beginning to learn some of the sorcerer's secrets.

In the drafting room there were rows of drafting tables for the Fellowship. The tables were Wright's design: very angular, simply constructed from a sheet of plywood, with crossed legs and plywood gussets which were painted red. The tops had a permanent slope and were just big enough for one large sheet of paper. Each of us had a toolbox under the table where we kept our drawing instruments. Wright was very critical of gadgetry; he believed in T-squares, not drafting machines. A 45-degree triangle and a 30/60-degree one were all we needed, along with a circle template and a compass; and we used Fs, HBs, and a soft Eagle drafting pencil on yellow trace for all the sketches.

In the studio were several lists of recommendations. One was for the colored pencils used in the Taliesin style of rendering, which consisted mainly of horizontal lines. For the grass we were enjoined to use "grass green"; for the trees another green. There was also a technique that used dots to show the curves in a circular building. We were self-taught. That was the Taliesin way. If you didn't want to do anything, nobody would press you. We learned from our fellow apprentices, many of whom were very experienced as architects, and from the seniors—the half dozen or so architects who

assisted Wright. A senior might come and ask you to help detail something, perhaps for a house that should have been ready that night. After a few months an apprentice could be working on details for live projects, but always as a junior member of a team. To work directly for Wright you had to be there for several years, unless you were highly qualified.

WRIGHT'S WORKING METHOD

Contractors were frequently calling up to say, "How can I build this house? There are no dimensions." A typical Usonian house would be laid out on a module, maybe 3 × 6 feet or 4-foot square, and the grid lines were numbered vertically in one direction and alphabetically in the other. All one had to do was to refer to and measure from the appropriate grid coordinate. However, a lot of contractors, and even some local architects, couldn't get the hang of a set of plans with few dimensions.

Wright's plans were bold and simple; he did not believe in endlessly complex details. At Taliesin, after breakfast, there would either be a list on the wall of things you were supposed to do for the next week, or else one of the seniors would be looking for volunteers to pour concrete or to cope with one crisis or another. During my first week at Taliesin East I was assigned each morning to a work party. I didn't realize yet that, as in the army, you have to learn to disappear to survive, because there is always one more emergency work party, and you would never have time to go to the drafting room or brush your teeth if you were always available. But being a new boy, and feeling fresh, I discovered that I was assigned to a work party down on the farm, and it was our job to repair the earth dam for the lake Wright had created. We went out in the cold wintry morning to cut rolls of turf to patch the erosion. I came from a big city; now I was experiencing directly the feeling of the grass, the nature of the earth. Each load weighed about 100 pounds and it was hard work. Afterward I said as much to one of the other apprentices. He laughed and told me that every year the dam leaks, and every year the new boys patch it up with turf.

FIRE

Hillside School, an early progressive school Wright had built for his aunts, was down the road from Taliesin East, and was used as the Fellowship school of architecture. Shortly before I came to Taliesin, its theater caught fire. Most of the apprentices were away on a farm project. Alarmed by a rising column of smoke, the apprentices ran toward the building to find the theater in flames. Nearby they found Mr. Wright sitting on a salvaged chair, already sketching the new theater design. With few regrets, he had seized the destruction of the old as the opportunity to design the new.

A problem as first-year students was to find the time to get to the drafting room. One morning the word suddenly went around that the clay tiles had arrived: after the fire, the theater and dining areas needed a new roof. Wright, a masterly showman, had called up one of the tile manufacturers and persuaded them what an excellent advertisement it would be if their tiles were used on the roof. And he was prepared to do that for them if they would provide the tiles free. An enormous semitrailer arrived, with thousands of tiles. We formed a human chain, probably 30 or 40 of us, catching the tiles and throwing them from the stack right up to the roof. The new theater roof had an enormous cantilever which reached out to just touch a large tree: very romantic. Closer inspection, however, revealed that the cantilever was in fact nailed to the trunk of the tree.

Taliesin was completely run by the apprentices. There were no servants, contractors, or state financing. The boys did every sort of building work for the school, and Taliesin was built and maintained by the apprentices. Some specialized in carpentry, joinery, plumbing, or electrical or concrete work.

The apprentices made the tables and furniture for Wright's Plaza Hotel apartment in New York. In the Taliesin workshop I was assigned to the group making the drafting tables and stools for this apartment. These were made from ¾-inch Douglas fir plywood in the form of intersecting planes, finished in matte black lacquer, which rather shocked me, as I preferred and expected the expression of natural wood finish. Each coat of lacquer had to be rubbed down with steel wool. The steel wool got under my fingernails and was unpleasant. Was I getting the Gurdjieff treatment?

I was busy working when suddenly I had a premonition that I was going to see Mr. Wright. My conscious mind said no, there was no reason to see him, and at that moment an apprentice came and said, "Mr. and Mrs. Wright want to see you." I joined two other apprentices and we were nervous, not knowing what it was about, but suspecting it might have to do with our reputation for being a bit too rebellious and independent. Sure enough, when we reached the meeting we were roundly criticized for our behavior by Mrs. Wright: we were not showing the right attitude (specific charges were not leveled). When she had finished, she looked to Mr. Wright, and obviously it was now his turn to discipline us. But equally obvious was that Mr. Wright was quite baffled about what the meeting was for. One of the boys said something about his being a conscientious objector against the army and authority, and Wright's face lit up with understanding. He boomed at us that he had been a conscientious objector all his life against the cultural establishment and authority. He spoke against the tyranny of easel painting and how a good architectural wall should never be cluttered by hanging Renaissance paintings on it. He talked about the correct relationship between the arts and the "Mother Art," architecture. We sat for an hour, enthralled by this private discourse on architecture. Everyone had long forgotten the original purpose of the meeting.

I remember finishing the last piece of furniture, outside, just as the first snow was beginning to fall at Taliesin East. It was time for the migration to Taliesin West: already most people had left. We finally shipped them off and awaited Wright's comments. Word eventually filtered back: "OK, but we need more." What Wright did with all this stuff we never found out. Years later I saw photographs of the furniture in his Plaza apartment in a book on Wright's life in New York.

One day I met Wright outside the drafting room. He had a keenly perceptive eye. Observing my English reserve, he said: "Son, to be an architect you cannot be an introvert. An architect must be extrovert, salesman, psychologist, diplomat, designer and builder." He knew, painfully, how difficult it was to sell an avant-garde project to a new client. With an uncanny sense of timing, he could seduce any client with his charm and forceful aura. When all else failed, he could be alternately humble, arrogant, innocent, guileful and endlessly patient. Demanding perfection, he could be as temperamental as a Karajan and had little tolerance for stupidity or incompetence. Anyone who tampered with his design would get short shrift, becoming the object of a powerful burst of anger.

One of the secrets of his success was his immediate, unequivocal response to the false. With a quick temper, he had a tendency to say what he felt, to shoot from the hip. On one occasion some seniors decided that a kitchen in Taliesin East had become tacky and worn out. Someone had the bright idea to give Mr. Wright a surprise. They had completely rebuilt the kitchen in his private quarters, working day and night so the kitchen was exactly as they thought he would like it. When Mr. Wright returned, he walked into the kitchen, took one angry look, and rhetorically demanded: "Who is the god-damn architect around here, anyway? You're fired!"

Olgivanna, in her feminine role as mother and peacemaker, would calm him down. "Oh Frank," she would say, "You can't fire them, we need them, it was all a misunderstanding!" He would be mollified and his anger would evaporate. The next day he would forget the incident.

Even with his friend Alexander Woollcott, the drama critic, he could get carried away in argument. The next day, filled with remorse, he would send a gift of some Japanese prints to Woollcott accompanied by a note and joke of apology.

TRICKSTER

No quotation of Wright does justice to, nor can it convey, his great sense of humor. The blood of the legendary trickster, Gwion Bach, still coursed in his veins, and particularly through the mischievous twinkle in his eye. (In American Indian myth, too, the trickster is an important character for change. Bach was Taliesin's original incarnation, the trickster who stole the witch's brew and was transformed by it into a magician.)

One afternoon Wright and apprentice Edgar Tafel were cutting branches from a street tree for decoration at Taliesin's Saturday night party. A woman came up to them and demanded to know what they were doing. "Madam," Wright replied, "we are taking samples for the department of agriculture!"

THE APPRENTICE GAMBLER

A rich man's son arrived at Taliesin in 1938 at a time when, as usual, there was a shortage of funds. Gene Masselink, the artist who also functioned as secretary and soulmate, asked him for the important $1,500 for tuition. "I want to see Mr. Wright first," was the reply. "No, first the money and then Mr. Wright," said Masselink. Finally, Mr. Wright appeared and the young man told his story. "On the way here I passed through Las Vegas and I thought it would be fun to try a little gambling at the casino. Well, first I won, but then I began to lose and I saw my tuition going down the drain, so I made one last attempt to recover my money—and lost it all!" There was a pregnant pause. Mr. Wright said, "Son, tell me just one thing. If you had to do it all over again what would you do?" The young man thought for a moment, and said, "Well, I guess I would do it just the same way." Mr. Wright smiled and said, "OK, you're in."

ANTHONY QUINN

Anthony Quinn, as a young man, wanted to study architecture at Taliesin and had an interview with Wright, who said, "You can never be a successful architect unless you can communicate well with a client—and you have a speech defect. Your speech is unintelligible because of the ligaments tied beneath your tongue. I can give you the name of a surgeon who can fix them so that you can speak properly." (Wright was a fund of knowledge.) Quinn had the operation and afterward went to a voice therapy class to learn to speak properly. There he met several actors and realized he wanted to be one too.

OLGIVANNA'S ROLE

One weekend we were told that Henry and Clare Boothe Luce, the publishers of *Life* and *Time* magazines, were coming. Possibly remembering some previous incident, Olgivanna warned us against attacking them with our liberal ideas. At the time we thought she was unduly apprehensive. Only later did I realize that her role at Taliesin was as both wife and mother. She had to see that the Fellowship kept going, could pay its bills and attract new clients. This meant hosting prospective clients and important people, to ensure publicity and new projects. Wright told me he had to earn over $50,000 a year to run Taliesin (equivalent to $500,000 today).

Some people found Olgivanna difficult. Probably her own early experiences fleeing the revolution in Russia, being jailed and threatened with deportation and vilified by the U.S. media as a foreign adventuress had left her apprehensive and suspicious of strangers.

RULES AGAIN

The different approaches taken by Wright and Olgivanna were evident, for example, when apprentice Jeremy was called before them because she claimed he had a wrong attitude. Mr. Wright still seemed unclear as to what the problem was, so Mrs. Wright explained: "Frank, he doesn't want to follow the rules!"

"Rules," boomed Mr. Wright, "there are no rules. When you have rules you start with policemen, judges and end up building jails! And there are not going to be any jails in Taliesin. There are no rules as long as I'm around."

Although we sometimes worked hard, like humble "slaves," as some critics claimed, we were treated as part of Wright's extended family and felt privileged to work and learn from the Master himself. Even though I was on a scholarship, paying nothing for board and tuition, I was treated no differently from anyone else. Indeed, I doubt if anyone knew of my status. We were older than the average college student. A number of us were graduates or had already worked in architecture. Like most students we were a high-spirited bunch with minds of our own. If we felt like going to a late-night movie or a local bar, we went. We didn't need to ask permission.

CAMELOT

During the summer Taliesin became an open house for musicians, writers and artists in residence. Frequent guests were the poet Carl Sandburg, the writer Alexander Woollcott, the actor Charles Laughton and the architect Erich Mendelsohn. Wright enjoyed the company of fertile minds. There were no barriers and we apprentices were considered a part of Wright's extended family.

Taliesin had become a Camelot for architecture. Almost every major foreign architect visiting America made it a part of his pilgrimage.

A Taliesin joke ran that if Wright was King Arthur, then certainly Wes Peters, 6'4" tall and his favorite apprentice, was Sir Lancelot. In 1933, Wes fell in love with Wright's sixteen-year-old stepdaughter Svetlana. Forbidden by the Wrights to marry, they eloped one night and for two years were exiled from Taliesin. Life, with irony, had reversed Wright's roles; no longer the rebel, he was now the authority. With the birth of their son two years later, they became reconciled with the Wrights and returned to Taliesin.

Wright thought he had reached the end of his architectural career, but instead, the Usonian house, Broadacre City and the Fellowship heralded his hearty rebirth. Wright said, "A change is as good as a rest." When his mind was exhausted he turned to physical work and chopped wood.

Wright in his studio at Taliesin East

The Fifth Age
TRIAXIAL SPACE

FALLINGWATER, THE HILLSIDE CASCADE

FOR MORE THAN A DECADE WRIGHT had remained submerged in the public consciousness. Then, with the publicity created by his autobiography and the creation of the Taliesin Fellowship, Wright's name was introduced to a new generation of Americans.

Wright's clients came through an invisible network of friends, clients, family and admirers. Empathetic with his work, they were a kind of collective unconscious. As in the allegorical *The Fisherman and the Genie*, it was a net that would trawl in a few new clients, and a genie.

A friend introduced Wright's book to Edgar Kaufmann, Jr. By reading *An Autobiography* young Kaufmann opened the door to a totally new direction to his life and an extraordinary adventure into architecture. Soon after visiting Wright he joined the Taliesin Fellowship. Intelligent and open to the new, Edgar, in his incarnation as youth, was destined to be the genie who would make the miraculous possible.

Edgar introduced Wright to his father, E. J. Kaufmann, Sr., wealthy owner of a Pittsburgh department store, not unlike a Venetian merchant prince—rich, successful and autocratic. Wright responded with an equally aristocratic manner. As equals they hit it off: Michelangelo had met his patron and shortly afterward E. J. Kaufmann sponsored an exhibition of Broadacre City in New York and at his store in Pittsburgh.

E. J. Kaufmann owned 2,000 acres of virgin land, some 60 miles south of Pittsburgh, that he used for a weekend retreat. His greatest pleasure was to walk and relax in nature. Taking Wright up to the site, he asked him to design a second home. They hiked all over the hills, ravines and forest looking for a site until Wright asked E. J., "What is your favorite spot?"

E. J. showed Wright the enormous boulder on which he liked to sit and meditate, looking down to the cascade and the glen below. Wright had found the key to E. J.'s world.

Wright was presented with a landscape as dramatic and as beautiful as the failed McCormick project; it was an extraordinary site that challenged the full extent of his imagination. With his uncanny sense of the *genius loci*, his photographic eye for its contours and forms, his empathy with the landscape, he absorbed it all: trees, rhododendrons, rock ledges, and above all the primal element of water. Water cascaded down its liquid stairway,

"Fallingwater has always been rightly considered one of the complete masterpieces of twentieth-century art."
Vincent Scully, Yale University

Fallingwater

interacting between rocks and trees, refracting the forest light and the sky above. The silence of the forest glade was broken by the sound of the stream and the cascade.

"Can you say, when your building is complete, that the landscape is more beautiful than it was before?" Wright challenged us.

Wright wanted a house that was not a conquest of nature but a symbiotic embrace, as integral a part of the landscape as the surrounding trees.

On his return to Taliesin he requested Kaufmann to send him a site survey showing contours and the location of the waterfall and certain rocks and trees. For several months nothing was to happen.

GERMINATION

Wright scorned those architects who, designing elevations and plans on a two-dimensional drawing board, attempt to create three-dimensional space out of two-dimensional images.

For Wright the inner vision of a project first took form in his mind. He said, "One must be able to walk around and inside the structure, know every detail, before putting pencil to paper . . . I never sit down to a drawing board—and this has been a lifelong practice of mine—until I have the whole thing in my mind. I may alter it substantially, I may throw it away, I may find I'm up a blind alley; but unless I have the idea of the thing pretty well in shape, you won't see me at a drawing board with it. But all the time I have it, it's germinating, between three o'clock and four o'clock in the morning—somehow nature has provided me with an hour or more of what might be called insight . . . so this design matter is not something to do with a drawing board. It is something that you do as you work, as you play. You may get it in the middle of the tennis court and drop your racket and run off and put it down. That is the kind of thing it is. It is fleeting, it is evanescent. It's up here where you have to be quick and take it."

The whole complex triaxial concept of Fallingwater, with all of its levels, cross cantilevers and interspatial relationships was taking form in his imagination before he put pencil to paper. It is a measure of the magnitude of his mind that he could hold this whole complex spatial structure in his imagination, adding to it day after day, clarifying the details, its relationship to the site, before committing it to paper. Wright, with cool head and incredible patience, was waiting until his vision, complete in every detail, was ready for birth. Wright's associates were nervous. Since his trip to the site, the summer before, nothing had appeared on the drawing board.

In the fall E. J. Kaufmann telephoned to say he would be traveling in the vicinity of Taliesin and asked Wright how the plans were progressing. Wright responded, "We are ready for you." A little later E. J. called from Milwaukee to say that in a few hours he would drop by to see the plans.

With only a few hours left before Kaufmann was due, Wright sat down by the plot plan on the drafting board and began to draw. My friend Edgar Tafel, who was assisting apprentice, described the actual passage from Wright's imagination to the drawing board: "First floor plan. Second floor. Section, elevations. Side sketches of details, talking sotto voce all the while.

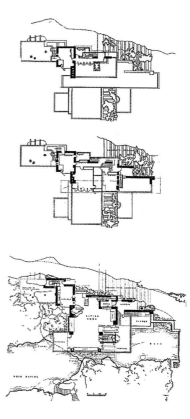

Fallingwater plans

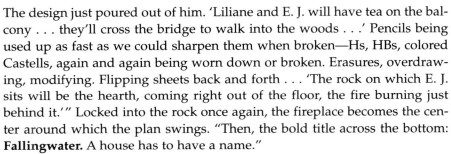

stairs at Fallingwater

concrete beam detours tree

The design just poured out of him. 'Liliane and E. J. will have tea on the balcony . . . they'll cross the bridge to walk into the woods . . .' Pencils being used up as fast as we could sharpen them when broken—Hs, HBs, colored Castells, again and again being worn down or broken. Erasures, overdrawing, modifying. Flipping sheets back and forth . . . 'The rock on which E. J. sits will be the hearth, coming right out of the floor, the fire burning just behind it.'" Locked into the rock once again, the fireplace becomes the center around which the plan swings. "Then, the bold title across the bottom: **Fallingwater.** A house has to have a name."

In front of the apprentices, Fallingwater began to take shape. They were entranced and amazed: the house was cantilevered over the waterfall itself. Tiered balconies spread in all directions. The architecture seemed to be an extension of the natural rock ledges and the falling cascade. It was breathtaking.

E. J. Kaufmann arrived just as Wright finished. Unaware of the drama that preceded him, he studied the drawing. He said, "I didn't realize it would be so close to the waterfall."

Wright responded, "I want you to be of the waterfall." He shrewdly took Kaufmann off to lunch, giving the draftsman apprentices time to complete the other elevations.

The vertical masonry mass emerging from the bedrock soars like an ascending tree to the sky above. From it, balanced and anchored in the rock, issues a succession of horizontal planes, roofs and balconies, like the branches of the surrounding trees. Wright had discovered that the relationship between horizontal planes generates energy, and now he discovered

Fallingwater

another energy, a different resonance, created by the counterpoint between the horizontal and vertical elements of triaxial space. Fallingwater represents a quantum leap in Wright's understanding of space, the full flowering of Wright's spatial imagination.

Drawing its inspiration from the stepped rock ledges that define the landscape, the stepped principle of the descending hillside cascade creates the form of Fallingwater, transforming its image into a multilayered structure of inner and outer space: becoming an integral part of the landscape, echoing the vertical trees, the horizontal branches, the ascending foliage, the descending cascade, the rhythm of the forest. A suspended stairway leads up from the stream below to the living room above. The structure steps back to match the hill, forming layers of terraces toward the sun.

Wright wanted a "natural house," built in nature for the natural man, who himself "shall be like a tree planted by the rivers of water." He played his love of technology against his love of nature: a pergola of concrete beams ties the rear of the house to the hillside, a concrete beam detours around a tree. The corners of the concrete parapets are softly rounded. A balcony cantilever is pierced to incorporate three trees and receives additional support from a rock. The fireplace hearth is cut from the living rock, the fireplace walls made from the same stone. A hollow hemisphere of space is cut into the stonework to receive a large spherical pot which swings out over a roaring fire.

In a forest glen, a fire upon a rock. Was it Wright's token to Caridwen's caldron of inspiration?

In his own mind alchemy was transmuting ancient elements into new form. Wright worked in sudden bursts of great energy. When he ran out of inspiration, he lay down in front of the flames of the drafting room fireplace and took a catnap. With a new insight he awakened refreshed and returned to complete the project. If creation is a quantum leap, the technical process is an uphill ramp of working drawings, details, calculations, engineering, and specifications. Wright, using the skills, crafts and tricks of a lifetime, labored to make Fallingwater a practical reality.

CONSTRUCTION

Now begins the complex process of translating the architect's vision into practical reality. At Taliesin working drawings were being completed, and at the site stone was quarried for the walls of the new structure. Using the native stone, the horizontal layers of the ascending walls reflect the natural rock outcroppings. The house would truly be of the site.

When the plans were sent to the steel company for determining the quantities of reinforcing rods required, the engineers were fascinated by the unusual balcony cantilever design. They were used to post and beam structures, where each element is calculated separately, and their figures for the stresses of the floor slab determined that the balcony cantilevers would not work. They sent a report to E. J. warning him that the house could not stand up. He immediately called Wright for his comments. Wright snorted, "Put that letter inside the wall and let posterity decide!"

Analysis takes the whole to pieces to understand its parts. Using synthesis, by fusing the parts together, the whole is stronger than its parts.

Wright used the three-foot-high balcony parapet walls as structural concrete beams, reinforced by the floor diaphragms and cross walls, and by continuing the reinforcing steel into a three-dimensional matrix, combined floor and walls into one integral structure; employing the holistic principle of continuity to distribute the stresses throughout the structure, he folded the concrete slab under the living room to stiffen the cantilevers.

Because of the isolated site, E. J. was forced to employ a local builder with little experience in building a modern reinforced concrete structure. When the time came for the builder to remove the post supporting the forms of the large cantilever balcony, he was so nervous about his poor workmanship he refused. Exasperated, Wright, standing beneath the balcony, demonstrated his faith in his design by grabbing a sledgehammer and knocking out the post.

The audacity of Fallingwater expresses Wright's supreme self-confidence, the fearlessness of youth to challenge and explore the new. As with every champion, it was faith in his own invincibility that made him invincible. Critics would read it as arrogance, but he was not alone: the architect Alvar Aalto said, "I'm the best!" The champion boxer Muhammad Ali proclaimed, "I am the greatest!" Wright's belief in himself was a self-fulfilling prophecy, fueling his victories.

Wright prided himself on his sense of engineering, and when he discovered that the job apprentice had added more steel to a cantilever, he was furious and sent him back to Taliesin.

GRAVITY

The cascade illustrates an invisible but tangible force: gravity, the ancient nemesis of architecture. Fallingwater is about defying gravity.

Like a chessmaster playing three-dimensional chess, Wright carefully placed his pieces on the board, playing gravity against gravity, cantilever against cantilever, horizontal by vertical mass, uplift by downlift. Maneuvering the forces of gravity into a balanced checkmate, Wright, like his "namesake" aviator brothers, demonstrated that gravity can be transcended. In Fallingwater man hovers above the falling water.

The reinforced concrete cantilever was born out of nineteenth-century technology; not all engineers approve of its use. The old Ecole des Beaux

Arts banned the use of the cantilever by students, but the Greek artist Yanko Varda claimed he only had to shout "cantilever!" for every architect in the room to experience an erection.

The engineers, worried about the length of Fallingwater's main cantilever, recommended reducing its span by extending its base wall four feet. E. J. persuaded the apprentice to get the mason to extend the wall, without informing the architect.

His son Edgar said, "Wright himself came around in due course of inspection and said nothing. Another month passed and Wright came again, went over the work with Father, and no word of the wall. At the day's end, over a comfortable drink in the half-finished shell of the house, Father confessed to Wright and said, "'If you've not noticed it in these last two days of inspection, there can't be anything very bad about it, architecturally.'

"'E. J.,' said Wright, 'come with me.' They went out to the spot in question and, behold, the top four inches of the additional wall were gone! 'When I was here last month,' Wright continued, 'I ordered the top layers of stone removed. Now, the terrace has shown no sign of falling. Shall we take down the extra four feet of wall?'"

Edgar was the genie that would make the miraculous possible and bring Fallingwater to a seamless perfection by mediating between his father and Mr. Wright, oiling the wheels, shaking money out of the Kaufmann tree. His understanding of Wright's architecture helped him translate Wright's vision for E. J.'s practical mind. A battle arose with E. J. over the cost of the suspended stair to the stream. With its hatch doors, it was complex and expensive, but Edgar persuaded his father that it was an essential element, linking interior space with the exterior stream below.

On one occasion, Wright, exasperated by E. J.'s foot-dragging attitude, exclaimed, "Fallingwater is too good for you; you don't deserve it!"

E. J., once he understood what Wright was trying to achieve, could be helpful. Wright's concept that the masonry line should continue uninterrupted from interior to exterior appealed to him, and Wright used his suggestion to set the glass flush into a slot in the masonry wall.

To get Fallingwater built, Wright used all his charm, authority, guile and humor, but there was a limit to how far Wright could press E. J. When it came time to choose the color, Wright suggested they cover the concrete in matte gold leaf, like the Golden Temple of Kyoto, Japan. It would have been hauntingly beautiful. E. J. couldn't go so far, and Wright dropped the suggestion and chose a light apricot color.

Wright's mastery of triaxial space is consummated at Fallingwater, where architecture forever defies its former limitations and effortlessly moves into the planes and vertical axis of the forest. The horizontal planes, transverse cantilevers and vertical axis fulfill Wright's vision of a triaxial architecture penetrating space.

Wright later said that Fallingwater "is a great blessing—one of the great blessings to be experienced here on earth."

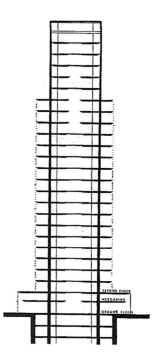

National Life Insurance Company
Skyscraper project

National Life Skyscraper section

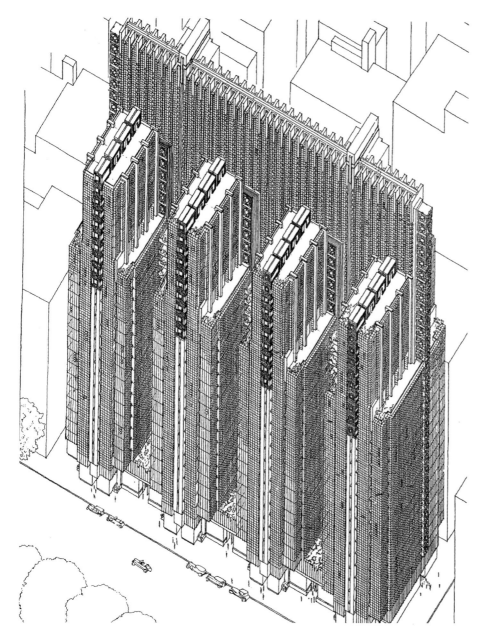

THE VERTICAL TOWERS

Wright's journey to verticality began with his innovative stressed skin, the eighty-foot windmill tower, Romeo and Juliet, and progressed through the Luxfer Prism Project, which expressed the structural frame in its fenestration. It moved on to the thrusting, vertical ribs, sweeping up to a great cantilevered roof, of the San Francisco Press Building Project. The openings in the great roof's overhang, by freeing the flow of space, enhance the feeling of height. But Wright was moving away from the conventional post-and-beam-frame skyscraper and seeking a new technology for spatial freedom.

"Wright felt that the soaring vertical shaft—expressing a line radiating from the earth's center—both defines and defies gravity. In his vertical architecture he sought a new freedom to express Sullivan's 'sense of tallness.'"
D. W. Hoppen

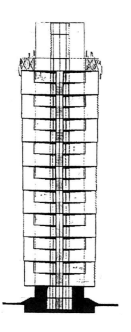

St. Mark's section

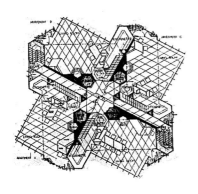

St. Mark's plan

The **National Life Insurance Company Skyscraper Project, Chicago, 1920–1924,** for A. J. Johnson, provided Wright with the time and money to research a new system for a high-rise building.

The traditional building began from the outside facade. What he had done for horizontal architecture, Wright now did for the vertical, stripping away the old system of exterior load-bearing walls and the post-and-beam box frame.

Wright's design began, as he created, from the center, centrifugally, growing and moving out. From the vertical structural core, incorporating elevators, stairs, and services, the floors cantilever out, balanced by reverse cantilevers.

He transformed the old massive exterior wall structural system into a transparent curtain wall of glass and lightweight copper panels, suspended from above. It is a major seminal concept and a beautiful design, a dramatic alternative to the conventional framed building.

Wright was able to show his drawings to his Lieber-Meister shortly before he died. Sullivan said, "I had faith that it would come. It is a work of great art. I knew what I was talking about all these years—you see? I could never have done this building myself, but I believe that, but for me, you could never have done it." Wright said, "I know I should never have reached it, but for what he was and what he himself did. This design is dedicated to him."

CONTINUITY

With the objective eye of a scientist, and the intuitive eye of an artist, Wright penetrated beyond outer beauty to observe the structural systems of nature. He saw in the tree a superb engineering. From its roots locked in the earth, a trunk can cantilever up over two hundred feet high, a branch can cantilever out forty feet. The tree achieves its strength through the continuity of its structural fibers, which, growing along the stress lines, join root to trunk to branch in one indivisible process: the sum is greater than the parts.

Wright used reinforcing rods as his steel fibers to carry the loads from cantilevered floor slabs to vertical core. These rods, bent and encased in concrete, became the tension fibers for the structural plasticity he sought.

THE TRIAXIAL TOWER

Wright finally achieved the "verticality" he sought with **St. Mark's in the Bowery, New York, 1929.** Fresh from the desert, Wright used a triangular grid and Indian swastika plan, expressing centrifugal energy. Inspired by the tall saguaro cactus, he employed its structural ingenuity in the design of the structural folded-plate core incorporating services and elevators.

From its central trunk, cantilevered from the earth, with cross fin-walls, the concrete floors cantilever out, like branches from a tree. Now, freed from exterior structure, the outer skin becomes a suspended curtain wall of glass and copper panels. It is a true triaxial structure, reaching out effortlessly in all dimensions, presaging a new approach and a new age in architecture.

In the **Chicago Towers, 1930,** the **Crystal Heights, Washington, D. C., 1939,** and the **Golden Beacon, Chicago, 1956** projects it evolved further. It

Price Tower

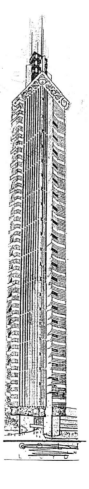

Golden Beacon elevation

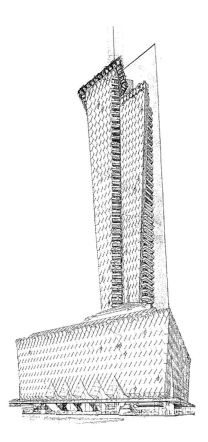

Lacy Hotel elevation

was finally realized as the **Price Tower, Bartlesville, Oklahoma, 1955.** In this constructed version, the four elevations are different, determined by the pattern of the solar vertical and horizontal copper shading fins.

Three of us apprentices, heading for Taliesin, decided to make a detour to visit the Price Tower, then under construction in Bartlesville, Oklahoma. We headed south, making about 400 miles a day along the straight monotonous roads. We arrived just as they had finished pouring the concrete for the Price Tower. Bartlesville at that time was a little town of wood frame houses in the middle of nowhere, and suddenly appeared this great concrete shaft soaring into the sky, looking like a science fiction rocket launching tower. Torroja, the Spanish engineer, was there then, and Joe Price, the owner's son, was supervising, and he had a few problems. The balconies were cantilevered some considerable distance, and a three-foot wall provided part of the structural support—similar to Fallingwater. Where the wall emerged from the main fins of the central support column, some hairline cracks were appearing. Torroja said, "Oh, that's nothing, it's just the steel taking up the slack." Joe told us that when they were pouring concrete into the foundation of the core, there was so much reinforcing steel that the problem was how to get the concrete around the steel.

We shot up in the construction elevator on the side of the tower, and it was just as Wright had envisioned: first the town, its rooftops spread out around, then suddenly the freedom of the surrounding landscape and the view of the horizon for miles around.

Joe Price was a good friend of Bruce Goff, and he had recommended Goff to his father to design a two-story office building for their company. Goff was busy and suggested Wright be asked to do it. So he introduced Price Sr. to Wright, who saw the small-town site as a perfect location for his St. Mark's project, which had never been built. He redesigned the plans as a combination office and apartment tower. The Price family—whose firm produced steel pipes for the oil industry—was very happy and gave Goff an office in it.

Johnson Wax Research Tower, Racine, Wisconsin, 1944. Wright always wanted to complement the Johnson Wax Building with a vertical element and when asked to add a research facility he designed this 14-story tower. A hollow structural core contains the mechanical services, elevator and exhaust ducts. From this core, visible at the first story, cantilever the alternating circular mezzanines and square floors. Fenestration is provided by bands of continuous Pyrex® tubing which wraps around the curved corners. Wright's original scheme showed each floor stepping out beyond the one below to provide a self-cleaning function. As the tower ascends the structure grows outward, creating a dramatic perspective.

Wright said, "one can see in the Japanese pagoda an abstraction of the pine tree." This structure represents his most perfect example of a tree and a taproot foundation.

Rogers Lacy Hotel Project, Dallas, Texas, 1946. Wright, having used the inward-sloping batter wall for Taliesin West, now reversed it to an outward

Johnson Wax Research Tower

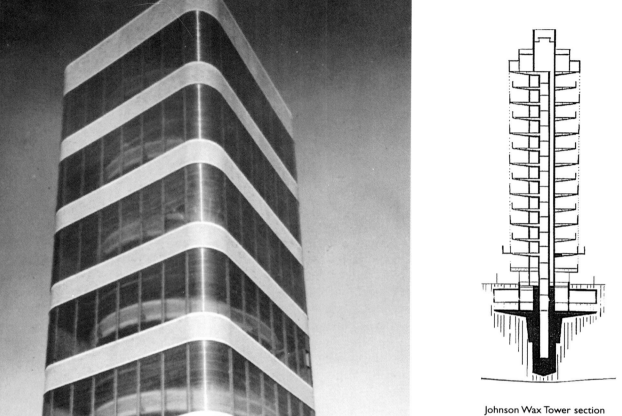

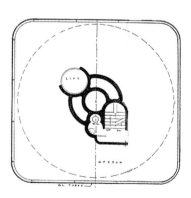

Johnson Wax Tower section

Johnson Wax Tower plan

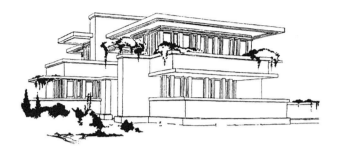

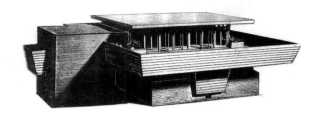

Gale House and Malcolm Willey
House #1 model

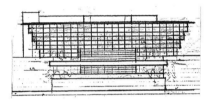

House on the Mesa section

*"The serious architect
comes closer to certain
secrets of nature if he is
master of organic form
than most artists and
even scientists."*
F.LL.W.

slope. Sheathed in magnesium diagonal panels, the Lacy Tower progressively becomes larger as it grows upward from a large inner court.

Olgivanna warned Wright that his design would be imitated and urged him to copyright his design, but he didn't approve of copyright. It was later copied and vulgarized with great success. Edgar Tafel said that when Wright finished the stunning drawing he was overheard to say, sotto voce, "I am a genius." Critics say this proved his conceit, but who hasn't said the same when achieving a breakthrough?

Another side of Wright was shown at the opening of one of his buildings. It rained, the roof leaked, and Wright was overheard saying, "Oh no, not again!" Water was his nemesis, the douche on his ego.

DISCOVERIES

The years of failure, the lean decade 1921–1931, allowed Wright to explore deeply the inner processes of architecture, structure and space. Rich in insights and visions, it was a fertile meditation that engendered his greatest successes.

The **Richard Lloyd Jones House 1 & 2, Tulsa, Oklahoma, 1929.** Fresh from the desert, Wright used the triangle for his angular plan. Too unorthodox for the client, its builder and its time, it was redesigned. Wright, looking for a way to convert the original angular plan to a more conventional right angle, transformed the angular line into a succession of digital steps: replacing the angular terminals of the first plan with a striking series of alternate glazed and masonry steps.

He had discovered the principle of the digital step, and he would take it further in the **Elizabeth Noble Apartments, Los Angeles, 1929.** Wright now moved the digital step into the fenestration elevation and plan, making the transition from large to small spaces through a series of layered steps. This window detail appeared in the **R. Levin House, Kalamazoo, Michigan, 1948.**

It appears strongly in the upwardly expanding profile of **The House on the Mesa, 1932.** This design demonstrates a new openness to light and

space. A vast living room is contained within a great window, which in profile becomes a series of rising steps, projecting outward. This window detail was realized in the **Walker House, Carmel, California, 1948.**

QUANTUM LEAP: DIGITAL STEP, ANALOG RAMP

Man's discoveries in science and art seem to parallel one another, as if both aspects of the mind, the scientific and the artistic, represent only different views of the same process.

Wright discovered the digital step in architecture, shortly before science discovered the same principle in the architecture of subatomic physics: "That a linear increase (a ramp) of electric current produced a digital (stepped) quantum increase in the resultant magnetic field." This discovery led to the Nobel Prize in science in 1933.

These principles, digital and analog, step and ramp, represent two expressions of the same energy.

The **H. Price, Sr., House, Paradise Valley, Arizona, 1954,** is a remarkable demonstration of a Roman villa reborn into the twentieth century. In the covered atrium with its central fountain, digital columns expand in a series of steps as they ascend. At the apex a slender steel shaft supports a vast, hovering roof plane. The materials are basic twentieth-century: standard concrete block, steel I beams, Heraclith® roof panels. Hinged decorative plywood screens allow the space to be closed when necessary.

THE VERTICAL HILLSIDE HOUSE

These converging discoveries: abstract form, structural core, cantilevered floor, roof, plane, balcony, and digital step, finally came together in the project of the first **Malcolm Willey House, Minneapolis, 1932,** revealing Wright's new solution for the hillside house.

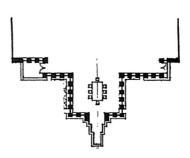

Richard Lloyd Jones plan

From a masonry mass emerging from the hillside cantilevers a large balcony. Continuous bands of windows and French doors open to the balcony and the view beyond. The balcony is framed by a band of stepped horizontal boards that progressively project outward. This detail of lapped digital boards appears hereafter as virtually a standard detail, in the balcony and frequently in the ceiling, in his residential projects.

In his early work, as in the Ross House, Wright's solution for a house on a sloping lot was to extend its walls down, as skirts to the sloping terrain, or create a flat site through large retaining walls. Although this version of the Willey residence was not built, Wright used its concept as the archetypal springboard for a whole new series of hillside houses.

Wright said that the abstract **Gale House, Oak Park, Illinois, 1904,** originally conceived with a reinforced concrete cantilevered balcony, was a discovery that led to Fallingwater. All of these different discoveries were converging into a new synergy, a triaxial architecture, a structural wholeness greater than its parts.

REDEMPTION

Fallingwater received enormous publicity and soon became the most famous modern house in America. With this one building Wright, at age 67, was back at the top.

Wright's projects would often take their owners for a rough ride, but equally transformed their lives, making their name famous. Among the guests who came to see the house were the architects Walter Gropius and Marcel Breuer. They invited Edgar Kaufmann to visit them and they became friends. Edgar entered the architectural world and became the head of the Department of Industrial Design at the Museum of Modern Art.

Major architects are fiercely competitive and rarely admit they are influenced by another. In fact they always seem au fait with the latest develop-

Pew House

ment. Alvar Aalto designed a house remarkably similar to Fallingwater, but he was never able to sell the idea of a forest location to his client.

THE TRIAXIAL HILLSIDE HOUSES

There was never another Fallingwater, but a whole series of variations followed, usually in wood, frequently overlooking a stream, river, lake or ocean.

The **Pew House, Shorewood Hills, Wisconsin, 1938,** shares the atmosphere and qualities of Taliesin East, with a similar great stone fireplace. It was built mainly with the Fellowship's labor and fits the forest glen as effortlessly and as magically as the surrounding trees. It is situated above a lake. The corner windows with their projecting plane roofs are striking and unique, an original concept that deserves further development.

The **George D. Sturges House, Brentwood, California, 1939,** with its great cantilevered balcony projecting on an angular bracket from a brick mass, is one of his most abstract and striking houses. An asymmetrical pergola roof hovers over an extraordinary cantilevered balcony supported by a giant bracket. From the street one is confronted with a form as powerful as a Mayan temple. There is no sign it is a residence. Sheathed in digital lapped horizontal wood siding, it is one of his most remarkable houses. (When I worked nearby in an architect's office in the Fifties I used to visit it during my lunchtime to restore my confidence in the potential and greatness of architecture.) The rear is beautifully detailed in brick and wood. It is an exquisite architectural interplay of vertical and horizontal elements.

The **Gregor Affleck House, Bloomfield Hills, Michigan, 1940,** is elevated above the landscape and a small stream. An inner court looks down on a reflecting pool. The interior walls are sloped and covered with lapped siding.

The **Arch Oboler House, "Eaglefeather," Malibu, California, 1940,** is built on the side of a mountaintop, with an extraordinary cantilevered balcony overlooking the Pacific Ocean and a mountainous landscape. The center of

Sturges House

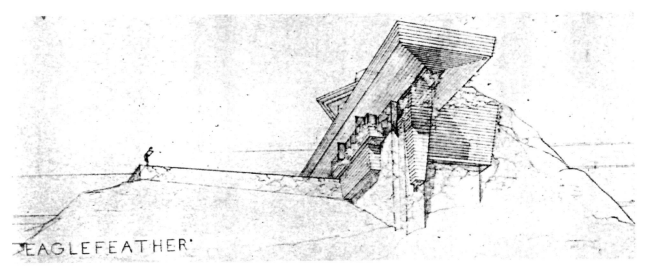

EAGLEFEATHER

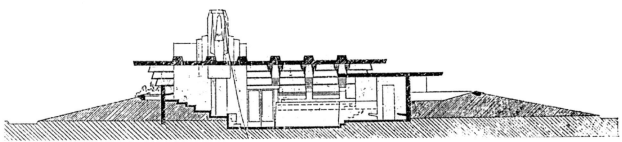

Arch Oboler House and
Chapel of the Soil

the balcony is pierced with an opening, within which are plantings. The axis
of the house rotates around the mountaintop in a play of geometric elements
matched against the rugged landscape.

The **Ayn Rand House, Hollywood, California, 1947,** is the closest design
to Fallingwater, but lacks its coherence and finesse. Ayn Rand was a super-
individualist and wrote the successful book *The Fountainhead*, loosely based
on Wright's career. It was turned into a movie, starring Gary Cooper. Wright
was asked to design the architectural sets but the studio refused to pay his
fee. Ayn Rand once asked to visit Taliesin East. When she arrived Wright
sent a message asking her to wait for him in the living room, so she stood by
the fireplace waiting. Meanwhile, Wright called up Ed, the old Welsh stonemason who was more than 70, and told him the fireplace had a loose stone
that needed fixing. Old Ed entered the living room and, finding only Ayn
Rand there, asked her what exactly needed fixing in the fireplace. This was
a rerun of the scene in the movie where Gary Cooper, playing the architect
working as a stonemason, is called in by Patricia Neal to fix the fireplace.
Ayn Rand evidently was not amused. She eventually bought a Neutra
house.

Chapel of the Soil, 1937. Wright designed this extraordinary chapel without a client. It expresses his own deep relationship with the earth. Here for
the first time he scooped out the earth and sank the building into its
embrace, berming the earth against its walls, as though he wanted the visi-

112

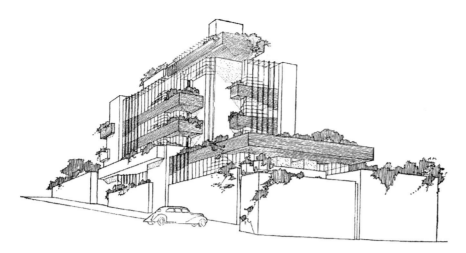

tor to be in the earth, of the earth, and experience its arcane spirits and invisible forces. Strange decorative forms are cast into the concrete columns.

The wall fenestration steps outward in a series of saw-toothed, angled steps. A reflection pool introduces the element of water. It is a chapel for the forest glade, where a passing stranger can meditate and commune with his gods. (Wright's son Lloyd Wright designed the Wayfarers Chapel in Palos Verdes, which in a different form follows the same function.)

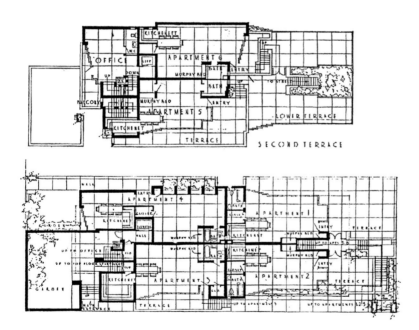

Noble Apartments plan

Wright at the Johnson Wax Building

The Sixth Age
CURVING SPACE

IN 1931 WRIGHT crossed from the linear square to the analog circle with his project for the **Capitol Journal Newspaper Plant** in Salem, Oregon. Within the squares of a 20-foot grid were centered circular "mushroom columns." The printing presses were to be installed on the ground floor, with mezzanine offices upstairs. The columns would support the mezzanine, roof garden and two-story penthouse apartments above. The corners of the building were curved.

There were two symmetrical entrances and behind each a circular stair led to the offices and roof garden above. A spiral service ramp at the rear ascended around a circular smokestack to the roof garden above. The outer fenestration of copper and glass was suspended from the roof slab above. The columns were visible from the outside.

The client, unable to obtain financing, abandoned the project, but for Wright something new had been discovered and set in motion.

In the spring of 1936 Taliesin had only a few residential jobs on the boards and was barely surviving. Not far away the Beaux Arts architect Matson was signing a contract for the new Johnson Wax Building. At this moment in time there seemed no connection between these events, but in Wright's life, events had a way of following a zigzag path.

In early summer one of Wright's friends organized a weekend at Taliesin for the Art Directors' Club. Present was Willis Jones, a young art director, who was deeply impressed by Taliesin East and Wright's work. When he returned to Racine he communicated his enthusiasm to his friend, W. Connolly, advertising manager of Johnson Wax, and showed him the Wasmuth book of Wright's work.

Herb Johnson had taken over the family business, and in spite of the Depression, the new discovery of carnuba wax polish followed by an audacious advertising campaign had been successful. The company was prosperous and rapidly expanding.

Meanwhile, Matson's drawings for the new building were nearing completion and the company was acquiring more land for the new expansion. Matson presented his plans to the client. In the entry he had provided niches for the placement of several realistic sculptures. These included a boy waxing a table and a woman waxing a floor.

Johnson Wax lobby and the
"Great Workroom" at the
Johnson Wax Building

When Johnson and his manager looked at the plans they were appalled, exclaiming, "It's just another building!" In an urgent search for a better architect they consulted Rafferty, a good architect of modern buildings and apparently something of a saint. He responded that certainly he would like a crack at it, but that such an exciting project belonged to the father of modern architecture, Frank Lloyd Wright, who lived not far away.

Connolly and general manager Jack Ramsey asked Willis Jones to set up a meeting with Wright. Ground for the new building was to be broken in July. Wright knew how to set the scene for an important potential client. Taliesin was spruced up for the visit of the Johnson Wax people.

Jones arrived early to explore the situation with Wright. After meeting Wright, Connolly and Ramsey were impressed by his ideas, but now came the task of persuading Johnson to discard Matson for Wright. They arranged a meeting between the two.

Johnson drove out to Taliesin to have a private lunch with Mr. and Mrs. Wright. Wright liked to be alone with the client during the first critical meeting. They met, argued and laughed. Johnson recalled, "He insulted me . . . I insulted him . . . I showed him pictures of the old office and he said it was awful . . . I said if that guy can talk like that he must have something. He had a Lincoln Zephyr, and I had one—that was the only thing we agreed on."

Wright described Matson's plan as a fancy crematorium. When Johnson suggested he did not want a building too unconventional, Wright replied, laughing, "You came to the wrong man . . . the building is not going to be what you expect. But I assure you of one thing—you'll like it when it is put up."

Beneath their jocularity lay a common bond: enlightened ideals to create a new kind of workspace for the workers. Johnson's family had a long tradition of concern for social progress. His father had introduced profit sharing, the 40-hour week and no layoffs.

When the check and letter arrived jubilation rang through Taliesin. It was Wright's first big check in a decade, Taliesin's first major, solid project. "When the sky at Taliesin was dark . . . Hib [Herb Johnson] and Jack came like messengers riding on white steeds trumpeting glad tidings . . . the pie thus opened, the birds began to sing . . . dry grass on the hillside waxed green . . ." Wright said, "held back outside the current of building for seven years . . . never ceasing to be glad that I have for friends the two men who came to see me that day. I knew the scheme I wanted to try . . . when I drew the newspaper plant."

Johnson recalled that as a child he lived only a few blocks from Wright's Hardy House. Perhaps something influenced him even then. He wanted Wright to begin drawing—as soon as possible.

Edgar Tafel drove Wright out to Racine to see the site, already cleared and ready for construction. It sat in the middle of an industrial wasteland of factories, run-down houses and bars. The environment was so depressing that Wright wanted to move Johnson Wax out to the countryside and make it a part of a Broadacre City project, but Herb Johnson resisted all his pressures. After yet another big argument over the location, Olgivanna said, "Give them what they want, Frank, or you will lose the job."

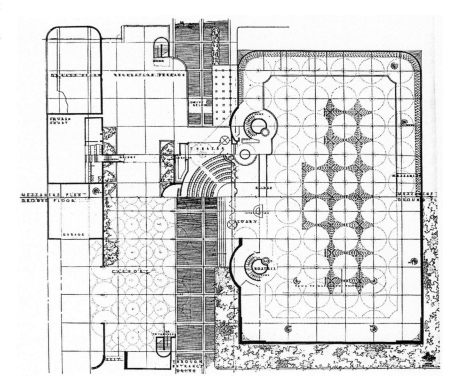

Wright realized that—as with the Larkin Building—he was stuck with an ugly environment and must create a luminous world within. He returned to Taliesin with his first conceptual sketch drawn on the back of Matson's discarded plans.

Hib (as Wright called him) Johnson became a good friend of Wright and a frequent guest at Taliesin weekends. With his enthusiasm, energy and power he would back his architect to the very end. It was just as well Wright had his concept already in mind, because Hib was impatient to begin construction immediately.

THE S. C. JOHNSON ADMINISTRATION BUILDING, RACINE, WISCONSIN, 1936–39

Wright sought a streamlined continuity in which curvilinear walls, fenestration, and roof become one continuous structure; where the parts become one indivisible whole, a luminous work place expressing a new sense of freedom, movement and flowing space. Like the physicist who designs a collision between two systems to create a new element and energy, so Wright employed the interreaction between two different geometric systems, square and circle, to generate new forms and energy. Beginning as a right angle, the brick corners metamorphose into a curved, luminous cornice. Above, the brick wall, now curved, ascends to a curved, larger, glass cornice.

The matrix of the glass tubes of the luminous ceiling follows the lines of the 20-foot-square-grid floor plan, and is framed by the circular petals of

Johnson Wax Building

the columns. The ceiling becomes a pattern of circles played against luminous crosses.

He was embarking on a new voyage of discovery into circular form, mass, space and light. Wes Peters said that Wright's progress evolved day after day as he discovered new ways to express fluid space. Each new discovery opened the door to another. From the moment the first concrete foundation was poured—one month later—Johnson Wax became an ongoing and ever-changing movement of creation, a fusion of discovery and invention.

Wright's vision was of a great work place supported by tall, slender columns. The first obstacle he encountered was the building regulations, which called for a minimum 30-inch-diameter concrete column. He said, "so thick you wouldn't be able to see across the room." First he would have to reinvent the column.

THE DENDRIFORM COLUMN

A tree trunk and its branches are circular. Observing that the trees in a forest generate space and create the magical light entering through the spaces between inspired Wright's design for the great workspace. Wright called his new columns dendriform (from the Greek, akin to a branched tree).

120

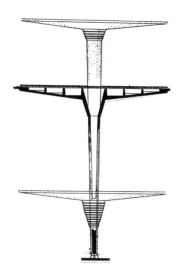

Johnson Wax column

Wright had designed a mushroom column for the **Richland Center Warehouse, Wisconsin, 1915.** Based on the standard engineer's design for supporting heavy loads, the thick cap transfers large shear loads. His version was 24 inches square, with the stresses transferred by an angular 6-foot-square capital decorated with a triangular motif.

The 18-foot-high concrete columns for the **Capitol Journal Building, 1931,** were 24 inches in diameter at the top, tapering to 18 inches at the bottom. To isolate the upper floors from the vibration and noise of the printing presses below, Wright placed the columns into a small metal shoe, resting on an independent foundation, to minimize contact with the ground-floor slab. He carried this detail over into his dendriform column.

Wright reinvented the column. Through structural continuity he transformed the massive shear cap into the 18-foot, 6-inch petal that cantilevers out to become the roof itself. The old elements of post-beam-joist-plank structure were rendered obsolete. The new column was 21 feet high—31 feet in the lobby—tapering from 22-inch diameter at the top to a 9-inch bronze crowsfoot base. (Within was hidden a rainwater pipe.) The transition from horizontal roof to the vertical column is made through a "calyx-capital," a series of digital stepped rings from "petal" to "stem."

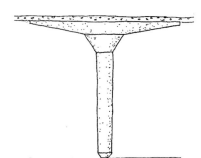

Capitol Journal column

Wright intuitively drew the conoid form that exactly follows the line of the stresses from roof to base. The continuity of structural steel makes roof and column one: the roof becomes the point. Form follows function, transferring 400 square feet of roof load, 20,000 pounds, down to a 9-inch-diameter bronze "tiptoe" point: an area ratio of 800:1. This graphically proves that the form itself is as structurally potent as its materials.

INVENTION

As alchemist Wright transmuted new technologies and materials to create his dendriform column: the steel form, high-strength 7,000-p.s.i. pumped concrete with vibrator, expanded steel mesh shaped to the form, high-strength steel, spiral reinforcement. He made the upper third of the column

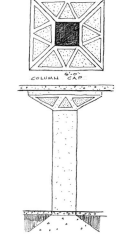

Richland Warehouse column

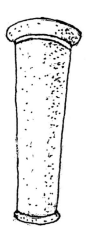

Knossos column

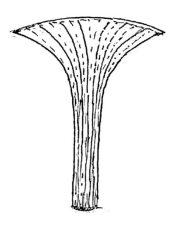

stone fan vault

hollow, its walls only 3½ inches thick, and continued them into the 2½-inch-thick petal with its supporting ribs.

THE TEST

Although Johnson had a good relationship with the local officials, they were anxious to cover their backs in case of failure. Refusing to accept the engineering calculations, the building department demanded that the new column be tested with a load of 24,000 pounds—twice the full design load.

The foundations were in when Wright built his test column, which would be loaded with pig iron to see if it could sustain the regulation load.

It was not only the column that was being tested, but Wright's vision and the fate of the project.

Surrounded by a crowd of officials, reporters, clients, and Taliesin workers, a crane dumped load after load of pig iron on the column. Wright stood by the column, unperturbed by the mounting tension around him, periodically tapping it with his cane. When the load finally reached the 24,000 pounds required, everyone sighed with relief, but Wright insisted they keep going and see how far it could go before the point of destruction. By late afternoon there was no more room to add any pig iron. At 60 tons, it was carrying five times the test requirements. Wright, seeing he had made his point, ordered the supporting braces removed. The calyx of the column broke, but the column stem itself was still intact. He had proved his vision in practice, and created a new column for the twentieth century. In the evolution of the column from the first simple tree trunk through Karnak, the Parthenon and the Gothic fan vaults of King's College Chapel, Wright had made a quantum leap. Wright said, "Greek or Egyptian found a revelation of the inmost life and character of the lotus and acanthus in terms of lotus or acanthus life." All this great architectural inspiration came from the understanding of nature.

Wright, by metamorphosing the ugly mushroom into the graceful dendriform, had achieved the delicate tall, slender column he envisioned, like a dancer poised on a point, balanced by the connecting arms between the petals. The dendriform columns became generators of space. There are no supporting walls. The freestanding columns support the whole structure: roof, mezzanine and suspended cornices.

THE LUMINOUS CORNICE

Wright hated the "trapped space," the dark corner where the cornice joins vertical wall to horizontal ceiling in the traditional house. At one Sunday talk Mr. Wright said to us, "Boys, you must learn to avoid the re-entrant angle—the acute angle in a ceiling terminating against a wall—which traps space and avoid an angle in which space cannot be released through an opening or a skylight."

The dark cornice has been transformed into a luminous cornice of light. Spliced transparent tubes allow an unbroken continuity of form. The suspended luminous cornice of glass tubing separates the non-load-bearing brick wall below from the ceiling plane above, allowing the ceiling planes to float above a continuous band of light.

Wright achieved his streamlined, sweeping curves by using special curved bricks. He rejected conventional windows and experimented with wedge-shaped glass blocks, but he found their joints broke the flowing continuity he sought. He needed a transparent material that could follow the curves, randomly spliced at the joints, to achieve a seamless perfection. He discovered it in the Pyrex® laboratory tubing that chemists use to transport liquids. He wrote to Corning Glass asking for samples and cost. Assembling a test section at Taliesin, he saw that through the glass tubing, a figure was transformed into a marvelous abstract, impressionist image. He had found his new medium. To make it watertight he designed a tube section indented top and bottom with a parallel groove for caulking. To support the stacked tubes he designed a curved metal casting. The extraordinary section of the luminous cornice shows it swelling out—like an eye— on the exterior. The rhythm of the glass tubing was varied by the use of different tube diameters.

Flowing in continuous bands around the building, the crystal tubing clarifies and diffuses the light. It was the organic system he sought, an audacious, revolutionary system.

THE GREAT WORKROOM

The great workroom expresses a new sense of freedom and movement. A luminous and magical space, it is an interior oasis of space and light within an industrial desert.

Beginning as points, the columns are so perfectly formed they seem to flow upward on their own accord, as if seeking the light above, spilling over the petals, outlined against the sky. The linear grid of the building is reflected in the Pyrex® tubes, veins of light etched against the sky. The ceiling plane floats above the glass cornice, which, suspended from the edges of the petals, flows in continuous bands of light.

Extending around all four sides of the work space, the mezzanine is serviced by circular elevators. The ceiling beneath is illuminated by a second luminous cornice. Concealed lighting provides a diffused illumination that reinforces the natural light.

Wright said that steel in tension makes "weight in this building appear to lift and float in light and air."

The unbroken bands of light beneath roof, mezzanine and petals convey a sense of weightlessness, so that the individual elements seem to float suspended in space and time. Within this clear refracted light Wright has created a mythical world suffused with light, or circular lily pads floating against the sky.

The curved form of the crystal tubes, refracting light as through the rippled surface of a stream, creates a pure and vibrant light. Johnson Wax takes its place among the great historic spaces of architecture. Instead of being a palace for an elite this building is a twentieth-century celebration of democracy and the individual. The great work space complements the Usonian house, bringing together the essential elements of Broadacre City.

"That lifelong endeavor to demolish the box . . . so I took the corners out. I came upon the elimination of the horizontal corner, the corner between walls and ceiling . . . I took off the cornice . . . thus light was let into the interior space where light had never been before." F.LL.W.

Guggenheim Museum at night

Wright said, "Johnson Wax is a feminine building sired by the masculine Larkin Building . . . a streamlined building." When the building opened in 1939 it received universal acclaim. *Life* magazine described the building as being "like a woman swimming naked in a stream." Johnson Wax received more than $2,000,000 of free publicity—more than the $700,000 cost of the building. When Wes Peters took the Finnish architect and master of flowing space, Alvar Aalto, to see the building he exclaimed, "This is greater than I."

INNER AND OUTER WORLDS: INTERFLOWING LIGHT AND SPACE

Night photos of Johnson Wax reveal light radiating from the cornices. In his renderings Wright would often have a reverse photostat made for a night view, which would show inner space—as light—streaming out of the windows and skylights. Those pictures showing light streaming out from the interior were used as graphic illustrations of the metaphor of interior space flowing out to the exterior.

SUNG VASE

In a glass window in the corridor by the Taliesin West living room a Sung vase partly projects, through a circular hole cut in the glass, to the exterior. The vase penetrates both worlds. It is a paradigm of Wright's insight into the relationship between inner and outer spaces.

Wright was always fascinated by the relationship between two worlds, between the interior and exterior worlds of architecture. He saw it as emblematic of man, who stands at the threshold between two worlds, the interior world of the psyche and the exterior physical world.

Sung vase, *left,* luminous cornice of Johnson Wax, *right*

He saw, like Marshall McLuhan, that the body is an extension of the mind, the house an extension of the body, the window an extension of the eye. To Wright glass was a membrane separating inner and outer space: the regulator and modifier of the flow of energy, space and light, between inner and outer worlds. He saw that the window that lets light and space in was equally the opening that allowed space to flow out.

THE GLASS HOUSE

One day Wes Peters was driving Wright back from a conference when Wright said, "We must be near my architect friend's new glass house. If he ever heard I had passed nearby without visiting him, he would never forgive me. Let's see if we can find it." They found the all-glass house situated in the middle of a green lawn. Wright walked up to the house and, peering in the window, saw his friend in bed with his lover. Wright, laughing, exclaimed, "Still at it, I see!" The architect and his companion dashed to the bathroom, the only enclosed space in the house. Reappearing, wrapped in a robe, the architect came to the door and said, "Oh, Mr. Wright, what a lovely surprise, do come in." Wright entered, paused, and said, "Wait a minute, am I outside or inside, where should I hang my coat?"

Contrary to expectations, Wright rarely used large California-style "picture windows." As if using a weir to control a river's flow, Wright modulated the flow between inner and outer space by a variety of devices. The evolution of the window began with the elimination of the "hole punched in the wall," moved from double-hung to bands of casement, to awning, mitered glass corner, and up to clerestory, from leaded glass to the decorative windows of the prairie house, the inserts of the block houses, the glazing muntin pattern of the Usonian, Pyrex® tubing of Johnson, canvas roofs of Taliesin West, fretwork plywood screens (an economical version of decorative ones), glass spheres of the Greek Church to the suspended plastic hemispheres of the Morris Shop. Always the interrelationship between inner and outer space is delicately balanced; in the Hanna House the windows are divided by several horizontal muntins to control the flow between inner and outer space. Wright described the Llewellyn House's alternate vertical bands of wall and glazing as a palisade.

THE WINDOW

One Sunday after Mr. Wright's breakfast talk I was standing in the Hillside School dining room, fascinated by the original window treatment: a double casement window floated, surrounded by six inches of glass, within the limestone wall. Suddenly I was aware of Mr. Wright behind me. With the intimacy of a friend he said, "Son, all my life I have been trying to solve the problem of the window in the wall and here I thought I had it!" I was struck by the simple, direct way he said this, for he revealed to me his inner self, forever open to the Muse, imbued with the quality of questing youth.

Taliesin East window

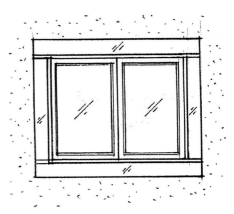

floating casement window

Johnson Wax carport ceiling

carport ceiling

*"Living in the desert
is the spiritual cathartic
many people need.
I am one of them."*
F.LL.W.

"Unity" petroglyph

SICKNESS

With one of those fresh insights, unexpected mutations, delightful surprises that prevent his buildings from ever becoming mechanical or repetitive, Wright changed the column spacing for the more intimate spaces at the Johnson Wax penthouse. In the rear entry he created a breathtakingly different rhythm in the spacing of the carport, where he punched hemispheres of space into the concrete ceiling, reversing the plastic form of the petals into negative forms.

Johnson's insistence to proceed with construction immediately, before Taliesin had time to complete the drawings and details, put enormous pressure on Wright. At one point during the construction, changes and additions to the penthouse necessitated replacing its foundations with larger footings. The pressure of work became relentless. Endless journeys to the site—165 miles—were required. In December the Midwest winter was hitting hard. After spending another long day at the freezing site, Wright came down with a bad cold. When it turned into pneumonia the doctor forbade him to work and ordered him to stay in bed. Peters, Tafel and the other workers were instructed to deal with vital decisions until his recovery. The doctor advised Wright, now 70 years old, to go to the dry desert to recover. Wright, with family members and some apprentices, took off for Arizona, taking drawing boards and plans along.

THE BIRTH OF TALIESIN WEST, PARADISE VALLEY, ARIZONA, 1937

Whenever he was sick, Wright found renewal in the desert. There, while recovering his strength, Wright made the decision to build a new camp. With the money from Johnson's advance he bought cheaply 400 acres of virgin desert 15 miles outside Scottsdale. At $3.50 per acre, it had no water, but Wright soon found it, and began to lay out the plan of Taliesin West directly on the site.

The first simple building, "the Suntrap," was constructed of wood and canvas for the Wrights. Olgivanna was quite tough, roughing it in the desert with only the simplest of plumbing facilities.

What is remarkable is that at the same time he was designing the most streamlined building in America, he was excavating a powerful, ancient vision. In the annals of architecture has there ever been an architect who simultaneously created two such totally different designs?

Taliesin now took another, fourth, form. The tiny, nascent germ of an idea—Ocotilla—now bloomed into magnificent reality.

When Edgar Tafel and some apprentices found a large boulder inscribed with Indian petroglyphs, Wright made sure they placed it at Taliesin in its original orientation. He said, "When the Indians come back 2,000 years from now to claim their land, they will note we had respect for their orientation."

If Wright could patiently wait for over a quarter of a century to see one of his designs built, he showed all the impatience of youth when it came to unwrapping the forms of his latest creation. A week after Tafel and others poured the concrete for Theater #1, Wright told him to take down the forms.

126

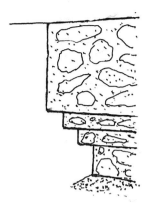

Taliesin West

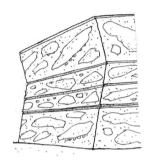

Theater #1

reverse-slope wall

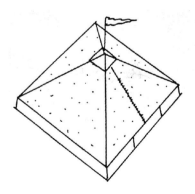

apprentice tent

Tafel reminded him that one is supposed to wait the standard 28 days needed for concrete to set. "No matter," said Wright, "I have a client coming and I want him to see the new space." Since the walls step outward as they ascend—as with the Mesa house project—Tafel very gingerly removed the supports, and was relieved to find the structure remained standing.

He was not always so successful. Wright's new idea was to go halfway up, then reverse the backward slope of the wall to slope outward. Wright invariably pushed his ideas to the limit. So impatient was he to see if his new concept was a success, he ordered the form removed after only a few days. After viewing and approving the result, Wright and Tafel sat down for lunch. Suddenly they heard a roaring crash! The unsupported wall had collapsed. No matter, after lunch they began to put it back up again.

When I arrived in 1954, Taliesin West looked as if it had existed forever. As a new apprentice, I inherited a pyramidal shepherd's tent to live in, eight feet square at the base. This I mounted on a revolving wooden platform, designed by Wright's grandson, Eric Lloyd Wright, which allowed a diverse choice of views: primal mountain or distant city lights.

The apprentices expressed considerable imagination in what they did with their pieces of canvas. One had built a massive stone base, another stretched the canvas by ropes from adjoining trees, creating a desert sheik effect. Around the camp about forty tents were scattered, some with pennants flying in the breeze. It looked like a scene from *Henry V.* One day, looking down on the camp from above, Wright observed that the tents looked like a bunch of chickens scattered across the landscape! Concerned about preserving the primal desert, he had them moved farther away from the mountainside.

We celebrated our reunion at Taliesin West with a party in J. R.'s tent. Drinking cheap Mexican rum brought back from El Paso, Bruce Pfeiffer and I drank toasts to Queen Victoria. After 2 A.M., somewhat inebriated, I departed but then lost my way. I seemed doomed to end up in the deadly embrace of a cholla cactus, but finally I saw my forlorn tent and was saved.

It was quite a leap from a London flat. I had to learn to watch out for spiders and snakes and remember to shake out my sleeping bag each night to oust lurking scorpions. The three-foot-high wall around the camp to discourage rattlesnakes was not always successful: Wes Peters, on entering his room one day, was confronted by a very big and angry one. Peters, a larger-than-life John Wayne character, simply grabbed his six shooter and blasted it.

My first few nights were spent in the library, before my tent had been sorted out. The library was the former Theater #1—there were finally three. Wright was always busy building a newer and bigger version. This was the earliest, a somewhat cubist structure of desert stone and concrete, unique in the way the outer walls step up and out. I was surprised to find several volumes of Edwin Lutyens dedicated to his "Good friend, Frank Lloyd Wright." Wright's taste in literature included Whitman, Thoreau, Viollet-le-Duc, Kropotkin and Lao Tse.

We were told to bring with us to Taliesin a sleeping bag, a T-square, a hammer and a saw. I had borrowed an ancient army sleeping bag from a friend in England, but no one had told me that at night the temperature in the desert drops below freezing. The joke of the hammer was that I had brought one of the finest English hammers, with a beautiful ash handle, but in the extreme dryness of the Arizona desert the hammer head flew off at the first blow.

I recall at Taliesin West getting up on the roof of the living room to replace some of the redwood beams—under the harsh desert sun the redwood just turns to papier-mâché. I could pull the nails out with my fingers.

WRIGHT'S WORKING METHOD

The contract would be signed, the plot plans would arrive, and Wright would go off and see the site. A twenty-minute visit was often all he needed. There are numerous accounts of his uncanny ability to view a site briefly, absorbing every detail of its character, and then be able to go back to Taliesin and draw up a building to suit the site exactly. He would just put a sheet of yellow tracing paper over the site plan and start to sketch the plans and elevations, and it would fit. This would usually take just a few hours, usually in short spurts of activity.

Each day he would be in the drafting room for maybe an hour or two. Everyone was facing the fireplace in the drafting room, and he'd be sitting at the front with his back to you. He had his own drafting board just like the others. He'd come in with his porkpie hat, cane, and cloak; or if you came late and saw the cloak and cane on the bench by his drafting table, you knew he was there. He'd sit down, with Jack Howe standing on one side and Wes Peters on the other, and show them conceptual thumbnail sketches of his ideas. The original sketch Wright did for the Mile High skyscraper was on an ordinary sheet of office typing paper, handed over to Jack Howe and some of the other seniors, who then worked it up. The original sketch for Trinity Chapel was made on the page of a brochure. Howe and Peters had a good rapport with Wright and a clear sense of what he wanted. He would get up after half an hour or so and leave them to begin drawing up his ideas. Jack Howe, who had been with Wright twenty years, would usually do the preliminary design from these sketches, spending the rest of the day on it.

Meanwhile Wright would be off into town for appointments. After lunch he would be back to check over what Howe had been working on. Then you might get a rumor in the afternoon. "Mr. Wright has changed it all—he's had a new idea."

The six or seven seniors would be doing working drawings and details—all for projects at various stages of development. If they needed help they would try to attract Wright's attention. If an apprentice was lucky, his project might also catch Wright's eagle eye while he was passing and he would stop off at your board. Howe usually went over the penciled working drawings and inked in the things he considered important. He was incredibly helpful to new apprentices.

Wright's details were bold and simple. His was a straightforward approach that also showed in his letters to clients, which were very informative, often with a sketch. One client sent back the preliminary plans of her house with a list of nitpicking corrections. Wright sent her a telegram: "Do you want a chicken on the nest or an eagle in flight?"

Toward the end of the year—if an apprentice showed any talent—he would be assigned, as clerk of the works, to coordinate with the contractor and ensure that he followed the drawings. This was excellent experience for the apprentice, and it ensured that the frequently unusual construction methods used by Wright were carried out. An apprentice did not dare change a detail. One day I was in the office when a telegram arrived from an anxious apprentice in another state: "CONCRETE BOND BEAM PASSES THRU CHIMNEY FLUE STOP WHAT SHALL I DO?" Someone on the drawing board, lacking the necessary three-dimensional perception, had gotten it wrong.

ENTERTAINING MR. WRIGHT

Wright had always enjoyed exotic cars. One day, exploring the garages of Taliesin East, I discovered his old Cord, a classic American car of the Thirties. It looked as though Wright might have designed it himself, and with its horizontal grille, belonged alongside the architecture of Johnson Wax. It was sitting up on blocks and obviously needed a lot of attention. (The car later was restored, and was listed for sale subsequently as Wright's automobile.) He insisted that apprentices park their cars as far away as possible, and disliked shiny chrome so much that most cars, including his Jaguars, were painted entirely with matte Taliesin red (an earth red). All the machines, steel and tools were given this treatment. He loved to be driven at high speed along the desert roads. One of the seniors had the job of also being Wright's chauffeur. Wright would suddenly announce that he wanted to see a John Ford movie in Phoenix—he particularly liked cowboy stories—and so they would jump in the Jag and take it up to 80 or 90 mph to get to the movie on time. Wright would spend the afternoon relaxing in front of the film. I remember one old English film based on a Dickens novel, in which, during a courtroom scene, the naive hero turns to his lawyer and says, "Don't worry, justice will prevail." The lawyer, turning, says, "Hm, that's an interesting idea." At this point Wright cracked up, roaring with laughter until tears ran down his face, remembering his own bouts with an unsympathetic law.

Sometimes during his favorite movie—or with a new movie he didn't like—he would just get up in the middle and walk out. I suspect that watching films was not only his form of relaxation but also his form of thinking and meditating, and when the time came he would cut out. One of Wright's favorite films was *Stagecoach*, particularly the location shots in Monument Valley. He loved foreign movies, especially French ones. Some films, if he liked them enough, would be bought and became part of the film library. One such favorite was the Russian fairytale *The Magic Horse*, the story of the mythic Firebird. Wright obviously enjoyed this story of renewal by fire, a Russian version of the phoenix myth.

On Saturday nights dinner was served in the Cabaret Theater, which had benches for seating, with a shelf at the back of the bench in front of you to hold your plate. After dinner a movie would be shown. Wright had the idea that watching the changing forms of the soundtrack of a movie was fun, and so this would appear on a vertical red screen alongside the film. Wright would have dinner at the back of the theater; generally he would be entertaining new clients, friends or visiting celebrities.

DAILY LIFE

We would buy cases of oranges from groves near Taliesin West. Wright had designed a shallow metal bowl which was placed on a wooden pedestal with a low-level lightbulb built into its base. We would pile these "lamps" high with oranges to be taken whenever we felt like eating one. Similar lights were set in the ceiling and walls, and in the floor, under toughened glass. Wright's approach to lighting was that it should be diffused like natural light: you should not be aware of a single source.

Breakfast would consist of three or four oranges fed into the juicer, toast and brew from a marvelous coffee machine. Lunch was generally good, but it would depend on who was assigned to cook. Dinner was served at six in the evening. You could sit wherever you wished; the food was usually basic, no wine. One week I was assigned kitchen duty and found it grueling: up at five in the morning to prepare breakfast, and then working all day until midnight before cleaning the last of the saucepans. It was like an initiation, a Taliesin rite of passage—I don't remember seeing the sun for a week.

During the week, for five or six days, we all lived in blue jeans: we never knew whether we would be pouring concrete, cooking meals, or drafting. But a nice change came on Saturdays and Sundays, especially in the evenings, when we put on our Sunday clothes and suddenly were gentlemen and no longer proletarian worker/students. We would appear in the living room, and the string quartet would play some Mozart, and the choir would sing. Then drinks and dinner would be served.

On Sunday mornings everyone dressed for a formal breakfast, and afterward Wright would give a talk.

There were always several cultural events going on. Boys were rehearsing a Shakespeare play; we could join the choir or the chamber quartet; there were dance groups; and some apprentices preferred the local bars or movie houses in Phoenix and Scottsdale.

Wright was a collector of people and enjoyed helping the underdog. One old man I knew asked Wright for help, and he said, "We are leaving for Wisconsin soon and you can be the caretaker of Taliesin West while we are away." My friend Roger Sommers told me that when he was unable to get an appointment to see Wright, he located his hotel, bribed the room service man, took his place, and served Wright's breakfast in his suite. When he revealed his impersonation, Wright just roared with laughter.

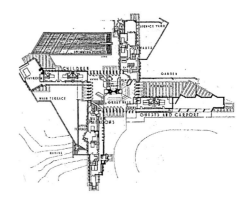

"Wingspread" plan

HERBERT JOHNSON HOUSE, WIND POINT, WISCONSIN, 1937—"WINGSPREAD," THE LAST PRAIRIE HOUSE

Wright used the pinwheel plan—an ancient archetype of the sun wheel—for this residence for Herb Johnson. The house indeed revolves around the central fireplace unit. There are five fireplaces in its brick core, serving the grand hall, dining room, library, music room and mezzanine. What Wright called the "wigwam" core is surrounded by a continuous skylight. It was Wright's most expensive house, employing the finest workmanship, exotic wood veneers and a spiral stair to the roof belvedere.

He called it "the last prairie house." Certainly it is a prairie house transformed into modern form, floating above the landscape, but why "the last"? Wright implied that the cycle of energy that brought a generation of prairie houses had reached the final flowering.

Frank Lloyd Wright with models

131

Celtic form

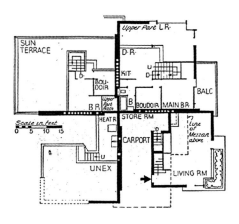

Suntop Plaza

In his design, he kept extending the cantilever of the master bedroom, as if testing how far he could go. Edgar Tafel and Wes Peters were concerned because there was little mass to counterbalance the cantilever and Wright seemed quite uninterested in this problem. Tafel tried another approach. When Wright was away he casually told Johnson that if he needed somewhere to store his trunks, there was a space beneath the bedroom wing that could be employed. Johnson said, "Tell Frank I like the idea." When Wright returned, Tafel relayed Johnson's message. "Good idea," said Wright. Tafel and Peters designed the foundation of the new trunk room as a massive concrete counterweight. The angular influence of the new Taliesin West can be seen in the forms of the playroom and carport.

One day when the house was three-quarters complete, a dove that had taken residence in the belvedere flew away. A carpenter saw it as an ill omen, and shortly afterward Johnson's young bride died.

THE SUNTOP HOMES, ARDMORE, PENNSYLVANIA, 1938–39

This two-story quadruplex employed an Indian swastika plan. During the war Wright used the design for his housing project of a hundred units for the federal government near Pittsfield, Massachusetts. A complaint from local architects that Wright was an out-of-state architect and the project belonged to local men resulted in his losing the job.

JESTER HOUSE PROJECT, PALOS VERDES, CALIFORNIA, 1938

In 1912 Wright designed a series of decorative windows for the Coonley Playhouse. Representing the forms of a children's parade, the circles are abstractions of balloons floating on strings, among flags and pennants.

In the unrestricted breadth of his imagination a form could effortlessly glide from vertical plane to horizontal plane, from two dimensions to three. He was well known for his gift of transposing an old form into a different context. Once, approaching the drawing board, he observed a horizontal window design and remarked to the draftsman, "That would make a better form vertically."

Wright had a direct access to every one of his past discoveries. These, like a seed, could remain dormant for years until some new challenge triggered them into the next stage of growth. Twenty-five years later, the circles and lines of the Coonley window are transformed into the plan for the Jester House; a play of circles set in a square matrix. Wright, with a new freedom, allowed the circles to become freestanding rooms of different diameters defined by use: living room, dining room, kitchen, bedroom, bath, valet. Like balloons floating in space, the rooms are tethered to the lines of the pergola grid. The house is mirrored in its largest circle, the swimming pool, expressing the natural form of water. Wright always enjoyed challenging a site, and placed the pool in a natural gully, instead of the usual hole in the ground. The outer edge wall of the pool is flush with the water level, allowing the water to cascade down to the gully below. He had artfully created a circular Fallingwater.

132

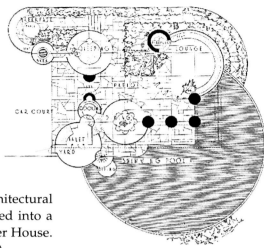

Coonley House window, *left*;
Jester House plan, *right*

Wright was adept in grasping new technology to further his architectural reach. Now utilizing the curved strength of plywood when formed into a cylinder, he used it as the material for the circular walls of the Jester House. (Aircraft designers use the principle for the stressed-skin fuselage.)

The circles become vertical towers arising out of the roof, which is supported by stone columns. A master of textures, Wright contrasted the rough stone surface of the columns against the smooth,˙sensuous surface of the plywood, the plastic curves of the walls against the orthogonal matrix of the roof. The windows follow the curved walls as wide horizontal slots. The bachelor client was an assistant film director. The balmy site was perfect for an open living style.

The project was a major, seminal work, but the design proved too challenging for the contractors of the time and was not built. Several variations followed, some with a pollywog bedroom extension. Fifteen years after Wright's death the house was finally built, in a modified form, for Bruce Pfeiffer and his father beside Taliesin West, 1974.

Ludd M. Spivey House Project, Ft. Lauderdale, Florida, 1939. Spivey said to Wright, "We choose you as much for your philosophy as for your architecture." Wright designed a circular house for Spivey, President of Florida Southern College, in 1938, as well as the new campus in Lakeland, where the library is also a large circular structure. The great fountain generates a hemisphere of water above a circular pool.

Herbert Jacobs House, "Solar Hemicycle," Middleton, Wisconsin, 1943, construction, 1948–49. Stories that Wright would force his designs onto unwilling clients are untrue. If they rejected his design Wright would take a pause and begin again with an entirely new concept. (However, he kept the original aside, to await an appropriate client.) When Herb Jacobs rejected Wright's orthogonal design for his house as too large and expensive, Wright sent Jacobs a note a month later. "We are about ready to make you 'the goat' for a fresh enterprise in architecture . . . if you don't get what is on the boards some other fellow will. So *watch out*. It's good. I think we have a real 'first' that you will like a lot. Only the picture remains to be done—suppose you come out next Sunday."

In the Jacobs Hemicycle, earth, berm, site and house become one indivisible entity, oriented to the solar cycle.

Taking his form from the shape and orbit of the sun, Wright designed the house as a part of a circle, completed by the earth itself, now an integral part of its architecture. His windows follow the orbit of the sun, the sunken garden becomes a sun trap, the concave form generates solar heating.

One enters through a cave, penetrating the outer earth berm to the sunken garden within. Wright echoes the circular forms, earth berms and solar orientation of the first Stonehenge, 2700 B.C. Drawing upon ancient archetypes of Druidic ancestors, he created an architecture expressing the eternal relationship between man, earth and cosmos. (The house and Stonehenge

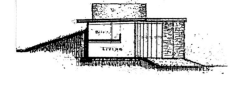

section

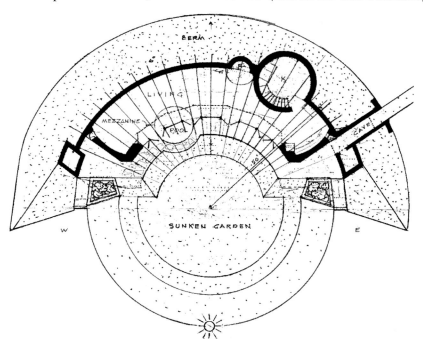

Jacobs Hemicycle plan

share similar diameter and spacing. The house columns are spaced at 6 degrees, the Stonehenge posts were 6.4 degrees.)

The berm along the north wall and the sunken garden shield the structure from the cold winter winds of the rural hilltop location. It is a house for the north, designed to utilize the maximum from the light and heat of the sun, and protected during the summer by a large roof overhang. The war introduced Wright to a world short of building materials. He used the most simple materials for the house: exposed post and beam construction, 2"-thick roof deck, and beams laminated out of the available 1 × 12 lumber. The Jacobses, short of money, found a group of Swiss immigrant farmers who doubled as stonemasons. They laid the stones in the Tcino fashion of their native country. Someone told Wright that the stonework was terrible. It was not. Meanwhile, Wright took exception to a note by Jacobs that he had assisted him with the new addition to his autobiography. A chill descended on their relationship and for several months the Jacobses received no word from Taliesin.

It was not unknown for clients to be awakened at home early in the morning by Wright touring a potential client through their house, so when the Jacobses heard Wright's voice extolling the beauty of their house to a prospective client one morning, they breathed a sigh of relief and knew all was well. Wright returned to supervise, along with his own bulldozer and operator, to form the earth berm to its correct 45-degree angle.

PARTY

Wright's relationship with his clients was generally as if they were part of his extended family. They would be invited to Taliesin, and if in turn they invited the Wrights to a party, it was assumed that his extended family, the sixty-man Fellowship, was included.

Arriving at one such party, I entered through the cave to be met by Herb and Katherine Jacobs at the entry, and passed into the interior of the hemicycle. Across a sea of people I experienced my first vista of curved and endless space. The curve of the living room, continuing in a parabola, swept out of sight. Another spatial twist was provided by the curving mezzanine hovering above; it had no support. Wright didn't want cross beams marring the flow of space. Unconditioned by a conventional college education, Wright recognized no rules, freely moving through dimensions, up or down. He hung the mezzanine bedrooms from the roof. Steel rods inside the walls hold the floor beams below, which then double as cantilevers, to support the balcony.

Wright provided a circular pool, half in the house and half outside. The glass window dips just below the waterline; the goldfish can pass from inside to outside. During construction the Jacobses changed it to a plunge pool.

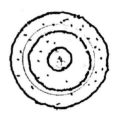

"Spring" petroglyph

THE ELEMENTS: EARTH

Beginning with the Chapel of the Soil project, Wright moved into creating the forms of the surrounding earth: earth and shelter soon became one indivisible entity. The section of the bermed house for the **Co-operative Homestead**

135

Thomas House

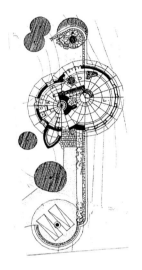

Friedman plan

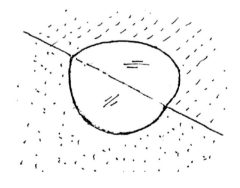

Loeb House window

Project, Detroit, Michigan, 1942, is a classic pyramid form. The 45-degree angle of the roof planes continues in the earth berms on each side. They provided added insulation to save fuel during the war years. The design was finally realized as the **Thomas House, Rochester, Minnesota, 1950.**

The **Cabaret Theater (#2), Taliesin West, 1949,** is sunk three feet into the desert for insulation. Constructed out of monolithic reinforced concrete and desert stone, it features exterior ribbed structural beams and a marvelous, intimate interior space. In the service kitchen the rubble stone wall is pierced by a circular three-foot hole. Crudely held in place in the hole—sealing is not a problem in the hot desert climate—is a large disk of glass. From three feet below the earth, one of Wright's surprising, intimate views of another world is provided: the floor of the desert, as seen by the small creatures that live in underground burrows, looking up to the desert vegetation above.

The **Friedman House, Pleasantville, New York, 1948–50,** is built in a wooded hillside, a Wrightian community of houses. In this small house "for a toymaker," the plan is formed by two interlocking circles, with a circular mezzanine overlooking the living room. It is an intimate house, the fireplace nook a cave. The circular carport roof is provided by a stone and concrete mushroom column. The rear of the house is dug into the hillside.

The **Gerald Loeb "Pergola" House Project, Reading, Connecticut, 1942,** is one of Wright's most extraordinary projects. This represents the elongated evolution of the Jester House, a play of linear and circular elements. With its long colonnades of stone columns it echoes a Greek temple for contemplation. The long covered walkway connecting the various living elements was a recurring theme in his work, but rarely built (the McCormick House project, among others). Ours is not a contemplative society.

The circle appears as both a column of mass and a skylight. A new approach to the glass cornice is introduced: in the wall/ceiling corner are glass folded circles, which begin in the ceiling and, like a Salvador Dali watch, continue down the wall plane. This detail was later used in the rear of the Guggenheim Museum. The garden-living room, like an open glass Greek temple, hovers above the pool and is reflected in the underwater garden below. As with the Johnson House pool, the pool walls are undercut to make them invisible.

In the Loeb pool he goes farther. The stone columns continue down into the pool to create a submarine garden world. It's like a submarine temple for Proteus, father of Taliesin. Water, Jung's symbol of the unconscious where all forms arise, was Wright's fountainhead. At this time his creative imagination was incandescent, centrifugally spinning off new ideas like solar flares, outpacing his critics, who could not understand new concepts that broke the "rules" of modern architecture.

Inspired by this submarine garden, a former apprentice, architect Alden Dow, submerged his new house three feet below the level of the lake outside. When Wright saw it he exclaimed, with a laugh, "This time I think we have gone too far!"

136

THE ELEMENTS: WATER

For Wright, water represented life. His love of water was expressed in the triangular pool and the cascading water at the entry to Taliesin West, where he converted the drafting-room fireplace into a waterfall.

In Johnson Wax, Wright created a mythical underwater palace beneath the sea. But water is not always easy to contain. With the advent of the first rain, the roof leaked in Herb Johnson's new office, right above where he was sitting. Furious, he called Wright, asking "What shall I do?" Wright, never at a loss for a one-liner, replied, "Move your chair!" According to Taliesin legend, Wright followed up this surrealistic scenario by designing special "Taliesin red" buckets to be placed under future leaks.

The **Huntington Hartford House Project, Hollywood Hills, California, 1947.** In this bachelor house the circle expands into the hemisphere, the upper portion formed by curved glass tubes. The living room becomes an atrium of light for entertaining guests.

Other circular projects followed, including **Park Point, 1947; Wieland Motor Hotel, 1956,** with circular units arranged as a crescent necklace; **Bramley Motor Hotel, 1957,** with three circular towers arranged in a triangle; and **Baghdad University Complex, 1957.**

A TOLSTOYAN ANARCHIST

With the advent of World War II many apprentices were drafted; others were in the Spring Green jail as conscientious objectors. Wright was against the war. He didn't want his emergent democratic "Usonia" infected by the old-world imperialism. He feared that America would be dragged once more into the corruption of Europe, with its feudal hierarchies, its endless wars of empire.

"Force and compulsion on the part of the State or any individual in it seemed hideous to me. Thoreau's 'That government is best government which governs not at all' I accepted as a truism . . ." Wright said. "The anarchist's idea, faith in the commonwealth based on voluntary instinctive respect for the other fellow's rights, I saw as the normal thing . . ." He was a lifelong rebel along the lines of Tolstoy, Paul Goodman and Kropotkin. His opposition to the war made him unpopular. Even good friends, like Lewis Mumford, deserted him. There was little work, a shortage of building materials; construction was trickling to a halt. He retreated inside the two Taliesins, finding inspiration and sustenance in the land, the farm; walking and riding through the woods; rebuilding and reforming Taliesin. He published a monthly *Taliesin News Letter,* with comments on architecture, society and war.

After the feverish pace of the past decade, in this fallow period, Wright had the time to reflect, to inwardly explore new worlds and experiment with new concepts, to plunge deeper into the meaning of architecture, space and form. He prepared himself for the final flowering of his last visionary years, but for the outside world, occupied with war, his name was once more sinking into obscurity.

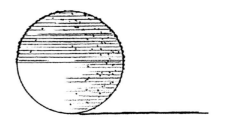

Huntington Hartford House

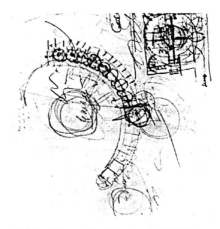

Wieland Motor Hotel drawing by F.LL.W.

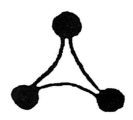

Celtic form

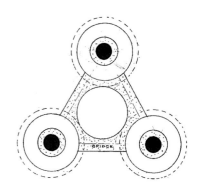

Bramley Motor Hotel plan

Wright at the Guggenheim Museum

The Seventh Age
A SPIRAL SPACE

THE ADVENT OF WORLD WAR II brought an end to the rich harvest of the Thirties, but this last fallow period allowed the seeds of the new plasticity to germinate in Wright's creative mind and bring forth the fruits of his last golden age.

Shortly after I arrived at Taliesin, and after Mr. Wright had finished his Sunday talk, I was intrigued by a picture of the logo of his red double spiral. Mr. Wright came up behind me and with the relaxed familiarity he enjoyed with his students, explained—with his pencil—"In the West, son, if you want to move from one point to another, you move in a straight line. But in the East no one ever moves in a direct line, so what you do is go past the thing, turn right and pass it again, and pass it again, until you have become the thing."

SQUARE LOGO

Wright incorporated the red square logo into his new double-spiral logo. The Southwest Native American spiral used one continuous line that doubles back on itself, whereas Wright's version is of one continuous space: a centripetal, clockwise labyrinth that at the center becomes transformed into the counterclockwise, centrifugal exodus. It is emblematic of the creative process, of the intake of energy that the artist transforms into art.

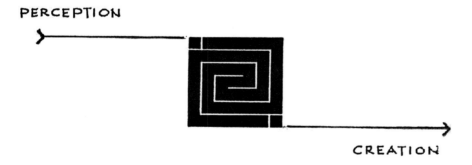

The double spiral represents a vortex of energy. Wright had discovered the eye of the storm, the still center from which creation springs.

"Architects were no longer tied to Greek space, but were free to enter into the space of Einstein."
F.LL.W., 1936

Pot design, Mimbres culture

Strong Planetarium

His sketch was complete. I think he picked up the design while in Japan. Wright began using this symbol as his logo about the time he was building Taliesin West in 1938, and the American Indian petroglyphs on the boulder by the entry display a simplified form of the symbol. (It is also similar to an ancient picture of the labyrinth of Knossos.) The spiral is one of man's oldest universal symbols. Every seashell helix expresses it as an archetypal form of growth and the double helix is the DNA principle of organic life. In his first model of the Guggenheim Museum, Wright employed a double spiral. His interest in spiral architecture began with the **Gordon Strong Planetarium Project,** a ziggurat of concrete for the automobile. Some time later, in 1929, he seemed prescient and asked the client for the return of the drawings, "For an art gallery to be built in Europe . . ."

In 1939, Wright designed the new Kaufmann guest house above Fallingwater. To cover the stairs down to the house below he designed a stepped, spiral roof, with almost no visible support. An astonishing tour de force, it presaged Wright's new entry into the world of spiral space. In keeping with the digital principle of Fallingwater it is composed only of horizontal and vertical elements, the latter cantilevered from slender steel posts and supported by the inner compression ring of the circular form. It was the bridge between the digital Fallingwater and the spiral plasticity of the Guggenheim, yet to come.

In 1943, Wright's two large housing projects had been canceled and there was little work on the boards. He was living a quiet life and the media no longer found him newsworthy. He was 76 years old and opposed the war; they chose to bury him in silence.

Guggenheim Museum

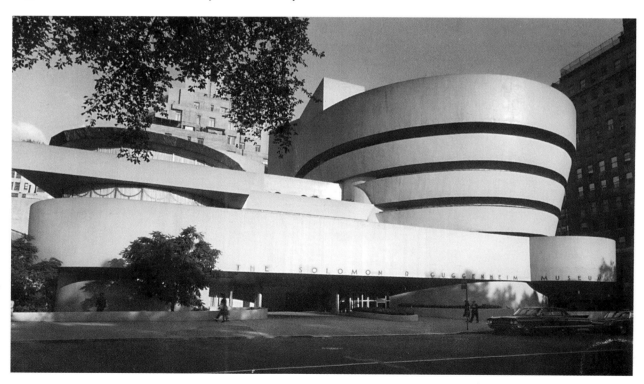

DEATH AND RESURRECTION

Solomon R. Guggenheim Museum, New York, 1943–1959. In 1943 Solomon Guggenheim asked his curator, the German baroness Hilla von Rebay, to select an architect to design a new museum to house his extensive collection of nonobjective art. She asked László Moholy-Nagy, a Bauhaus intellectual icon, to draw up a list of possible architects. His list included fellow modernists—Le Corbusier, Gropius, Neutra, Lescaze, Aalto—and himself. He omitted any mention of Wright, a founder of modern architecture. When Rebay told a friend she was disappointed with the response, he expressed surprise that Frank Lloyd Wright had not been included in the list of notable architects. "But surely he is dead!" Rebay exclaimed. When she was told that he was very much alive she immediately sent him a letter. "Dear Mr. Wright, could you ever come to New York and discuss with me a building for our collection of non-objective paintings. I feel that each of these great masterpieces should be organized into space and only you, so it seems to me, would test the possibilities to do so . . . I need a fighter, a lover of space . . . I want a temple of spirit . . . Hilla Rebay, Curator."

"But surely he is dead!"
Baroness Rebay

Interior of the Guggenheim, looking down

In 1943, the middle of the war, there was virtually no work at Taliesin. The invitation was a gift from the gods. Wright, assuming Rebay was a man, replied with an invitation to visit Taliesin. "Bring your wife. We have room and the disposition to make you comfortable." Rebay met the Wrights and they soon became friends on a first-name basis. Olgivanna and Rebay, both European, found they had much in common. After Wright met Guggenheim in New York, a contract rapidly followed.

Wright did not like the proposed urban site on 39th Street, and a search was begun to find a better location. He wanted nature and space and found it on Fifth Avenue by Central Park.

> *"I want something completely different."*
> Solomon R. Guggenheim

It was a challenge guaranteed to evoke Wright's best work. His first designs were low and linear, following on the lines of Johnson Wax, but the move to the small, expensive site on Fifth Avenue indicated the building would go upward. A hexagonal tower appeared, soon followed by a ziggurat. The tapered centripetal ziggurat was inverted to become the expanding spiral of the final scheme.

The grid of the floor plan is an eight-foot square, in-filled with circles, expressed in the surface of the terrazzo floor. The plan, beginning as a circle, is transformed into a living, changing form as the great helical plane of the gallery coils slowly upward, centrifugally expanding both outward and inward: an expanding vortex, coiling around, and generating the great, invisible, spiral space.

Wright's experiment with structural continuity now advanced further. The concrete floor plane continues upward, becoming both parapet wall and outer wall—all three planes acting in unison become a structural U-channel, expanding as it winds its way as a giant helical spring to the top. An unending flow of continuity spirals up from the ground to the great apex. (Wright said that if a bomb hit New York the structure would bounce back like a spring.)

The coils were separated by a continuous spiral band of light—a luminous cornice of crystal tubing, similar to those designed for Johnson Wax—illuminating the paintings displayed on the tilted gallery wall.

Wright has left behind the linear world and entered a spiral universe of space, filled with linear contradictions: the floor below where I stand is the ceiling plane above; each revolution returns to the beginning; far is close. Forward movement is transformed into centrifugal, helical movement: a warped, sloped, curving floor, steeper on the inside than the outside, continues to the roof.

Ascending the great ramp of the Guggenheim, one is aware of different levels of subliminal experience, some verbal and others nonverbal. Something is happening to one, but one cannot say what. One is in a great wave, moving simultaneously forward and upward.

Wright said, "The impression made upon one is of complete repose similar to that made by a still wave, never breaking."

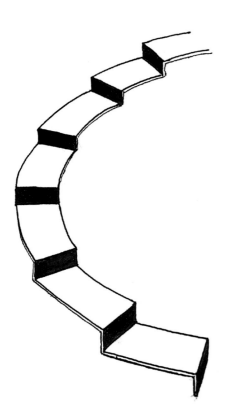

stepped canopy to Fallingwater House

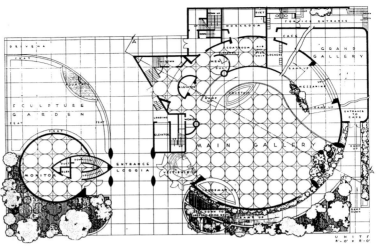

Guggenheim floor plan

The great dome of crystal glass is extraordinary, diffusing the light to the galleries below. The double hollow-glass tubing provided both thermal insulation and space for interior lighting.

Upon entering the great space, one looks upward and sees concentric, expanding circles, the compounded curves of endless, unwinding waves, the tunnel of afterlife experience. Walking up the ramp, one ascends around six expanding circles. No simple geometry of parallel forms, but a spiral complexity of warped space and interacting curves moving outward like the circles in the vortex of a pool or an expanding spiral universe.

THE VORTEX

The hollow dendriform column of Johnson Wax resembles a spinning top suspended in time—a Midwest twister, a cyclone, a vortex of spatial energy that, beginning as a point on the ground, expands outward as it ascends. The linear centrifugal plans of the St. Mark's Tower and the Johnson House enter a new dimension of expression with the Guggenheim, a centrifugally expanding vortex revolving around a hollow core, without central support, only an invisible core of space.

Wright drew on the ancient Persian ziggurat, a giant screw of adobe to heaven, turning it upside down and inside out, transforming its core of mass into a spiral gallery of space and light, a modern vortex of spatial energy, its structure cantilevered inward from its outer spiral shell. Within this vortex lies the still center, the eye of the storm.

In the Guggenheim space and light flow in through the ground floor windows from outside, and are modulated by the spiral clerestory and released through the great dome skylight at the roof. Space is alternately compressed and expanded; it is released through windows, cornice and the great skylight above. The space is alive, charged with energy, by the spatial interflow between inner and outer worlds. (The night view of the building shows light—inner space—flowing from the cornice and skylight.)

The conception of invisible space requires an extraordinarily subtle mind. Wright saw that space is not simply a negation of mass, but a form of ener-

144

gy like light, with which it has a deep affinity: that the architect determines spatial interflow by modulation, compression, expansion and release—its energy charged by the interflow between inner and outer polarities.

SPACE

"The building . . . may only be seen 'by experience within' the actual structure . . ." Wright said. "The depth-plane defies the flat camera eye . . . The essence of organic building is space, space flowing outward, space flowing inward (not necessarily by the use of the picture window). Only when the buildings are comprehended from within . . . its own special environment . . . are they really seen. If trees or mountains are round about, they will come to join and enrich the building . . . any true sense of the whole edifice is seldom found in a photograph." Wright explained, "The ceaseless overtones and intones of space, when developed as the new reality in architecture, go on, tone upon tone, as they do in the music of Beethoven or Bach, Vivaldi or Palestrina."

Music, as with architecture, depends on space: in wind instruments the form and volume of the pipe determine its harmonic resonance. In the Gothic church both the perfect architectural space and its acoustic resonance enhance the Gregorian chant of the monks. Architectural space has its own resonant energy. (As a child Wright worked the air bellows of the church organ, generating the invisible energy that his musician father transformed on the organ into Bach.) Music provided Wright both with relaxation and his profound insight into the architecture of space and depth.

The first model of the Guggenheim was breathtaking—a vision of perfection from another world of being. When the working drawings were completed in 1946, Platonic perfection entered an imperfect world and began to make waves.

> *"Rightly to be great is not to stir without great argument."*
> Hamlet

Today the Guggenheim is one of New York City's most popular art museums. As many people come to experience the architecture as to see the art, making it difficult to realize the hostile opposition it received that almost prevented its ever being built. As soon as it became a viable package—perfect site, brilliant architecture, good collection and money—it became the target of power and controversy. Critics either loved or hated it with a passion. Mounting pressure forced Hilla Rebay, Wright's champion, to resign.

The New York City Buildings Department lacked the flexibility and goodwill of Racine, which had allowed the Johnson Wax building to reach its full potential. New York's building code measured Wright's expanding spiral of space against an archaic list of regulations developed for traditional, rectangular structures. Their response to Wright's magnificent glass dome was to destroy it, demanding that a large safety net be suspended beneath it, though glass domes are in common use throughout the world. Suffering from this lack of communication, as with the Tower of Babel, Wright might have recalled a passage from Robert Graves's description of an earlier incar-

Celtic form

fascia ornament

145

nation of Taliesin as Nimrod, its master builder: "One called for stones, they brought him tiles."

The project was stalled, and neither side would make a compromise. Meantime building costs were going up and Guggenheim's budget of $2,000,000 was becoming pitifully inadequate for such a building. Contractors, with no precedents for building a helix design, raised their bids accordingly.

In 1949, Solomon Guggenheim died. In a desperate effort to save the project, Wright traveled to London to meet with one of Guggenheim's daughters.

*"The rectilinear frame of a painting has more to do
with the frame than the painting."*
Solomon R. Guggenheim

The development of the rational analytic brain led to the invention of the vertical/horizontal rectilinear frame of reference, the tri-axial coordinates of navigation and the laws of perspective to locate the position of any point in a three-dimensional framework. The master of linear building, Mies van der Rohe, confessed that he would never design a dome since he would never feel comfortable if he did not know the position of every point and what sort of space he was creating. It says much for Wright's spatial imagination that in the Guggenheim the location of every point in space is unique.

THE FLAT-EARTHERS

Used to conventional rectangular galleries, artists and critics were unprepared for a revolutionary approach to a museum: a spiral with tilting floor and walls, suffused with natural light, where every painting was visible and part of one vast space.

In every age there are those who feel threatened by the new. Critics of the Guggenheim fought Wright's tilted floor, with the hostility that flat-earthers once reserved for those who discovered the world was round and revolved around the sun. Sweeney, the new, modernist curator who replaced Rebay, wanted a sterile, white interior. Wright's organic design called for a warm, light sand color. Wright tilted the outer wall to follow the angle of an easel, the way prints, drawings and paintings are best displayed. Sweeney wanted the pictures vertical, projected out on rods. Wright was himself an artist, with 60 years of experience in the display of his extensive collection of Japanese prints and sculpture. He was not against modern art and had long admired Picasso's ability to create a three-dimensional image on a two-dimensional surface. Wright said, "The trouble with Picasso is that he has no respect for humanity."

A group of artists picketed the site of the Guggenheim to protest the design. At the age of ninety Wright was still fighting the battle of the box! A thousand miles away his supporters in Madison, Wisconsin, were picketing the statehouse to demand construction of his Monona Terrace project.

Time was running out and costs were rising. To proceed Wright was forced to sacrifice the crystal glass tubing of the dome and cornice. But positive forces were also at work. He was related by marriage to Robert Moses, a powerful commissioner in New York City. Moses called the head of the Buildings Department and said, "If those plans are not ready and upon my desk tomorrow you better start looking for a job!" The plans were approved.

When the bids finally came in they were far over the budget. Wright called former apprentice Edgar Tafel for help. Tafel introduced him to the freeway builder George N. Cohen, who was familiar with constructing curved concrete forms. Cohen got the job and asked Wright for a favor, to place his name on the cornerstone. Wright replied, "A round building doesn't have a cornerstone, George." On a curved stone his name accompanied the architect's.

"It breaks every rule. It is so astonishing as a piece of architecture, of course, that it makes you feel that rules hardly matter. But the very way in which Wright's building breaks the rules of urban design becomes its own rule," said Paul Goldberger in the *New York Times* in 1992. Every new culture brings its own rules, and Wright made his own. Those who measure his work with an outdated yardstick are unable to enter its world.

THE FOURTH DIMENSION

Like Einstein, Wright had left the old Newtonian concepts of three-dimensional space to move into a far-reaching understanding of the subtle relations of mass, energy, vibration, light—and space. It was a new, mysterious universe of quantum mechanics, Heisenberg's uncertainty principle, black holes, anti-gravity and spiral galaxies, where, as Wright said, "Sometimes 6 plus 6 equals 36."

In 1941, when asked if he had been influenced by Ouspenski's and Gurdjieff's theory of the fourth dimension, Wright replied, "No, three dimensions are enough for me." By 1957 his understanding of space had evolved further, and he wrote, "To sum up, organic architecture sees the third dimension never as weight or mere thickness, but always as 'depth.' Depth an element of space: the third (or thickness) dimension transformed to a 'space' dimension. A penetration of the inner depths of space in spaciousness becomes architectural and a valid motif in design. With this concept of interpenetrating depth comes flowering a freedom in design which architects have never known before but which they may now employ in their designs as a true liberation of life and light within walls."

Perhaps only Wright could talk about "depth interpenetrating space" and explore further this new dimension.

As Einstein was master of relativity, Wright was the master of space and continuity. Wright treated space as tangible, living energy—a fourth dimension that can neither be measured nor described in three-dimensional terms. No two-dimensional photograph can reveal the depth and quality of space. As Aalto said, "With instruments you can measure a building—but only man can experience its architecture." Man is the link that completes the circle of architecture, made by him and for him.

EVOLUTION OF SPIRAL

At a time when the Guggenheim project was mired in a myriad of conflicts, Wright continued his exploration of the spiral with projects like the Morris

Shop, David Wright House and others. In the spiral **Park Point Parking Garage Project, Pittsburgh, 1947,** the ramps are cantilevered and suspended on steel cables from a central mast. It is an extraordinary project, deserving construction today. The adjacent Community Center is a visionary spiral, a megastructure of the future, incorporating symphony and opera halls, convention rooms, cinemas, an arena, restaurants, shops, parking and other facilities.

V. C. MORRIS SHOP, MAIDEN LANE, SAN FRANCISCO, 1948

An opportunity to test the spiral presented itself with a smaller project, when Mr. and Mrs. V. C. Morris asked Wright to design their new gallery for objets d'art. Maiden Lane is now a prestigious lane off Union Square, but its name evokes its history when treasures of a less reputable nature were available.

The project involved the transformation of an existing building—which included an ugly skylight—into a gallery. The building was close to a cube. The opportunity to play the circle against the square, the spiral against the cube, proved irresistible. Most architects at that time would have made the facade one large piece of glass, but Wright did the reverse, making the entry a mysterious cave which would draw people's curiosity to explore within.

In *A Thousand and One Nights,* Ali Baba discovers the "open sesame" to the magic treasure cave. It is a Sufi parable for man's discovery of his own rich inner world. In this design for a gallery of objets d'art Wright retells the myth eloquently through architecture, in symbol, form and space.

A great wall of golden Roman brick is pierced by a single arched opening, framed by four concentric brick arches radiating out like the widening rings in a pool. One is drawn into a tapering, wondrous cave of paradoxical arches: the left side dark, the right side transmuted into transparent glass through which one glimpses, as in a revelation, the treasure cave beyond.

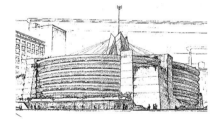

Park Point Parking Garage

148

From the compressive cave one enters the expansive space of a great circular shaft filled with exquisite treasures arrayed on circular and semicircular walnut tables, as at a feast. Within the circle, its walls filled with niches and art, a spiral ramp ascends, winding its way around the interior space up to the mezzanine above. The mezzanine, another circle set within a square, provides a superb overview of the great space below. Smaller displays are exhibited in fine walnut cabinetwork; the scale is intimate and exquisitely detailed.

The luminous ceiling above is formed by a matrix of large and small translucent hemispheres suspended beneath an existing skylight, like the

interior of the Morris Shop

bubbles on the surface of a pool, seen from below. Descending the ramp around the shaft—as in *Alice in Wonderland*—one passes displays of objets d'art set in niches within the walls.

The space is enhanced by a large, shallow bowl filled with plants, their foliage dripping over the edge, a hanging garden of Babylon, suspended over the ziggurat. The floor is covered with a square flagstone pattern like a medieval vault.

Wright, drawing on the Sullivan and Dana arches of his beginning, developed further his entry design for the early Chauncey Williams House.

THE BURLINGHAM HOUSE PROJECT, EL PASO, TEXAS, 1942
A modified version was built in 1986 (C. Keotsche)
Santa Fe, New Mexico

The Burlinghams have a place near El Paso piled with sweeping sands, continually drifting in swirling lines that suggest waves of the sea ... This is a design for a pottery house, that is to say, adobe ... the walls are molded accordingly.

Wright was inspired by the plastic, flowing forms of the shifting sands of the landscape. He liked to quote Heraclitus, "The only thing permanent is change," and expressed it in this pottery house, saying, "It will always be changing, like a stone emerging from shifting sands."

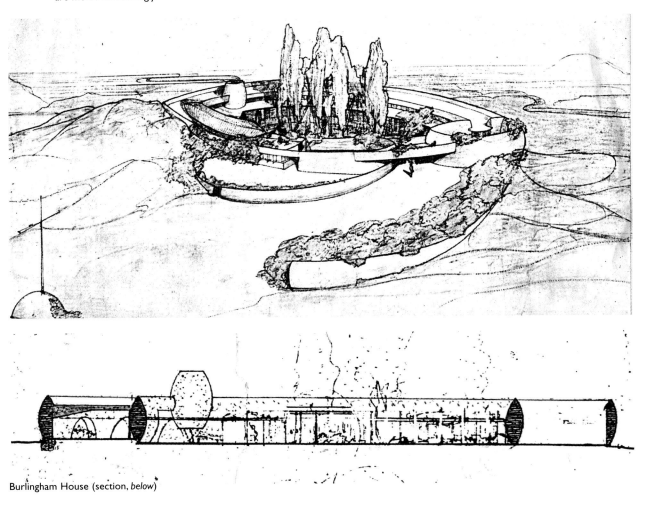

Burlingham House (section, *below*)

150

The plan is turned in on itself, for protection from the elements, around an atrium garden court. Made from adobe brick, the free-form shape presaged the plasticity of the Guggenheim Museum yet to come. The plan is a reflex eclipse formed by two radii, like the shadow on the moon cast by the earth, also known as the ancient "Vesica of Pisces"; and when he used its form for the entry pool of the Guggenheim he used the Celtic description, "the seed form." The curved wall section of adobe brick employs the same form as the plan and is shaped like a pot. (Wright called Gaudí, the master architect of art nouveau plastic form, "the son of a potter.")

This is a seminal building; here, for the first time, plasticity expresses a continuous flow from floor to wall to roof. Wright, moving from the geometric circles of the Jester House into the freer form of the reflex eclipse, comes closer to his vision of plasticity.

Benjamin Adelman Laundry Project, Milwaukee, 1945. The seed form moves into the roof section in this design for a laundry. Utilizing the form of the appropriate, bowstring truss, the upper curve becomes the roof and the lower curve the ceiling: the space within becomes a plenum for the air-conditioning system. Poised like an airfoil, above a continuous band of clerestory windows, the roof-ceiling seems to float in space and light, the curved ceiling diffusing the light into the great work space below. The roof completes itself, as a semicircular form, at the ends, above the drive-in entry.

In the **Marin County Civic Center Post Office, San Rafael, California, 1957–62,** the plan follows the seed form. A Plexiglas® globe of the earth is situated at the entry, half inside and half outside. (I know, I helped place the gold leaf map of the earth upon it.) It is Wright's only building constructed for the United States government.

SHALLOW DOMES

Wright's journey through the world of plastic form took him from the saucer-shaped petals of the Johnson Wax columns to the reflex eclipse of Burlingham and on to the shallow disks and domes of the Huntington Hartford Sports Complex project, a play of cantilevered saucers capped by tubular glass domes. This was followed by the **Daphne Mortuary Project, San Francisco, 1948,** where five chapels were capped by shallow domes arranged in a pentagram plan (in the Middle Ages the pentagram was a symbol of man, and the occult) and by the circular **Greek Orthodox Church,**

Celtic seed form

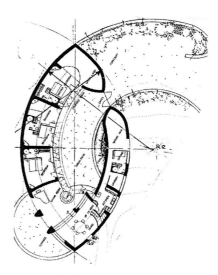

Burlingham House plan

Daphne Mortuary plan

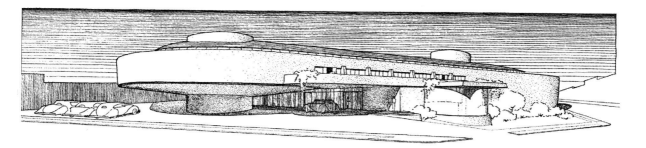

Adelman Laundry project

151

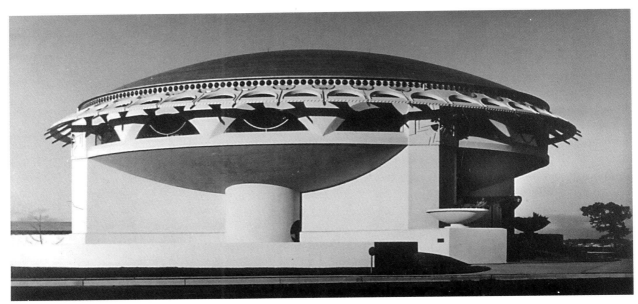

Greek Orthodox Church

Wauwatosa, Wisconsin, 1956, which is a clamshell sandwich, the upper dome supported on a continuous band of glass spheres floating on a luminous cornice. By taking a section out of the center of a sphere—transforming it into the form of a convex lens filled with space and light—he achieves a new dimension of spatial energy. The lower saucer is the mezzanine, open to the floor beneath. The "seed form" section is created by two intersecting circles generated from two radii. Olgivanna was a member of the Greek Orthodox Church and advised her husband on its symbolism, which he used as an integral part of the form and structure of the building. Wright had always admired the Byzantine church of Hagia Sophia with its great dome. Here he used modern engineering to create a shallow concrete dome, supported by an extraordinary circular truss that wraps around the building; its

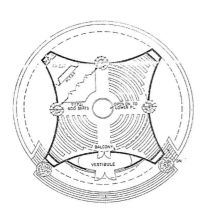

plan

Bailleres House

152

arched openings provide the fenestration, in an engineering tour de force. The four supporting columns form the Greek cross. Drawing on the richness of the Byzantine culture, Wright reaffirmed it in terms of the modern age.

Kaufmann House project

The **Bailleres House Project, Acapulco, Mexico, 1952.** An extension of the circles of the Jester House, it used a complex interplay of circle and dome forms. The chimney is the central pivotal mass of the structure. Wright reversed the fireplace, transforming it into a curved chamber of space,

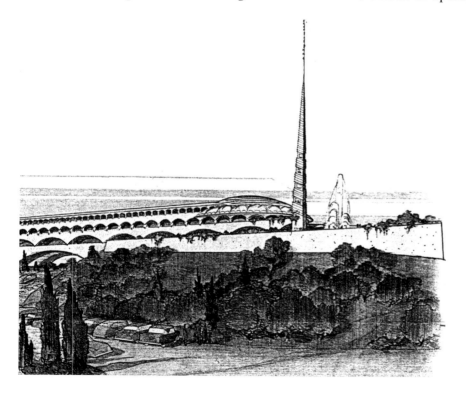

Marin County Civic Center

153

light—and water. The chimney scoops in fresh air which is cooled by passing across the waterfall pool set into the hearth. The element of fire is replaced by the element of water.

The **Edgar Kaufmann House Project, Palm Springs, California, 1951,** shows an asymmetrical copper shell roof over a crescent plan. The shell is a vertical reflex eclipse, creating a spinal ridge, and the articulated ribs of the copper roof seem to echo the curve and texture of some legendary creature. The spheroid boulders provide an appropriate material for this curved desert house. The "moat" that girdles the house is in fact a long, slender "lap" pool requested by Mrs. Kaufmann for her morning swim. It anticipates a new freedom of residential design.

Marin County Civic Center, San Rafael, California, 1957–62. The rolling hills of Marin inspired Wright to bridge the hills and express their form with his design. The seed form provided the archetype: the form of the concrete barrel vault roofs, the great dome of the library, the recurring shallow arches, the section of the columns. (Some critics described the design, pejoratively, as looking like a Roman aqueduct; apparently they were unable to differentiate between load-bearing Roman masonry arches and the suspended "pendant crescent" arches of the Civic Center.)

The great tapering spire provides a terminal, balanced by the hill where the structure begins and the prow where it ends. Wright designed sand-color walls and a gold-color roof to match the tawny golden hills of Marin. The manufacturer of the plastic roof membrane was unable to guarantee this color and a blue color was substituted.

Wright finished the conceptual drawings and handed them to his seniors, saying, "Now you can fill in the offices." It was originally designed for poured concrete. Built very economically ($23/sq. ft.) of prestressed concrete elements and standard acoustic ceilings, the design incorporates movable partition walls for future departmental expansion. The second wing includes the Hall of Justice, Sheriff's Department and jail. Only democratic America has a Frank Lloyd Wright jail.

David Wright House

154

V. C. Morris House Project, "Seacliff," San Francisco, 1945, 1955. Like some Arthurian watchtower, the house projects from a cliff, its floors descending to the sea. It is a stunning and visionary project, ahead of its age.

TILTING FLOORS AND WALLS

David Wright House, Phoenix, Arizona, 1950. Dismembering the last element of the "box" in 1943, Wright left the horizontal plane and began to move upward with the sloped floor plane of the Guggenheim Museum. In this house for his son, David Wright, the floor is raised above the desert floor to capture the breeze and the view above the orange grove. The entry winds up a sloped spiral ramp. Matching this slope, the traditional "horizontal" courses of the concrete-block wall system now leave the earth plane to follow both the angle of the ramp and the winding stair to the roof. When the house was completed Wright was not happy; he felt it seemed to be spinning, and added a linear horizontal wall to ground it.

Anderton Court Shops, Beverly Hills, California, 1952. To overcome the limited street exposure of an expensive site, Wright continued the street into the building, as a linear spiral ramp, to provide each shop with window frontage. Wright was away in Florence during its construction and it lacks his guiding eye. The elevation has been destroyed by a proliferation of L.A. signs.

Taliesin living room

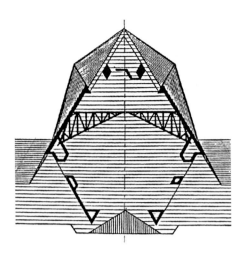

Second Unitarian Church ceiling

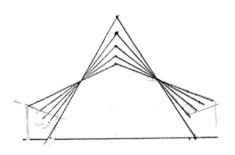

Unitarian Church warped ceiling

In the **Trinity Chapel Project, Norman, Oklahoma, 1938,** the floor has been elevated above the earth and access is by six intersecting ramps. In the Greek Orthodox Church the floor is concave. Wright said, "One is held in the hand of God." The floor of the Beth Sholom Synagogue is a concave hexagon.

TILTING WINDOWS

In the **D. M. Stromquist House, Bountiful, Utah, 1958,** the window transom bars leave the horizontal plane to follow the sloping roof above. In the Taliesin West living room windows the mullions leave the traditional, vertical axis and tilt 90 degrees to the sloping roof line. Together with the angled rafters of the projecting canvas screen, it creates an extraordinary perspective.

WARPED SPACE

Second Unitarian Church, Madison, Wisconsin, 1947. As the instrument of his creative power Wright's hands were eloquent, whether in drawing or describing his architecture. He derived the form for the Unitarian Church from observing his hands while held in prayer. The Unitarian Church does not use the steeple, but Wright saw that in prayer the hands themselves aspire to heaven: the angle, beginning low, progressively rises to form two warped planes.

In another departure from the linear past, Wright moved further into the world of plasticity with the warped plane, the form generated by the relationship between two planar systems. Photographs give a false impression of an A-frame roof, but in fact the roof has two ridges and three slopes. The roof is in the form of an offset pyramid with the top a sloping plane bordered on both sides by steep planes; the three planes converge at the apex. Below is the prow-shaped glass screen. The pitch of the gable ceiling, beginning low at the wide entry, increases as it proceeds toward the point of the prow, creating a warped surface. The two warped ceiling planes are created by the chords of a succession of trusses which support the roofs above. The angular glass screen is reflected in the pointed prow.

When the client ran out of funds, Wright brought in the Fellowship to complete the building.

VISIONARY PROJECTS
PLASTICITY AND SPIRAL SPACE

Frequently, as in the Unitarian Church and the Mile High Building, an angular form penetrates and reforms space like the prow of a moving ship. Like a great space marker heralding the twenty-first century, the Mile High is a haunting image of a new age. The concept received enormous publicity; it was one of Wright's most audacious projects.

Buildings such as the Lacy Tower, Park Point, Huntington Hartford Sports Complex, the Mile High, and Lenkurt were visions of the future, demanding the evolution of a culture and technology yet to come.

In 1948, E. J. Kaufmann financed Wright to prepare some visionary concepts, as seeds to encourage the redevelopment of Park Point in Pittsburgh.

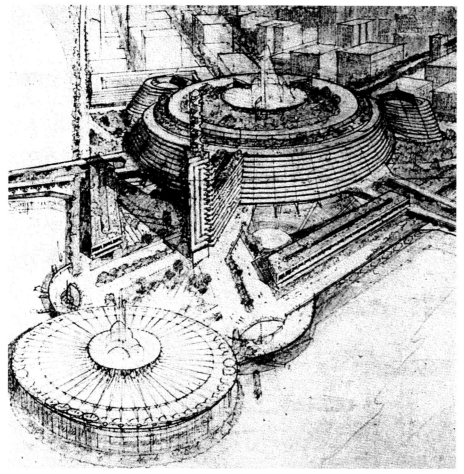

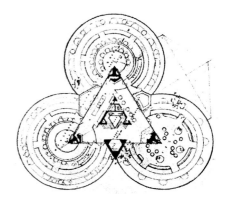

Huntington Hartford Sports Complex
plan

The Community Center, with its extraordinary domed caverns, is a visionary megastructure with its challenging, spiral form. The drawings of the
adjacent twin suspension bridge outpace Leonardo da Vinci. That year saw
the completion of the Huntington Hartford Sports Complex and other projects. Freed to stretch his imagination beyond limitations, Wright enjoyed a
banner year, bringing forth many of his most visionary concepts.

TRAGEDY

In 1947 Taliesin was rocked by another tragedy. Svetlana Peters, accompanied by her two children and their kitten, was driving her Jeep across a local
bridge when the cat leaped on her, causing her to lose control of the vehicle,
which smashed through the guardrail into the icy river below. Only her son
Brandock survived. Svetlana was Olgivanna's daughter from her first marriage, and wife of Wes Peters. She had been closer to her sister, Iovanna, than
anyone. It was a tragedy for all concerned. Wright designed a memorial
fountain from three harrow disks mounted on a triangular concrete base,
inset with a crystal.

Looking at the fountain, he transformed its simple form into the audacious design for the Huntington Hartford Sports Complex. A great crystal

Garden fountain

Huntington Hartford Sports Complex

form emerges from the earth and from its triangular core three great saucer disks cantilever into space. Wright drew on an ancient Celtic archetype—three circles centered on the points of an equilateral triangle. Within the core of the crystalline pyramid are located elevators, services, and accommodations. At the top is a circular sunbathing terrace. On the side, the three saucer-disks, with crystal glass domes, contain a lounge, a cinema and a dining room with dancing. The lower saucers contain gateway, tennis court and swimming pool, its water spilling over into the canyon below. In the alchemy of his art he transmuted tragedy into a celebration of life.

Celtic cross

THE ARCHETYPES

"Primitive American architecture, Toltec, Aztec, Mayan, and Incan, stirred my wonder, excited my imagination. I wished I might someday go to Mexico, Guatemala and Peru to join in excavating those long slumbering remains of lost civilizations," Wright declared. In the great cultures of Greece, Egypt and the Gothic, architecture communicated easily through a language of sign and symbol, icon and myth. "You can't get into the riches and depths of human expression unless you're born with something that is rich enough and strong enough to get there," he said. He tapped the universal forms that provide the profound resonance to his buildings.

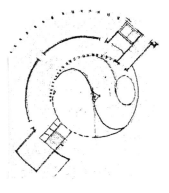

Strong Planetarium

Wright was unique in his capacity to encompass a universal array of forms. As Pygmalion, he brought to life the geometric archetypes: square, triangle, circle and spiral. Those forms provided the armature around which, like a growing crystal, his art took form. The spiral and sun wheel are among man's earliest archetypal symbols. The Chinese Yin/Yang symbolizes the feminine/masculine principle, the energy generated by the polarities: "All that comes to be." Wright wove his architecture out of an epiphany of opposites such as Reason/Emotion, Analysis/Synthesis, Classical/Romantic, Order/Disorder, Mass/Space, Subjective/Objective, Gravity/Pendant. Wright's signs and symbols speak a visual language that preceded words.

CREATION

Perhaps the creative process must forever remain a mystery beyond the reach of reason. Wright's best work is shrouded in such mystery. Of this creative process he said, "A thrilling moment in any architect's experience. He is about to see the countenance of something he is invoking with intense concentration. Out of this inner sense of order and love of the beauty of life something is to be born . . . Reality is spirit, the essence brooding just behind all aspect. Seize it! . . . the pattern of reality is super-geometric. Casting a spell or charm over any geometry."

His friend Gurdjieff said that there is creative energy that moves toward us, but when we lie, withdraws. No matter how outrageous his vision seemed, Wright was always true to the Muse; sharpening the cutting edge of his creativity with truth kept him youthful and renewed.

Asked by an apprentice about the fire and tragedy of his early life, Wright replied, "God may have been judging my character, but He knew that in architecture I always did my best."

Early one morning, Wright knocked on Jack Howe's door, with sketches for three new projects that he had conceived during the night—the hat trick.

As he grew older, like a movie played in reverse, his architecture became younger. (This is in contrast to the conventional architect, who, beginning as an avant-garde student, becomes conservative with age, ending his career designing a classic villa—one of Wright's first works.)

One day I saw the apprentices just completing the forms of the new Music Pavilion chimney and preparing to pour concrete when Mr. Wright appeared. Pointing with his cane (Shouldn't every architect have one?) he exclaimed, "It's too high, take it down three feet." At the age of 88 he was still working with the fine tuning of scale—the drawing-board solution versus the reality of construction. Even when it was finished he was dissatisfied with the scale of the structure; he demanded perfection.

TALIESIN

When the Museum of Modern Art in New York had an exhibition of one of Wright's houses, he loaned them his own Oriental stone lions (which he had brought back from Japan) to decorate the entry. Wright arrived at the museum to discover that the lions had been put in the wrong positions, so he went across to some hefty workers and asked them to move them. The workers gave it a try and said the lions were much too heavy—it would take a forklift to shift them. Wright was furious and called for his apprentices. He roared, "Boys, move the lions here." To general amazement the lions moved. And the apprentices didn't know how or why they were able to budge them, but as someone remarked, you couldn't refuse Mr. Wright.

A rich judge invited the Fellowship to his house near Phoenix. It was Saturday night, and beforehand we were admonished by Mrs. Wright not to make fools of ourselves or drink too much, for the Fellowship was on show. We all dressed up and endeavored to behave correctly when we arrived, though the waiters served us with large scoops of ice cream well spiked with brandy. Although the house was bourgeois by our standards, we enjoyed being in a luxurious house after our simple tents.

I had the impression that the judge was more interested in being immersed in the unique Taliesin social scene than he was in commissioning a new house. Toward the end of the evening the word was passed that Mr. Wright was pressing for the grand piano. (He seemed addicted to grand pianos, and there were already two at Taliesin.) Eventually there was an announcement that the judge had kindly donated the grand piano to Taliesin.

For Wright a piano was an essential instrument of inspiration and relaxation. The next day was spent in moving the three pianos to new locations in the library, theater and living room. At first twenty apprentices pitched in, but numbers dwindled as the day wore on. As we struggled with the last piano through a narrow doorway, there were only four of us, and with three holding it up, I slid underneath and screwed on the last of the legs. The judge would come to dinner maybe once a month. He never did get around to commissioning a house, but it did cost him a grand piano.

YOUTH

Asked by an apprentice if he was afraid of death, Wright replied, "Not at all. There is not much you can do about death. What is immortal will survive, but youth is a quality and once you have that it can never be lost." He shared the enthusiasm and openness of youth. He loved young students, and the best praise was when he said, "Son, I think we've got something there!" Although some apprentices saw Wright as a kind of god, he was endearingly human. Like many who suffered poverty in childhood, he would alternate between bouts of extravagance and a strong distaste for paying everyday bills. Temperamental and forgiving, he enjoyed jousting with his friends, teasing the pompous, but he was never vindictive, or mean-spirited. Introduced as a speaker at the University of California, Berkeley, by architect William Wurster, Wright saw hanging on the walls of the auditorium many large blowups of the architect's work. Wright couldn't resist saying, "Still doing the same old stuff I see!"

ARCHITECTURE FOR HEAVEN

One Sunday morning in 1956 after Wright's breakfast talk, apprentice Nezam Khazal (who introduced Wright to the Baghdad project) found himself working alone in the drafting room. Mr. Wright entered the room and came down the aisle, jauntily tapping his cane, and came alongside his table. Rhythmically tapping his cane, he was speaking aloud to himself, "Today [tap-tap] the architect will [tap] design his tomb. Nezam, fetch me a pencil and paper."

Khazal laid out the paper and, enthralled, watched as Wright sat down at the drafting board and began drawing his own tomb—a square plan, with semicircular windows, under a large, flat roof plane. The design included niches for the Lloyd Jones family.

A THOUSAND AND ONE NIGHTS

The "Arabian Nights" tales opened young Wright's imagination to mythic visions. Like Aladdin, he had grown up in a poor family. In 1957 myth became reality when he was invited by the king to Baghdad to design the new opera house. Iraq's young king was determined to use the oil revenues to spark a renaissance, a new city of culture, and commissioned Wright to design the opera house. Like a modern Aladdin flying in an airplane over Baghdad, Wright chose the island site on the Tigris. Inspired by the ancient structures of Sumer, he created an architecture of myth and imagination: a giant ziggurat topped by the opera house. On the concave cone top Wright placed "a golden figure of Aladdin and his wonderful lamp, the symbol of human imagination." Included in his commission was the design of the new post office, Sumer Museum and university complex.

Visiting the ancient buildings and museum, Wright felt a strong affinity with the ancient culture of Sumer. (The Celts are believed to have originated in this region.) Four thousand years after the first ziggurat was built here, he returned the form to its beginning.

"The Sculptor. Wind and water ceaselessly eroding . . ."
F.LL.W.

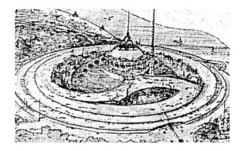

Baghdad Opera House

REVOLUTION AND ASSASSINATION

The completed presentation plans were delivered to the king in Baghdad in 1958. On the radio Wright heard his client had been assassinated. The revolution by Saddam Hussein had destroyed the regime and the project. The project itself endured, realized in a simplified form as the **Gammage Memorial Auditorium, Arizona State University, Tempe, Arizona, 1959.** The external crescent arches became pedestrian bridges that cross the parking area.

NEGATIVE FORM

In the **Lenkurt Project, San Mateo, California, 1955,** for an electronics factory, Wright developed further the dendriform columns of the Johnson Wax Building. Here the columns become a pure plastic form, flowing in one unbroken line from floor to roof. The ribbed calyx "capital" has disappeared within the pure form.

Lenkurt project

Lykes House (*left*) and
Robert Llewellyn Wright House

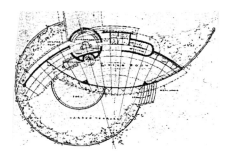

R. Llewellyn Wright plan

In Johnson Wax the negative form of the multiple spatial domes, impressed in the carport ceiling, created an extraordinary effect, as if space itself was pressing up, seeming to support the thick concrete ceiling above. In the Lenkurt skylights he took the negative form further. The interstices between the quatrefoil circular petals rise upward into a quadrant, concave skylight of Pyrex® tubes, where even the section is concave, as if the skylight had been formed by the pressure of four invisible spheres pressing on its surface. From above, the skylights appear like waves, formed by a windswept sea. Here Wright defines form and space as an expression of outer and inner forces. From the apex of a giant skylight a tall spire expands, like a butterfly's antenna.

The West is a masculine culture, choosing convex forms of mass. Wright's experience in the East introduced him to the feminine form of space discovered by Lao Tse. The educator/architect Rudolf Steiner said that the form of a plant reflects the equilibrium between the inner forces of growth and the outer elements pressing in. In his design for the concrete Goetheanum, 1926, he expressed concave negative forms, as in the concave surfaces of Islamic and Baroque architecture.

The **Robert Llewellyn Wright House, Bethesda, Maryland, 1956,** is a play between a concave plan and convex balconies. In one of Wright's last works, the **Lykes House, Phoenix, Arizona, 1959,** the balconies have become concave, and the prow is created by the meeting of two concave forms. While other architects were content to reshuffle the same basic elements, at the age of 91, Wright continued unabated his exploration of a new world of negative form and warped space.

TALIESIN

Wright seemed to embody several different architects, though he apparently had little trouble moving from one period to another. He would surprise us by sketching a detail straight out of a prairie house for Taliesin East, while in the same day designing a futuristic civic center.

In the last decade Wright had mellowed and had found the tranquil center, "the eye of the storm," within the vortex. He was enjoying his autumnal years and reaping the fruits of his fallow years; the harvest was coming in. The **Monona Terrace Civic Center Project, Madison, Wisconsin, 1938,** was again under way. A new vote on its construction was approaching. We were all enlisted for a *charrette* to complete a new model for presentation to the city. I found myself carving arches and forming tunnels. (The Civic Center was not constructed until the 1990s; it was completed in 1997.)

Wright, at 88, was beginning to relax and enjoy the fruits of a lifetime struggle. In his living room he had a small pagoda-like structure of stacked boxes, each holding a gold medal (including the R.I.B.A. medal from King George VI, two from the A.I.A., the De Medici medal from the city of Florence, and the Honorary Doctor of Fine Arts from Harvard, Princeton, Wisconsin and other universities). There was never any display of his awards.

Returning to Taliesin, I came upon Mr. Wright opening his mail one morning, and he passed a letter to me to read. It was from the National Academy of Arts and Letters, announcing that he had been elected a member of their elite fifty-member Academy. He said with a laugh, "Son, if you stick around long enough these things just come to you," and he tossed it into the wastebasket.

He was now in the final period of his work. The Guggenheim took much of his time and energy; he no longer had the raw physical energy to push through and supervise the execution of every complex structure, and some later works lacked the exquisite detailing of, say, the Johnson Wax Building done at the height of his power.

Marin County Civic Center, California, 1957, constructed 1962. Toward the end of his life Wright was chosen by the board of supervisors to design the Marin County Civic Center. He did the conceptual drawings and handed them over to the seniors. Unfortunately, he died before the building was finished, and it lacks his touch in the detailing. We missed Wright's genius for the unexpected; his setting up a module of rules and, just as you were getting used to it, breaking up the pattern with an inspired new direction.

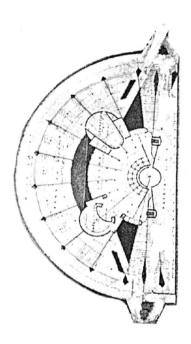

Monona Terrace Civic Center original plan

interior courts

The real magic in the building resides in the spatial organization, particularly in the interior courts. Although it appears to be one building, it is actually two buildings in parallel, with a Plexiglas®-covered court between them, which is planted at the bottom—rather like a miniature Guggenheim: from the third or fourth floor one can look right down through the building. It is in fact a pair of gigantic bridges spanning the four hills of the site. Each floor becomes successively shorter as it grounds against the grade of a hill.

When I first visited Marin County I found the unfinished Civic Center becalmed among the hills. Certain supervisors opposed to its construction had brought work to a halt. Architects and their wives were picketing outside with signs reading, "Vote for Recall and Wright." The recall movement was successful and the new supervisors voted to resume construction. It was emblematic of Wright's concern: developers versus environment.

In 1962 the Civic Center was nearing completion. The day before the grand opening, all the men in Aaron Green's office (Wright's representative, and the branch office in San Francisco) were on a crash program to help get the building finished. At midnight on the last evening the whole Civic Center was alive with activity. The great space made me feel I was inside a living organism, imbued with a dynamic sense of energy, filled with the sounds of hammering, power saws and whirring polishers. Two of us were given the job to fix the red square tile embossed with Wright's signature. He had signed "F.LL.W." in the soft clay of a tile about four inches square, which was then fired and glazed in his favorite red. There was a large bronze plaque at the entry listing all the dignitaries and the prime contractor involved in the building; in the bottom corner was a small recess. So with a tube of epoxy glue we pressed the red tile into the plaque and Mr. Wright's building was graced.

EDUCATION

In the summer and at Christmas the apprentices had the opportunity to present their work to Mr. Wright for his criticism. Generally, there was a suggestion about what kind of scheme to present. This year it was the low-cost Usonian Automatic, a concrete-block house—but in fact we were free to present whatever we felt was a good project.

The Christmas Box (as it was called) took place at Taliesin West on Christmas Day, as though the projects were presents. Ideally, one would spend two or three months on the Christmas Box. However, everyone was geared to the idea of *charrettes*, so it would all get completed in the last few days and nights. There was always a crisis in the drafting room the night before, and by 2 A.M. a tremendous clatter of colored pencils on paper as the apprentices practiced the Taliesin system of rendering, using many dotted textures to create shades and curved surfaces.

The whole Fellowship gathered around Mr. Wright on Christmas Day as he went through the schemes and made his comments. He could be devastatingly honest. He would open up the plans an apprentice had spent months working on, and say, "Hm, looks kind of familiar"—which could be crushing to the student who expected praise for his homage.

164

An Indian student presented a project which was a central building surrounded by twelve smaller ones connected by passageways, and he explained to Mr. Wright that this was a harem for an Indian prince: in each of the buildings was one of his concubines. Mr. Wright had a slow smile on his face, and he said, "Well boys, they have a different kind of culture to what we have here." As part of the Christmas celebrations, Mr. Wright gave each apprentice a present of locally made Indian silver jewelry, set with turquoise. In earlier eras apprentices were given one of his Japanese prints.

A TOUCH OF TARTNESS

The two Austrian architects, Neutra and Schindler, worked for Wright in the Twenties on the Barnsdall house. When Wright was asked for permission to display his work at an exhibition of California architecture, he replied with a laugh, "As long as I am not hung between the two thieves!" (Neutra had taken two of his clients, E. J. Kaufmann and Ayn Rand.) But when Schindler asked for help to support his application for a license, and later when he was dying, Wright showed his affection and wrote two very good letters of support.

THE WRIGHT STUFF

"I still hope to see these basic principles more comprehended. No man's work need resemble mine. If he understands the working of the principles behind the effects he sees here, with similar integrity he will have his own way of building," said Wright in *Architectural Forum* in 1950. "Personally, I believe architects are born. And I don't think they can be made . . . This is good soil in which it can sprout. Instead of imitating effects, search for the principle that made them original and own your own effects." Those who followed in his tradition became craftsmen continuing his work, while those who resonated with his energy were awakened to discover their own Muse. Wright was direct with those who sought to work with him. He replied to architect H.T.H. Widjeveld, "You were right in your conclusion that I would be difficult to work with. In fact I am impossible to work with." If we are to understand Wright it is necessary to explore the spatial consciousness that creates great architecture.

GRASS ROOTS

In many offices architects waited eagerly for the next issue of *Architectural Forum* devoted to a new Wright building. In the "work horse" office churning out dull projects it would stimulate the creative juices, and some Wrightian detail would enter into the plans of a current project.

In 1916 Bruce Goff, at the age of 12, was apprenticed to a big firm. He noticed that the chief designer would frequently refer, for inspiration, to a copy of a magazine he kept in a drawer of his desk. When he left for lunch Goff opened the drawer and discovered the work of Wright in the magazine, *Architectural Record*, 1908. Goff wrote to Wright for help and advice. Wright was always generous to youth and he sent the unknown teenager, as a gift, one of his few remaining copies of the Wasmuth Edition. Years later, Wright

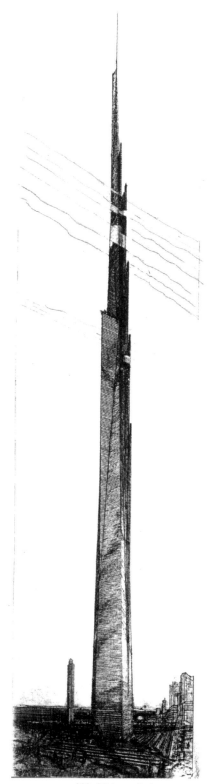

Mile High rendering

stated that Goff was the most imaginative architect of his time, one of the best American architects. Story has it that when Wright asked Goff to be his chief assistant, Goff turned him down, saying, "No, then I would become just another of your men."

AMERICA

Like Thoreau and Whitman, Wright was a quintessential American rebel who believed in freedom and democracy. He regretted that his country had never honored his work. (Some time after his death his portrait appeared on a U.S. postage stamp.)

At one of Mr. Wright's Sunday morning talks I sensed he was upset. He said, "I have just heard that the government has given the commission for the new Air Force Academy to the architectural firm Skidmore, Owings and Merrill—Skittles, Owes More and Sterile—the three blind mice." This was a pun on their tendency to imitate architect Mies van der Rohe.

But when an apprentice asked if he felt he was a prophet without honor in his own country, Mr. Wright replied, "Where else on this earth would I get to build some 600 revolutionary buildings and design 1,600 projects?"

The new architectural fad of hanging all the air-conditioning ducts and utility pipes on the outside had made its appearance. Wright said, "The architecture of exposed pipes and ducts is like your lover wearing her entrails on the outside."

Some wealthy clients might come for the weekend, and he would design them a house, but they would never build it. A few years later they might sell that site and buy another, and commission yet another design from him. They liked to be around the architect, but lacked the courage to go further. Some new clients arrived in a Rolls-Royce. I had the feeling these precursors of the yuppies were more interested in prestige designer labels than in content.

There were marvelous clients like the Kaufmann family, who would commission projects simply to engender extraordinary designs, much in the way Renaissance princes commissioned paintings and sculpture.

Wright's directness and penchant for publicity brought him in contact with future clients and filtered out the people he would not want to work with.

Wright had never been busier. Work was pouring in. The Guggenheim was nearing completion.

The Mile High Project, Chicago, 1956. A Chicago promoter came to see Wright, and asked him if he could design a TV tower that could be used to beam TV over a vast area. "Pity to go all that height for an antenna," Wright replied. "Why not go all the way and make it a mile?" The drawing was so large that it had to be mounted on a 4' × 8' sheet of plywood and turned on its side so Wright could work on it!

It could be any height, but he relished the challenge to devise a technology to make the ultimate verticality. Starting at the base with a kite-shaped plan, it changes to a triangle at its apex. Shaped like an upturned tapered rapier, with its hilt locked in the bedrock, its slender angular blade soars up into space. Along its sides, the external elevators emerge like Gothic spires.

166

Like a great space marker heralding the twenty-first century, it is a haunting image that heralds a technology and culture yet to come. It is Wright's most audacious project.

END OF AN ERA

One weekend there was much activity because Mike Todd and Elizabeth Taylor were visiting. Todd wanted to build a chain of cinemas to show his new wide-screen process, and was trying to get Buckminster Fuller and Wright to team together. Taliesin was on TV, which had the camera crews cursing as there were no power lines or telephone lines at Taliesin West.

The television interviewer was given the grand tour. Wright was incredibly gracious; he told some jokes, then showed him around the buildings, taking him finally into the drafting room where all projects were out on the tables with everyone pretending to be at work on them. It was a funny sight. Out there in the hot desert climate sat the apprentices at the drafting tables, pencils poised, every one of them dressed in their Sunday best suit and tie.

In the drafting room stood his latest work, a 10-foot-high rendering of the Mile High skyscraper, ready for presentation to the TV cameras and the press. At the far end of the room were giant photo blowups of drawings of Mr. Wright's early projects. He had been busy correcting details directly on the photos—the body of his work had to be perfect from beginning to end.

Being with Wright, like flying too close to the sun, could be dazzling, destroying one's individual expression.

A year after I left Taliesin I returned to visit Mr. Wright and showed him some photos of my first project. "Very good!" he said with a smile. Had I finally learned something during my time with him?

Pete Guerrero said that shortly before Wright's death he was invited to lunch with the Wrights. Mr. Wright had not appeared and Mrs. Wright asked him to go and find him.

Pete found Mr. Wright sitting on a bench in his room. Looking up, he said, "Pete, I must be getting old, I seem to have trouble getting up. Give me a hand."

Olgivanna had a wife's concern for her husband's health, saying, "Frank, take a nap, you look tired." The battles to save the Guggenheim were draining his health. To help him relax she took him out for Fellowship picnics in the desert he loved.

On April 4, 1959, Mr. Wright complained of a pain and was taken to the local hospital for surgery for an abdominal blockage. Although the operation was deemed a success, a few days later, on the evening of April 9, he died.

He had once said to us, "I daresay an idea is as close to God as we are likely, on this earth, to come."

By his grave in the family cemetery at Taliesin is a large standing stone, Celtic emblem of ancient Wales, and on his gravestone are inscribed his own words:

"Love of an idea is the love of God."

"A fine and good man has passed on. He was a genius not only of the building art of America but also in his life and art in general and has in his creations shown a passion for humanity. His forms in art will surely retain their greatness more than 100 years ahead. Personally I have lost a real friend."
Alvar Aalto,
in a telegram sent to
Architectural Forum

Appendix
THE ARCHETYPES OF ARCHITECTURE

THE FUNCTION OF architecture is to transform timeless archetypes into a new language for the age, and this was Wright's genius. He could raise the simple forms of a ziggurat into a breathtaking spiral of space, an apotheosis of form. His mastery of twentieth-century technology gave him a magician's ability to transform ancient elements into modern form.

Wright's architecture, like music, is a journey through magical experiences—a movement from compression to expansion, darkness to light, simplicity to complexity. A dark tunnel leads into magnificent luminosity, a labyrinth opens into breathtaking and endless space.

Frank Lloyd Wright transports us into new worlds through an odyssey of discovery.

THE ARCHITECTURAL POLARITIES

Narrow	/	Wide
Low	/	High
Ascend	/	Descend
Beneath	/	Above
Mystery	/	Revelation
Mass	/	Space
Asymmetry	/	Symmetry
Digital	/	Analog
Horizontal	/	Vertical
Compression	/	Expansion
Dark	/	Light
Centrifugal	/	Centripetal
Gravity	/	Pendant
Inner	/	Outer
Organic	/	Mechanical
Romantic	/	Classical
Feminine	/	Masculine
Straight	/	Indirect
Synthesis	/	Analysis
Intuitive	/	Rational
Direct	/	Labyrinth
Order	/	Disorder
Earth	/	Cosmos

A New Appraisal

IN AN AGE of cynicism Wright reaffirmed the power and range of the human spirit. He gave architecture back its soul once again, imbued with the energy of life. His work is as relevant today as ever. He traveled without charts into the unknown, on a lifelong voyage of discovery.

As in the words of Hamlet, "I could be bounded in a nutshell, and count myself a king of infinite space," Wright expanded the spatial frontiers of architecture into curved and warped space. Gifted with an extraordinary four-dimensional imagination, he outpaced the modernists, saying, "They speak, think and work in two dimensions while idealizing the third, and vice versa." He discovered the interflow of inner and outer space as a flow of energy and used it as a generator of form.

LIGHT

Wright called light "the great beautifier," transforming the gloomy workplace into a crystal palace and the dark Victorian residence into a new luminosity. Revealing the extraordinary relationship between light and space, his lighting enhances the quality of space. This fusion of natural and interior lighting gave his architecture its unique luminosity: daylight, introduced through skylight and clerestory, from north and south, was fused with interior lighting diffused through concealed lighting. Daylight and artificial light share a similar source. Every fixture matched the grammar of each project.

He modulated light through every kind of material: using decorative glass, perforated concrete blocks and plywood grilles on the exterior he broke the light into a musical play of light and shadow, through ornament, texture, and mass.

His driving revolutionary energy broke the mold of nineteenth-century eclecticism to create a new architecture for the twentieth century. Responding to every challenge in more than a thousand designs, he created a form for every function, a unique expression for every site.

With his mastery of technology he transmuted ancient archetypes into a new language for the age. He transformed the masonry architecture of compression into a dynamic structure of tension. He replaced outer load-bearing walls with an inner structural core and cantilevered floors, and freed the outer walls into becoming lightweight, freestanding planes of glass and

At the moment when both my money and visa were running out, fortune offered me work and a permanent visa through a friend in California. It meant leaving Taliesin. Working with someone as inspired as Wright could overwhelm one's individual expression and I felt the need for distance so I could observe Taliesin more objectively.

I went to say good-bye to Mr. and Mrs. Wright. They were sitting on their chairs in their magnificent living room, like a king with his queen. At the end of our talk I noticed the fluttering of a bird trapped inside the room. I caught it in my hand and released it through the window and our meeting ended. I, too, was free.

In California I found work and began freelancing to begin my own practice. Eventually, in San Francisco, I found work with Aaron Green, the only architect to share an office with Wright. Aaron was currently supervising the construction of Wright's Marin County Civic Center along with his own excellent projects, which included two hemicycle houses. I was back

copper. Thus he replaced the old post-and-beam system with structural continuity. His architecture effortlessly seemed to defy gravity, as he removed the old boundaries between floor, wall and roof, anticipating man's move to outer space.

IN THE NATURE OF MATERIALS

Wright had an uncanny sense of the earth and the nature of its materials: stone, and brick; steel, copper and bronze; glass, wood and textile. He revealed the intrinsic nature of every material and with integrity celebrated its virtues. Nothing was ever faked. I am always surprised by the number of people who were awakened when they first saw a Wright building. He was a lens that brought into focus a whole new world of truth and beauty.

INVENTIONS

As with his radiant floor heating hidden in the floor, so many of Wright's inventions—air-conditioning, the wall-hung toilet, the mitered glass corner window (Freeman House)—have been so seamlessly incorporated into the mainstream of architecture that few remember their origin. Others, like Wright's removal of the traditional corner and ridge post, are conspicuous by their absence. Sixty years ago, his first triangular structures were rejected by the establishment. Now I. M. Pei and other avant-garde architects employ the very forms he pioneered.

Pioneer of energy conservation and passive solar energy, he introduced the first earth berm and energy-efficient houses, passive-solar-energy architecture and the hemicycle house oriented to the solar cycle.

Wright destroyed the prison of the "box" and liberated man from its prison, transforming a closed system of compartments—and social classes—into a new sense of freedom and space.

Some minds prefer a secure prison to the insecurity of freedom, but when C. G. Jung, lying at the brink of death and experiencing a marvelous vision of heaven, was told he must return to earth, he complained, "Now I must return to the 'box system' again. For it seemed to me as if behind the horizon of the cosmos a three-dimensional world had been artificially built up, in which each person sat by himself in a little box."

INTERNATIONAL MODERNISTS

"Reason is modern man's most dangerous illusion."
C. G. Jung

The international modernists cobbled together a curious amalgam of revolutionary movements: Calvinism's puritan morality with its distrust of beauty; rationalism's naive belief in scientific progress and its worship of the machine; and a Marxist-style doctrine Wright called "left-wing modernists. The break between myself and them has widened."

Reason is but one facet of man; acknowledged or denied, the deeper levels of the psyche are ever present. Architecture, once the product of passion and inspiration of giants like Gaudí, Mackintosh, Richardson and Sullivan, became the provenance of clever intellects playing a "chess" game. When Wright's buildings conformed to their rules, as with the Unity Temple and Fallingwater, he was admired. When he introduced myth and decoration, he was condemned. With the decline of international modernism, one postmodernist critic pronounced Wright a good modernist, in the manner of the Pope proclaiming Buddha a good pre-Christian.

"THE AIR-CONDITIONED NIGHTMARE"

"What use to us are miraculous tools until we have mastered the human cultural use of them? We do not wish to live in a world where the machine has mastered the man! Much of the 'modern,' makes factories of our studios, churches and schools."
F.LL.W.

International architecture has become dominated by technology, emblematic of a mechanistic consumer society that threatens human values. Some modernists create, like advertising, impersonal skyscrapers crowned by corporate logos. Stripped of human sign and symbol, much modern architecture presents a sleek facade of technical perfectionism. Its slick use of glass, plastic, and steel has created a bland world, an irredeemable Megalopolis. Its technological exhibitionism masks an absence of content by a virtuoso display of its parts, flaunting its pipes and entrails suspended from a circus of structural engineering.

But where is man in all this?

The dehumanization of man was anticipated by such as Goethe, Kafka, and Henry Miller. The exaggeration of the rational has left man out of touch with his feelings. Without a rich inner experience, unable to create, he has nothing to give. That technology has outstripped our art is evident by the emptiness of much of our architecture. Arthur Drexler said, "A skyscraper is a machine for making money." Today, as developers compress more and more boxes into high-density structures, the box has become even more sterile, and man seems fated to spend his life living, working (and terminating) in a box. The horizontal ghetto is upended into the vertical tower. Wright called it "the sanitary slum." Now, more than ever, Wright's work, with all its richness and humanity, offers a hopeful, significant alternative.

THE INTERNATIONAL STYLE

"A civilization is just a way of life, and there have been many thousands of them in the world. But a culture is the way of making that life beautiful, and that we haven't got. We've never even started on that road in this country."
F.LL.W.

The International style, by imposing its standard design throughout the world, ignores the uniqueness of local culture and geography. Its high-rise towers dominate and destroy the fragile landscape, like the banners of medieval barons or multinational corporations, aggressive emblems of territorial conquest. Albert Camus said that certain cities, such as the ugly town of Oran in Algeria where he was born, "exorcised the landscape."

architecture, but when he was asked about Santa Barbara he was in a mellow mood and replied, "It's a lovely place, everything grows so well here." That was the last time I saw him.

Throughout the world, in New York, London, Paris and elsewhere, whole areas of redevelopment—high-rise office blocks and low-cost housing—have become wastelands devoid of spirit of place and human scale.

Wright's Broadacre City is a solution more valid than ever, as it is inspired by the nature of the site. It is more than just another garden city. Its architecture, following the contours of the landscape, nourishes the ecological balance between man and nature. Man himself is as much a part of the *genius loci* as the geography and will reflect its presence or absence. With his love of the earth and nature, Wright built in harmony with the landscape: He called his architecture "organic" because it was indeed a living element rooted in the landscape. In contrast to the white modernism that dominates and destroys the fabric of the landscape, organic architecture symbiotically enhances nature and allows nature to enhance the architecture. Modern architecture, by attempting to look forever young, ages badly, with its peeling white walls, cracking concrete and rust-streaked chromium. Its hard, unremitting surfaces destroy the delicate aura of the land.

While the chromium gloss of modernism is overstated, organic architecture achieves its power through subtlety and presence. Wright's buildings age well. Cypress boards develop the silver glow of weathered wood. Nature claims it as one of her own; vine, plant and tree enwrap his buildings. Roof shingles turn silver, copper develops its green patina, reflecting the changing sky and the passage of seasons. An unseen presence fills the air, an interchange with nature, a sense of spirit from the natural world. Fashionable icons, such as modernism and postmodernism, may come and go, but time washes away the superficial, and Wright's work will continue to endure.

At age 91, Wright was still the incarnation of Taliesin; his creativity reached its peak, as the fecundity and diversity of "the seventh age" testifies. The body of his work is awesome. He seemed like a force of nature, a four-dimensional visionary in a two-dimensional world. Like Proteus, historical father of Taliesin, maker of all form and Greek god of the sea, Wright was a giant without equal.

BIBLIOGRAPHY

An Autobiography, Frank Lloyd Wright, Longmans Green & Co., New York, 1932
An Autobiography, revised second edition, Duell, Sloan & Pearce, New York, 1943
An Autobiography, third edition, Horizon Press, New York, 1977
In the Nature of Materials, Henry Russell Hitchcock, Duell, Sloan & Pearce, New York, 1941
Frank Lloyd Wright on Architecture, edited by Frederick Gutheim, Duell, Sloan & Pearce, New York, 1941
An American Architecture, E. Kaufmann, Horizon Press, New York, 1955
A Testament, Frank Lloyd Wright, Horizon Press, New York, 1957
The White Goddess, Robert Graves, Farrar, Straus & Giroux, New York, 1966
Memories, Dreams, Reflections, C. G. Jung, Vintage Books, New York, 1965
Frank Lloyd Wright's Usonian Houses, John Sergeant, Whitney Library of Design, New York, 1976

(Quotations in this book were drawn largely from the above sources.)

Buildings and Projects
(a complete list)

Wright's architecture covered nearly every conceivable kind of building, including: low-cost housing, kindergartens, universities, farms, factories, offices, stores, banks, hotels, restaurants, country clubs, sports centers, health centers, observatories, museums, art galleries, theaters, opera houses, post offices, radio stations, civic centers, courthouses, a jail, gas stations, parking garages, bridges, fairgrounds, churches, a mortuary, urban and lakefront developments. A true architect of the world, Wright designed buildings in Italy, Iraq, Japan, Mexico, India, Egypt, Canada, and El Salvador.

Title	Status	Descr.	Location
1885 Civil Eng. Drgs	pjt	eng	
1887 Drawings for LHS	pjt	res	
1887 Unitarian Chapel	pjt	chpl	Sioux City, IA
1887 Country Residence	pjt	res	Hillside, WI
1887 HHS Home Building	dmd	schl	Spring Green, WI
1888 Auditorium Drg(s)	EXE	ornmt	Chicago, IL
1889 FLLW Oak Park Hse	EXE	res	Oak Park, IL
1890 Charnley, James	EXE	res	Ocean Springs, MS
1890 Sullivan, Louis	EXE	res	Ocean Springs, MS
1890 Macharg, W. S.	dmd	res	Chicago, IL
1890 Copper, Henry	EXE	res	Chicago, IL
1892 Blossom, George	EXE	res	Chicago, IL
1892 Clark, W. Irving	EXE	res	La Grange, IL
1892 Emmond, Robert	EXE	res	La Grange, IL
1892 Gale, Thomas	EXE	res	Oak Park, IL
1892 Harlan, Dr. Allison	dmd	res	Chicago, IL
1892 McArthur, W.	EXE	res	Chicago, IL
1892 Parker, Robert	EXE	res	Oak Park, IL
1892 Roberts, C. E.	pjt	res	Oak Park, IL
1892 Sullivan, Albert	dmd	res	Chicago, IL
1892 Victoria Hotel	dmd	(LHS)	Chicago Hts, IL
1893 Fisherman & Genie	EXE	mural	Oak Park, IL
1893 Gale, Walter	EXE	res	Oak Park, IL
1893 Lamp, Robert, ctg	dmd	res	Madison, WI
1893 Library & Museum	pjt	mus	Milwaukee, WI
1893 Mendota Boathse	dmd	boathse	Madison, WI
1893 Monona Boathse	pjt	boathse	Madison, WI
1893 Winslow, William	EXE	res	River Forest, IL
1893 Wooley, Francis	EXE	res	Oak Park, IL
1893 FLLW Oak Pk Playrm	EXE	res	Oak Park, IL
1894 Bagley Cmmn Rm	pjt	sclp	Chicago, IL
1894 Bagley Baptis. Font	EXE	sclp	Chicago, IL
1894 Bagley, Frederick	EXE	res	Hinsdale, IL
1894 Bassett, Dr. H. W.	dmd	res	Oak Park, IL
1894 Belknap Apts	pjt	apts	Austin, IL
1894 Candlesticks/Metal	pjt	vase	
1894 Flowerholder	EXE	china	
1894 Goan, Orrin	pjt	res	La Grange, IL
1894 Goan, Peter	EXE	res	La Grange, IL
1894 McAfee, A. C.	pjt	res	Kenilworth, IL
1894 Monolithic Con. Bk	pjt	bnk	
1894 Roloson Houses	pjt	res	Oak Park, IL
1895 Baldwin, Jesse	pjt	res	Oak Park, IL
1895 Francis Apartments	dmd	apts	Chicago, IL
1895 Francisco Terr. Apts	dmd	apts	Chicago, IL
1895 Hanging Vases	pjt	china	
1895 Luxfer Prism	EXE	prism	Chicago, IL
1895 Luxfer Prism Off. Bldg	pjt	offc	Chicago, IL
1895 Moore, Nathan	dmd	res	Oak Park, IL
1895 Residence, Arch Rev	pjt	res	June 1900
1895 Waller Aptments	EXE	apts	Chicago, IL
1895 Williams, Chauncey	EXE	res	River Forest, IL
1895 Wolf Lake Amus. Pk	pjt	amuse	Chicago (near)
1895 FLLW Oak Park Studio	EXE	stdo	Oak Park, IL
1895 Young, H. P., rem	EXE	res	Oak Park, IL
1896 Devin, Mrs. David	EXE	grph	River Forest, IL
1896 Goodrich, H. C.	EXE	res	Oak Park, IL
1896 Heller, Isadore	EXE	res	Chicago, IL
1896 House Beautiful	EXE	grph	River Forest, IL
1896 Perkins Apts	pjt	apts	Chicago, IL
1896 Roberts Clock	pjt	furn	Oak Park, IL
1896 Roberts, C. E., rem	EXE	res	Oak Park, IL
1896 Roberts, C. E., stbles	EXE	res	Oak Park, IL
1896 Roberts, C. E., housing	EXE	hsng	Ridgeland, IL
1896 Roberts, C. E., smr hse	pjt	res	
1897 All Souls (studies)	pjt	relig	Chicago, IL
1897 Factory Chic Screw	pjt	fcty	Chicago, IL
1897 Furbeck, George	EXE	res	Oak Park, IL
1897 Roberts Block Plan	pjt	blkpl	Oak Park, IL
1897 Romeo & Juliet Tower	EXE	wndml	Spring Green, WI
1897 Wallis, H., boathouse	dmd	boathse	Lake Delavan, WI
1898 Furbeck, Rollin	EXE	res	Oak Park, IL
1898 Mozart Gardens Rest	dmd	clbhs	River Forest, IL
1898 Smith, George	EXE	res	Oak Park, IL
1898 Vases & Flwerhldrs	pjt	china	
1898 Waller, E. C.	pjt	res	River Forest, IL
1899 Cheltenham Resort	pjt	amuse	Chicago, IL
1899 Eckhart, Mrs. Robert	dmd	res	Chicago, IL
1899 Ornamental	pjt	sclp	Chicago, IL
1899 Residence Arch Rev	pjt	res	June 1900
1899 Waller, E. C., rem	dmd	res	River Forest, IL
1900 Abraham Lincoln Cen.	pjt	relig	Chicago, IL
1900 Adams, Mrs. Jessie W.	EXE	res	Longwood, IL
1900 Adams, William	EXE	res	Chicago, IL
1900 Blossom, George Gar	EXE	stbl	Chicago, IL
1900 Bradley, B. Harley	EXE	res	Kankakee, IL
1900 Children of the Moon	EXE	sclp	Springfield, IL
1900 Dana, Susan L.	EXE	res	Springfield, IL
1900 Flower/Crannied Wall	EXE	sclp	Springfield, IL
1900 Foster, S. A.	EXE	res	Chicago, IL
1900 Hickox, Warren	EXE	res	Kankakee, IL
1900 Hills, E. R. (Moore Gir)	EXE	res	Oak Park, IL
1900 Jones, Fred B., boathse	dmd	res	Lake Delavan, WI
1900 LHJ Home in Prairie	pjt	res	Feb. 1901
1900 LHJ Quad. Block Pln	pjt	blkpl	Feb. 1901
1900 LHJ Small Hse/Room in	pjt	res	Jun. 1901

1900 McArthur, W., res rm	EXE	res	Chicago, IL	1904 Larkin Workmen's H.	pjt	hsng	Buffalo, NY
1900 McArthur, W., gar	EXE	res	Chicago, IL	1904 Martin, D. D.	EXE	res	Buffalo, NY
1900 Pitkin, E. H., smr lodge	EXE	res	Sapper Island, CN	1904 Martin, Frank (DDM)	pjt	res	Buffalo, NY
1900 Residence for Oakld	pjt	res	Oakland, CA	1904 Owens, O. D., rem	pjt	res	
1900 Unid. Ornament	EXE	ornmt		1904 Residence (wd & plas)	pjt	res	Highland Park, IL
1900 Unid. Lights, Lamps	EXE	lamp		1904 Scudder, J. A.	pjt	res	Ontario, CN
1900 Unid. Screens, Grilles	EXE	scrn		1904 Smith Bank #1	pjt	bnk	Dwight, IL
1900 Unid. Furniture, Early	EXE	furn		1904 Soden	pjt	res	
1900 Unid. Architecture	EXE	cbntwk		1904 Study/Bldg, Brick, Con.	pjt	stdy	
1900 Unid. Glass Designs	EXE	glass		1904 Ullman, H. J.	pjt	res	Oak Park, IL
1900 Unid. Glass Designs	EXE	glass		1904 Unity Temple	EXE	relig	Oak Park, IL
1900 Wallis, Henry, #1	pjt	res	Lake Delavan, WI	1905 Adams, Mary	EXE	res	Highland Pk, IL
1900 Wallis, Henry, #2	EXE	res	Lake Delavan, WI	1905 Adams, M. H., rem	pjt	res	
1901 Davenport, E. Arthur	EXE	res	River Forest, IL	1905 Baldwin, Hiram, #2	EXE	res	Kenilworth, IL
1901 Fricke, William	EXE	res	Oak Park, IL	1905 Brown, Chas. (model)	EXE	res	Evanston, IL
1901 Henderson, F. B.	EXE	res	Elmhurst, IL	1905 Buckingham, C.	pjt	offc	Chicago, IL
1901 Herbert, Dr. A. W., rem	dmd	res	Evanston, IL	1905 Chair (Taliesin type)	EXE	furn	publ. MOMA
1901 Jones, Fred. B.	EXE	res	Lake Delavan, IL	1905 Cinema San Diego	pjt	cnma	San Diego, CA
1901 Lexington Terr. Apts	pjt	apts	Chicago, IL	1905 Cummings, E. A., rl. est.	dmd	bldg	River Forest, IL
1901 Lowell, M. H., studio	pjt	res	Matteawan, NY	1905 Darrow, Mrs.	pjt	res	Chicago, IL
1901 Metzger, Victor	pjt	res	Desbarats, CN	1905 Double res., b/b type	pjt	res	Oak Park, IL
1901 River Forest Golf	dmd	clbhs	River Forest, IL	1905 E-Z Polish Factory	EXE	fcty	Chicago, IL
1901 Thomas, Frank	EXE	res	Oak Park, IL	1905 Gale, Mrs. Thos., smr	EXE	res	Whitehall, MI
1901 Universal Port	dmd	expo	Buffalo, NY	1905 Gilpin, T. E.	dmd	res	Oak Park, IL
1901 Village Bank, Concr.	pjt	bnk		1905 Glasner, W. A.	EXE	res	Glencoe, IL
1901 Waller, E. C., gatehse	dmd	gatehse	River Forest, IL	1905 Hardy, Thomas P.	EXE	res	Racine, WI
1901 Wallis, Henry, gatehse	EXE	gatehse	Lake Delavan, WI	1905 Heath, W. R.	EXE	res	Buffalo, NY
1901 Wilder, T. E., stables	dmd	stbls	Elmhurst, IL	1905 House on a Lake	pjt	res	
1901 Willits, Ward W.	EXE	res	Highland Park, IL	1905 Johnson, A. P.	EXE	res	Lake Delavan, WI
1902 Delavan Yacht Club	dmd	boathse	Lake Delavan, WI	1905 Lawrence Mem. Lib.	EXE	liby	Springfield, IL
1902 Dial Office, rem	pjt	offc	Chicago, IL	1905 Martin, D. D., grdenr's	EXE	res	Buffalo, NY
1902 Gerts, G., dbl cott.	EXE	res	Whitehall, MI	1905 McArthur Apt. Bldg.	pjt	apts	Chicago, IL
1902 Gerts, W., cottage	EXE	res	Oak Park, IL	1905 Moore, Nathan	pjt	res	Oak Park, IL
1902 Heurtley, "Les Cheveux"	EXE	res	Marquette I., MI	1905 River Forest Tnnis Cl	EXE	clbhs	River Forest, IL
1902 Hillside Home School	EXE	schl	Spring Green, WI	1905 Rookery Remod.	EXE	offc	Chicago, IL
1902 Lake Delavan Clbhse	pjt	boathse	Lake Delavan, WI	1905 Smith Bank #2	EXE	bnk	Dwight, IL
1902 Little, F. W.	EXE	res	Peoria, IL	1905 Study 1905	pjt	stdy	
1902 Little, F. W. (Ross)	pjt	res	Wayzata, MN	1905 Sutton, Harvey, #1	pjt	res	McCook, NE
1902 Martin, W. E.	EXE	res	Oak Park, IL	1905 Sutton, Harvey, #2	pjt	res	McCook, NE
1902 Mosher, John	pjt	res		1905 Sutton, Harvey, #3	EXE	res	McCook, NE
1902 Residence Bd/Bttn	pjt	res	Oak Park, IL	1905 Varnish Factory	pjt	fcty	Buffalo, NY
1902 Ross, Charles	EXE	res	Lake Delavan, WI	1905 Yahara Boathouse	pjt	boathse	Madison, WI
1902 Skyscraper Vase	EXE	vase		1906 Beachy, P. A.	EXE	res	Oak Park, IL
1902 Spencer, George	EXE	res	Lake Delavan, WI	1906 Blossom, G., gar adds	EXE	garage	Chicago, IL
1902 Terracotta Flwrhld	EXE	vase		1906 Bock, Rich., studio	pjt	stdo	Maywood, IL
1902 Waller, E. C., smmr #1	pjt	res	Charlevoix, MI	1906 Brown, Harry, #1	pjt	res	Genesco, IL
1903 Abraham Lincoln Ctr	EXE	relig	Chicago, IL	1906 Brown, Harry, #2	pjt	res	Genesco, IL
1903 Barton, George (DDM)	EXE	res	Buffalo, NY	1906 Derhodes, K. C.	EXE	res	South Bend, IN
1903 Cement Vase	EXE	vase		1906 Devin, Mrs. Aline	pjt	res	Eliot, ME
1903 Cheney, Edwin H.	EXE	res	Oak Park, IL	1906 Frazer	pjt	res	
1903 Freeman, W. H.	dmd	res	Hinsdale, IL	1906 Fuller, Grace	dmd	res	Glencoe, IL
1903 Jones, Fred B., res etc.	EXE	res	Lake Delavan, WI	1906 Gerts, Walter	pjt	res	Glencoe, IL
1903 Lamp, Robert, res #1	pjt	res	Madison, WI	1906 Gridley, A. W.	EXE	res	Batavia, IL
1903 Larkin Co. Adm. Bldg.	dmd	bldg	Buffalo, NY	1906 Hoyt, P. D.	EXE	res	Geneva, IL
1903 Prairie House Type D	pjt	res		1906 LHJ Fireproof House	pjt	res	April 1907
1903 Railway Stations (3)	pjt	trns	Chicago suburbs	1906 Ludington, R. S.	pjt	res	Dwight, IL
1903 Roberts Quad. Plan	pjt	blkpl	Oak Park, IL	1906 Millard, George M.	EXE	res	Highland Park, IL
1903 Scoville Park Fnt.	EXE	sclp	Oak Park, IL	1906 Nicholas, Frederick	EXE	res	Flossmoor, IL
1903 Studio-Res, Artist's	pjt	stdo	Oak Park, IL	1906 Pettit Memorial Chpl	EXE	chpl	Belvedere, IL
1903 Waller, E. C., smmr #2	pjt	res	Charlevoix, MI	1906 River Forest Tnnis Cl.	EXE	clbhs	River Forest, IL
1903 Walser, J. J.	EXE	res	Chicago, IL	1906 Robie, Frederick C.	EXE	res	Chicago, IL
1904 Baldwin, Hiram, #1	pjt	res	Kenilworth, IL	1906 Rug Designs, Early	pjt	crpt	
1904 Barnes, Charles	pjt	res	McCook, NE	1906 Seidenbecher, Jos.	pjt	res	Chicago, IL
1904 Clark, Robert	pjt	res	Peoria, IL	1906 Shaw, C. Thaxter, rem	dmd	res	Montreal, CN
1904 Hanging Lamp	pjt	lamp		1906 Shaw, C. Thaxter	pjt	res	Montreal, CN
1904 Lamp Post in Conc.	pjt	sclp		1906 Stone, Elizabeth	pjt	res	Glencoe, IL
1904 Lamp, Robert, res #2	EXE	res	Madison, WI	1907 Coonley, Avery	EXE	res	Riverside, IL

Year/Name	Type	Cat	Location
1907 Coonley, Avery Chhse	EXE	res	Riverside, IL
1907 Fabyan, Col. Geo.	EXE	res	Geneva, IL
1907 Fox River Country C.	dmd	ctycb	Geneva, IL
1907 Hunt, Stephen M. B.	EXE	res	La Grange, IL
1907 Lake Delavan Cott.	pjt	res	Lake Delavan, WI
1907 Larkin Co. Exhibition	dmd	expo	Norfolk, VA
1907 Martin, Emma	EXE	res	Oak Park, IL
1907 McCormick, Harold	pjt	res	Lake Bluff, IL
1907 Pebbles-Balch Shop	dmd	shop	Oak Park, IL
1907 Porter, Andrew T.	EXE	res	Spring Green, WI
1907 Porter, A., Smmr #1	pjt	res	Spring Green, WI
1907 Tomek, F. F.	EXE	res	Riverside, IL
1907 Westcott, Burton	EXE	res	Springfield, OH
1908 Baker, Frank, #1	pjt	res	Wilmette, IL
1908 Boynton, E. E.	EXE	res	Rochester, NY
1908 Brigham, E. D., stables	pjt	stbl	Glencoe, IL
1908 Browne's Bookstore	dmd	shop	Chicago, IL
1908 Como Orchards Smmr	EXE	rsrt	Darby, MT
1908 Copeland, Dr. W. H., #1	pjt	res	Oak Park, IL
1908 Davidson, Walter V.	EXE	res	Buffalo, NY
1908 Evans, Ray W.	EXE	res	Chicago, IL
1908 Gilmore, E. A.	EXE	res	Madison, WI
1908 Guthrie, William N.	pjt	res	Sewanee, TN
1908 Horner, L. K.	dmd	res	Chicago, IL
1908 Horseshoe Inn	pjt	inn	Estes Park, CO
1908 Japanese Print Exhibit	dmd	exhibn	Chicago, IL
1908 Little, F. W., smmr hse	pjt	res	Wayzata, MN
1908 Martin summer cott.	pjt	res	Lake Erie, NY
1908 May, Meyer	EXE	res	Grand Rapids, MI
1908 Melson, J. G.	pjt	res	Mason City, IA
1908 Roberts, Isabel	EXE	res	River Forest, IL
1908 Stockman, Dr. G. C.	EXE	res	Mason City, IA
1909 Baker, Frank, #2	EXE	res	Wilmette, IL
1909 Bitter Root Inn	dmd	inn	Darby, MT
1909 Bitter Root Town	pjt	twnpl	Darby, MT
1909 City Dwelling/Glass	pjt	res	
1909 City National Bank/Hot.	EXE	bnk	Mason City, IA
1909 Clark, Robert (Little)	EXE	res	Peoria, IL
1909 Coonley, Avery, study	pjt	res	Riverside, IL
1909 Copeland, Dr. W. H., #2	EXE	res	Oak Park, IL
1909 Copeland, Dr. W. H., gar	EXE	res	Oak Park, IL
1909 Gale, Mrs. Thomas	EXE	res	Oak Park, IL
1909 Ingalls, J. Kibben	EXE	res	River Forest, IL
1909 Larwell	pjt	res	Muskegon, MI
1909 Lexington Terr. Apts	pjt	apts	Chicago, IL
1909 Martin, D. D., Lake Erie	pjt	res	Lake Erie, NY
1909 Martin, W. E., pergola	EXE	res	Oak Park, IL
1909 Parker, Lawton, stud.	pjt	res	
1909 Puppet Playhouse	EXE	furn	Oak Park, IL
1909 Roberts, Mary	pjt	res	River Forest, IL
1909 Screen (MOMA) (HSSR)	pjt	glass	
1909 Steffens, Oscar	dmd	res	Chicago, IL
1909 Stewart, George	EXE	res	Montecito, CA
1909 Stohr Arcade Shops	dmd	shop	Chicago, IL
1909 Study for Conc. Box	pjt	stdy	
1909 Thurber Art Gallery	dmd	glry	Chicago, IL
1909 Waller Bathing Pavilion	pjt	bathhse	Charlevoix, MI
1909 Waller Rental Hsing	pjt	hsng	River Forest, IL
1910 Amberg, J. H.	EXE	res	Grand Rapids, MI
1910 Blythe-Markley Off.	EXE	offc	Mason City, IA
1910 Irving, E. P.	EXE	res	Decatur, IL
1910 Schoolhouse	pjt	schl	Crosbyton, TX
1910 Universal Prtlnd Cem.	dmd	expo	New York, NY
1910 FLLW Fiesole	pjt	stdo	Fiesole
1910 Ziegler, Rev. J. R.	EXE	res	Frankfort, KY
1911 Amer. Homes Twnhse	pjt	twnhs	first studies
1911 Angster, Herbert	dmd	res	Lake Bluff, IL
1911 Balch, O. B.	EXE	res	Oak Park, IL
1911 Balloons & Confetti	EXE	glass	Riverside, IL
1911 Banff Pavilion	dmd	rsrt	Alberta, CN
1911 Banff Railway Sta.	pjt	trns	Alberta, CN
1911 Booth, Sherman, #1	pjt	res	Glencoe, IL
1911 Booth, Sherman, smmr	pjt	res	
1911 Booth Art Gallery	pjt	glry	Glencoe, IL
1911 Booth Park Features	pjt	pkftr	Glencoe, IL
1911 Booth Station #1	pjt	trns	Glencoe, IL
1911 Booth Station #2	pjt	trns	Glencoe, IL
1911 Booth Town Hall	pjt	twnhl	Glencoe, IL
1911 Christian Catholic C. #2	pjt	relig	Zion, IL
1911 Coonley Gardnr's Cott.	EXE	res	Riverside, IL
1911 Coonley Greenhouse	pjt	res	Riverside, IL
1911 Coonley Kindergarten	pjt	kdgn	Riverside, IL
1911 Coonley Playhouse	EXE	thtr	Riverside, IL
1911 Cutten, Arthur E.	pjt	res	Downer's Grove, IL
1911 Esbenshade, E. E.	pjt	res	Milwaukee, WI
1911 Gerts, Walter, rem	pjt	res	River Forest, IL
1911 Lake Geneva Inn	dmd	inn	Lake Geneva, WI
1911 Madison Hotel	pjt	htl	Madison, WI
1911 Porter, Andrw, smmr #2	pjt	res	Spring Green, WI
1911 Schroeder, Edward	pjt	res	Milwaukee, WI
1911 Suburban House	pjt	res	
1911 Wright, Anna Lloyd	EXE	res	
1911 FLLW Goethe St. Stud.	pjt	stdo	Chicago, IL
1911 FLLW Oak Park St., rem	EXE	res	Oak Park, IL
1911 FLLW Taliesin I	dmd	res	Spring Green, WI
1912 Adams, Harry, #1	pjt	res	Oak Park, IL
1912 Booth, Sherman, stable	pjt	res	Glencoe, IL
1912 Florida Cottage	pjt	res	Palm Beach, FL
1912 Greene, William	EXE	res	Aurora, IL
1912 Kehl Dance Academy	pjt	schl	Madison, WI
1912 Little, F. W. "Northme"	dmd	res	Wayzata, MN
1912 Mendelson, Jerome	pjt	res	Albany, NY
1912 Park Ridge Cntry Cl.	dmd	ctycb	Park Ridge, IL
1912 Press Building	pjt	offc	San Francisco, CA
1912 School Hse La Grange	pjt	schl	La Grange, IL
1912 Urban House	pjt	twnhs	Milwaukee, WI
1912 FLLW Taliesin Cotts.	pjt	res	Spring Green, WI
1913 Adams, Harry, #2	EXE	res	Oak Park, IL
1913 Carnegie Library	pjt	liby	Pembroke, CN
1913 Chinese Restaurant	pjt	rest	Milwaukee, WI
1913 Double Residence	pjt	res	Ottawa, CN
1913 Hilly, M. B.	pjt	res	Brookfield, IL
1913 Kellogg, W. J.	pjt	res	Milwaukee, WI
1913 Midway Gardens	dmd	rest	Chicago, IL
1913 Post Office Canada	pjt	p.o.	Ottawa, CN
1913 Richard Co. Off. Bldg.	pjt	bldg	Milwaukee, WI
1914 Embassy for the USA	pjt	emby	Tokyo
1914 Frmrs & Mrchnts Bk	pjt	bnk	Spring Green, WI
1914 Imperial Hotel #1	pjt	htl	Tokyo
1914 Jaxon, Honore, 3 res	pjt	res	
1914 Kiosk Park Feature	pjt	pkftr	Ottawa, CN
1914 Mori Orientl Art Shp	dmd	offc	Chicago, IL
1914 Spring Green Frgrnd	pjt	fair	Spring Green, WI
1914 State Bank S. Green	pjt	bnk	Spring Green, WI
1914 Vogelsng Dnnr Grdn	pjt	rest	Chicago, IL
1914 FLLW Taliesin II	pjt	res	Spring Green, WI
1915 Amer. Homes Twnhse.	pjt	hsng	Milwaukee, WI
1915 Bach, Emil	EXE	res	Chicago, IL
1915 Barnsdall, Olive Hill	pjt	thtr	Los Angeles, CA
1915 Booth, Sherman, #2	EXE	res	Glencoe, IL
1915 Brigham, E. D.	EXE	res	Glencoe, IL
1915 Chinese Hospital	pjt	hspl	
1915 Christian Catholic C. #1	pjt	relig	Zion City, IL
1915 German, A. D., warehse	EXE	wrhs	Richland Center, WI

1915 Imperial Hotel #2	dmd	htl	Tokyo
1915 Jensen, Jens	pjt	grph	
1915 Lake Shore Residence	pjt	res	
1915 Model Quarter Section	pjt	blkpl	Chicago, IL
1915 Ravine Bluffs Bridge	EXE	brdg	Glencoe, IL
1915 Ravine Bluffs Hsing	EXE	hsng	Glencoe, IL
1915 Wood, M. W.	pjt	res	Decatur, IL
1916 Allen, Henry J.	EXE	res	Wichita, KS
1916 Bagley, Joseph	EXE	res	Grand Beach, MI
1916 Behn (Voight)	pjt	res	Grand Beach, MI
1916 Bogk, F. C.	EXE	res	Milwaukee, WI
1916 Carr, W. S.	EXE	res	Grand Beach, MI
1916 Converse, Clarence	pjt	res	Palisades Park, MI
1916 Duplex Apt. Munkwitz	dmd	dplx	Milwaukee, WI
1916 Duplex Apt. Richards	EXE	dplx	Milwaukee, WI
1916 Imperial Hotel	EXE	vase	Tokyo
1916 Imperial Hotel Annex	dmd	htl	Tokyo
1916 Imperial Hotel Pwr Hs	pjt	htl	Tokyo
1916 Richards Co. smr hse	EXE	hsng	Milwaukee, WI
1916 Vosburgh, Ernest	EXE	res	Grand Beach, MI
1916 White, William Allen	pjt	res	Emporia, KS
1917 American Homes Bung'w	EXE	hsng	Milwaukee, WI
1917 American Homes Bung'w	EXE	hsng	Wilmette, IL
1917 American Homes Bung'w	EXE	hsng	Lake Bluff, IL
1917 American Homes Dupl.	EXE	hsng	Milwaukee, WI
1917 American Homes Smr	EXE	hsng	Milwaukee, WI
1917 American Homes 2 Sty	EXE	hsng	Chicago, IL
1917 Barnsdall Hollyhock	EXE	res	Los Angeles, CA
1917 Fukuhara	dmd	res	Hakone
1917 Hayashi, Aizaku	EXE	res	Tokyo
1917 Hunt, Stephen M. B.	EXE	res	Oshkosh, WI
1917 Odawara Hotel	pjt	htl	Nagoya
1917 Powell, William	pjt	res	Wichita, KS
1918 Imai (Immu), Count	pjt	res	Tokyo
1918 Inouye, Viscount	pjt	res	Tokyo
1918 Mihara	pjt	res	Tokyo
1918 Motion Pic. Theatre	pjt	cnma	Tokyo
1918 Yamamura	EXE	res	Ashiya
1919 Monolith Hms, Hardy	pjt	hsng	Racine, WI
1919 Shampay, G. P.	pjt	res	Chicago, IL
1919 Spaulding Gallery	pjt	glry	Boston, MA
1919 Wenatchee Twn Pln	pjt	twnpl	Wenatchee, WA
1920 Auto w/cant'd top	pjt	auto	
1920 Barnsdall res. A	EXE	res	Los Angeles, CA
1920 Barnsdall res. B	dmd	res	Los Angeles, CA
1920 Barnsdall Motion Pic.	pjt	cnma	Los Angeles, CA
1920 Olive Hill Alphabet	EXE	grph	Los Angeles, CA
1920 Porter, Andrew, rem	pjt	res	Chicago, IL
1920 Staley, C. R.	pjt	res	Waukegan, IL
1920 Taliesin Hydro Hse	dmd	plnt	Spring Green, WI
1921 Barnsdall Little Dpr	dmd	kdgn	Los Angeles, CA
1921 Block Hse for LA Rav.	pjt	res	Los Angeles, CA
1921 Block House	pjt	res	Los Angeles, CA
1921 Block House 2 Story	pjt	res	Los Angeles, CA
1921 Department Store	pjt	dept	Tokyo
1921 Goto, Baron	pjt	res	Tokyo
1921 Imperial Hotel Orn.	dmd	sclp	Tokyo
1921 Jiyu Gakuen School	EXE	schl	Tokyo
1921 Johnson Comp. Shrine	pjt	res	Mohave, CA
1921 Study for Cal. Blck Hs	pjt	res	Los Angeles, CA
1921 FLLW Desert Cmpnd	pjt	stdo	Mohave, CA
1922 Barnsdall Bev. Hills	pjt	res	Beverly Hills, CA
1922 Butterfly Roof Hse	pjt	res	
1922 Lowes, G. P.	pjt	res	Eagle Rock, CA
1922 Merchandising Bldg	pjt	dept	Los Angeles, CA
1922 Sachse, Arthur	pjt	res	Mohave, CA
1922 Tahoe Summer Colony	pjt	rsrt	Lake Tahoe, CA
1922 FLLW Harper Av. Grph	EXE	stdo	Los Angeles, CA
1922 FLLW Harper Av. Stud.	EXE	stdo	Los Angeles, CA
1923 Commrcl Bldg, Conc.	pjt	offc	Los Angeles, CA
1923 Doheny Ranch Rsort	pjt	pln	Los Angeles, CA
1923 Ennis, Charles	EXE	res	Los Angeles, CA
1923 Foster, Dorothy M.	pjt	res	Buffalo, NY
1923 Freeman, Samuel	EXE	res	Los Angeles, CA
1923 Millard La Miniatura	EXE	res	Pasadena, CA
1923 Moore, Nathan Rebld.	EXE	res	Oak Park, IL
1923 Storer, John	EXE	res	Los Angeles, CA
1924 Gladney, Mrs. S. W., #1	pjt	res	Fort Worth, TX
1924 Gladney, Mrs. S. W., #2	pjt	res	Fort Worth, TX
1924 Nakoma Country Cl.	pjt	ctycb	Madison, WI
1924 Nakoma Sculpt Basin	pjt	sclp	Madison, WI
1924 Nakoma Sculptures	EXE	sclp	
1924 National Life Ins.	pjt	offc	Chicago, IL
1924 Phi Gamma Delta Frat.	pjt	frat	Madison, WI
1924 Skyscraper	pjt	offc	
1924 Strong, Gordon, obj.	pjt	pltrm	Sugar Lf Mt, MD
1925 Gladney, Mrs. S. W., #2	pjt	res	Fort Worth, TX
1925 Herron, Mary, rem	pjt	res	Oak Park, IL
1925 Republic Dis. Window	pjt	signs	Chicago, IL
1925 FLLW Taliesin III	EXE	res	Spring Green, WI
1926 Commrcl Arts Fest.	pjt	fair	New York, NY
1926 Kindersymphonies	pjt	kdgn	Oak Park, IL
1926 Liberty Mag. Cvers	pjt	grph	
1926 Skyscraper Reg.	pjt	offc	
1926 Steel Cathedral	pjt	relig	New York, NY
1927 Arizona Biltmore Htl	EXE	htl	Phoenix, AZ
1927 Jewelry Shop Window	EXE	grph	
1927 Martin, D. D., Greycliff	EXE	res	Darby, NY
1927 Ras El Bar	dmd	rsrt	Damietta
1928 Blue Sky Burial Terr.	pjt	fnrl	Buffalo, NY
1928 Chandler Block Hse	pjt	res	Chandler, AZ
1928 Colonial Equivalent	pjt	res	
1928 Cudney, Ralph & Well.	pjt	res	Chandler, AZ
1928 HHS for Allied Arts	pjt	schl	Spring Green, WI
1928 Rosenwald School	pjt	schl	
1928 San Marcos-in-Desert	pjt	htl	Chandler, AZ
1928 Sun, Moon and Stars	pjt	exhibn	Buffalo, NY
1928 Wedding Annment	EXE	grph	La Jolla, CA
1928 FLLW Ocotilla Camp	dmd	stdo	Chandler, AZ
1928 Young, Owen D.	pjt	res	Chandler, AZ
1929 Chandler Cmp Cabns	dmd	hsng	Chandler, AZ
1929 Jones, Rich. Lloyd, #1	pjt	res	Tulsa, OK
1929 Jones, Rich. Lloyd, #2	EXE	res	Tulsa, OK
1929 Leerdam Glassware	pjt	vase	Holland
1929 Millard, Alice, house	pjt	res	Pasadena, CA
1929 Noble, Elizabeth, Apts.	pjt	apt	Los Angeles, CA
1929 St. Mark's Tower	pjt	apt	New York, NY
1929 San Marcos Glf Clbhse	pjt	clbhs	Chandler, AZ
1929 San Marcos Polo Stble	pjt	clbhs	Chandler, AZ
1929 San Marcos Wtr Gard.	pjt	mtel	Chandler, AZ
1930 Cabins for YMCA	pjt	rsrt	Chicago, IL
1930 Corner Sta. Prototy.	pjt	srvst	
1930 Exhibition USA	EXE	exhibn	USA
1930 Grouped Tower	pjt	apttr	Chicago, IL
1930 Millard, Alice, gallery	pjt	glry	Pasadena, CA
1931 Capitol Journal Off.	pjt	bldg	Salem, OR
1931 Century of Prgrss	pjt	fair	Chicago, IL
1931 Longmans, Green (pub)	EXE	grph	New York, NY
1931 House on the Mesa	pjt	res	Denver, CO
1931 Monolithic Filling Sta.	pjt	srvst	
1931 New Theatre (3 schms)	pjt	thtr	
1932 Chase, Dr., sm. fctry	pjt	fcty	Madison, WI
1932 Cinema & Shops	pjt	cnma	Michigan City, IN
1932 Conventional House	pjt	res	

176

1932 Norm of Prefab Hse	pjt	res	
1932 Pre Fab Farm Units	pjt	farm	sheet metal
1932 Pre Fab Roadside Mkt	pjt	mrkt	sheet metal
1932 Stand. Overhd Ser. Sta	pjt	srvst	
1932 Taliesin Brochure	EXE	grph	Spring Green, WI
1932 Taliesin Fell. Complex	EXE	schl	Spring Green, WI
1932 Willey, Malcolm, #1	pjt	res	Minneapolis, MN
1933 Chicagoan Mag. Grph	pjt	grph	Chicago, IL
1933 Hillside Furnishings	EXE	furn	Spring Green, WI
1933 Hillside Playhouse #1	dmd	thtr	Spring Green, WI
1933 Hillside Th. Curtn #1	dmd	texti	Spring Green, WI
1933 Willey, Malcolm, #2	EXE	res	Minneapolis, MN
1934 Broadacre City Modl	EXE	pln	Spring Green, WI
1934 Broadacre City Plan	pjt	city	
1934 BC, Arena	pjt	arena	
1934 BC, Ball Park	pjt	fair	
1934 BC, Broadacre Hses	pjt	hsng	
1934 BC, Cathedral & Cem.	pjt	relig	
1934 BC, Community Cntr	pjt	cvctr	
1934 BC, County Office Bldg	pjt	offc	
1934 BC, Education Center	pjt	educ	
1934 BC, Highway Lighting	pjt	roadway	
1934 BC, Highway Overpass	pjt	brdg	
1934 BC, Hospital Group	pjt	hspl	
1934 BC, Industrial Park	pjt	fcty	
1934 BC, Little Factory	pjt	fcty	
1934 BC, Stable & Polo Fld	pjt	clbhs	
1934 Hillside L. R. Rug	pjt	crpt	Spring Green, WI
1934 Hillside Murals	dmd	mural	Spring Green, WI
1934 Machine Age Screen	EXE	mural	Phoenix, AZ
1934 Memorial to the Soil	pjt	chpl	Cooksville, WI
1934 Millard, A., hse/cple	pjt	res	Pasadena, CA
1934 Taliesin Farmlands	EXE	res	Spring Green, WI
1935 German Warehse rem	pjt	wrhs	Richland Center, WI
1935 Kaufmann Fallngwtr	EXE	res	Mill Run, PA
1935 Marcus, Stanley	pjt	res	Dallas, TX
1935 Marcus Housing	pjt	hsng	Dallas, TX
1935 Zoned Houses	pjt	hsng	
1936 Hanna, Paul & Jean	EXE	res	Stanford, CA
1936 Hillside Gatehouse	pjt	schl	Spring Green, WI
1936 Hillside Road Sign	pjt	schl	Spring Green, WI
1936 Hoult, C. R.	pjt	res	Wichita, KS
1936 Jacobs, Herbert, #1	EXE	res	Madison, WI
1936 Johnson Admin. Bldg	EXE	bldg	Racine, WI
1936 Little San Marcos	pjt	rsrt	Chandler, AZ
1936 Lusk, Robert	pjt	res	Huron, SD
1936 Roberts, Abby B.	EXE	res	Marquette, MI
1936 San Marcos Hotel rem	pjt	htl	Chandler, AZ
1937 Borglum, Gutzon	pjt	stdo	Santa Barbara, CA
1937 Bramson, L., dress shp	pjt	shop	Oak Park, IL
1937 Johnson, Wingspread	EXE	res	Wind Point, WI
1937 Kaufmann Office	dmd	offc	Pittsburgh, PA
1937 Parker, G.	pjt	garage	Janesville, WI
1937 Rebhuhn, Ben	EXE	res	Great Neck Est., NY
1937 Steelcase-Johnson Wax	EXE	furn	Racine, WI
1937 Wright, Frances, gift	pjt	shop	
1937 FLLW sleeping boxes	dmd	res	Scottsdale, AZ
1937 FLLW sun trap	dmd	res	Scottsdale, AZ
1937 FLLW Taliesin West	EXE	schl	Scottsdale, AZ
1938 All Steel Houses	pjt	hsng	Los Angeles, CA
1938 Bell, L. N.	pjt	res	Los Angeles, CA
1938 Bell, L. N. (Feldman)	EXE	res	Berkeley, CA
1938 FSC Block Details	EXE	educ	Lakeland, FL
1938 FSC Master Plan	EXE	educ	Lakeland, FL
1938 FSC Pfeiffer Chapel	EXE	relig	Lakeland, FL
1938 FSC Theatre	pjt	thtr	Lakeland, FL
1938 Jester, Ralph	pjt	res	Palos Verdes, CA
1938 Johnson, H., farm unit	pjt	farm	Wind Point, WI
1938 Johnson, H., gatehse	pjt	gatehse	Wind Point, WI
1938 Jurgenson, Royal	pjt	res	Evanston, IL
1938 Kaufmann Guest Hse	EXE	res	Mill Run, PA
1938 Life House for $5000	pjt	res	Minneapolis, MN
1938 Manson, Charles	EXE	res	Wausau, WI
1938 McCallum, George B.	pjt	res	Northampton, MA
1938 Midway Barns & Farm	EXE	farm	Spring Green, WI
1938 Monona Terr C. C. #1	pjt	cvctr	Madison, WI
1938 Pew, John C.	EXE	res	Shorewood Hills, WI
1938 Standrd Usonian Det.	EXE	res	
1938 Sun Top Homes	EXE	quhse	Ardmore, PA
1939 Armstrong, Andrew	EXE	res	Ogden Dunes, IN
1939 Bazett "Fir Tree Type"	pjt	res	Hillsborough, CA
1939 Bazett, Sydney	EXE	res	Hillsborough, CA
1939 Brauner, Erling, #1	pjt	res	Lansing, MI
1939 Carlson, Edith	pjt	res	Superior, WI
1939 Crystal Heights	pjt	htl	Washington, DC
1939 Dinky Diner	EXE	atmtv	Taliesin Fellow
1939 Euchtman, Joseph	EXE	res	Baltimore, MD
1939 FSC Dorm/Faclty Hse	pjt	educ	Lakeland, FL
1939 Garrison, J. J.	pjt	res	Lansing, MI
1939 Goetsch-Winckler #1	EXE	res	Okemos, MI
1939 Hause, C. D.	pjt	res	Lansing, MI
1939 Kaufmann Uson. Hse	pjt	res	Pittsburgh, PA
1939 Lewis, Lloyd	EXE	res	Libertyville, IL
1939 Lowenstein, Gordon	pjt	res	Cincinnati, OH
1939 Mauer, Edgar	pjt	res	Los Angeles, CA
1939 Newman, Sydney	pjt	res	Lansing, MI
1939 Panshin, Alexis	3pjt	res	Lansing, MI
1939 Pauson, Rose	dmd	res	Phoenix, AZ
1939 Pope, Loren	EXE	res	Mount Vernon, VA
1939 Rentz, Frank	pjt	res	Madison, WI
1939 Rosenbaum, Stanley	EXE	res	Florence, AL
1939 Schwartz, Bernard	EXE	res	Two Rivers, WI
1939 Smith, E. A.	pjt	res	Piedmont Pines, CA
1939 Sondern, Clarence	EXE	res	Kansas City, KS
1939 Spivey, Dr. Ludd M.	pjt	res	Fort Lauderdale, FL
1939 Stevens Auldbrass	EXE	plnt	Yemassee, SC
1939 Sturges, George	EXE	res	Los Angeles, CA
1939 Taliesin Frnt Gates 3	pjt	gates	Spring Green, WI
1939 Usonia I Master Plan	pjt	hsng	Lansing, MI
1939 Van Dusen, C. R.	pjt	res	Lansing, MI
1940 Affleck, Gregor, #1	EXE	res	Bloomfield Hills, MI
1940 Baird, Theodore	EXE	res	Amherst, MA
1940 Christie, James, #1	pjt	res	Bernardsville, NJ
1940 Christie, James, #2	EXE	res	Bernardsville, NJ
1940 Community Church	EXE	relig	Kansas City, MO
1940 Exhibition MOMA 1940	EXE	exhibn	New York, NY
1940 FSC Seminar Bldgs	EXE	educ	Lakeland, FL
1940 Kaufmann Farm Unit	pjt	farm	Mill Run, PA
1940 Kaufmann Gate Ldge	pjt	gatehse	Mill Run, PA
1940 Model Hse for MOMA	pjt	res	New York, NY
1940 Nesbitt, John	pjt	res	Carmel, CA
1940 Oboler, A., Eaglefeather	pjt	res	Malibu, CA
1940 Oboler, A., gatehse	EXE	res	Malibu, CA
1940 Pence, Martin, #1	pjt	res	Hilo, HI
1940 Pence, Martin, #2	pjt	res	Hilo, HI
1940 Slumber Bus Terr. Fur	pjt	furn	Scottsdale, AZ
1940 Taliesin mag grph	EXE	grph	Spring Green, WI
1940 Watkins, Franklin	pjt	stdo	Barnegat City, NJ
1941 Barton, John	pjt	res	Pine Bluff, WI
1941 Dayer, Walter, studio	pjt	stdo	Detroit, MI
1941 Ellinwood, Alfred	pjt	res	Deerfield, IL
1941 Field, Parker B.	pjt	res	Peru, IL
1941 FSC Roux Library	EXE	liby	Lakeland, FL
1941 Guenther, William	pjt	res	East Caldwell, NJ

Year	Project	Type	Type	Location
1941	Horlick-Racine Airprt	pjt	bldg	Racine, WI
1941	Nesbitt, Sijistan/E.	pjt	res	Los Angeles, CA
1941	Oboler, A., retreat	EXE	res	Malibu, CA
1941	Peterson, Roy	pjt	res	Racine, WI
1941	Peterson, Roy (H.)	EXE	res	Ann Arbor, MI
1941	Richardson, Stuart	EXE	res	Glen Ridge, NJ
1941	Schevill, Margaret	pjt	res	Tucson, AZ
1941	Scott Radio Cabinets	pjt	furn	
1941	Sigma Chi Fraternity	pjt	frat	Hanover, IN
1941	Sundt, Vigo	pjt	res	Madison, WI
1941	Wall, Carl, Snowflke	EXE	res	Plymouth, MI
1941	Waterstreet, Mary	pjt	res	Spring Green, WI
1942	Burlingham, Lloyd	pjt	res	El Paso, TX
1942	Circle Pines Resort	pjt	rsrt	Cloverdale, MI
1942	Cloverleaf Hsing	pjt	quhse	Pittsfield, MA
1942	Co-op Homesteads	pjt	hsng	Detroit, MI
1942	Foreman, Clark	pjt	res	Washington, DC
1942	FSC Indust. Arts Bldg	EXE	educ	Lakeland, FL
1942	Lincoln Cont. rem	EXE	auto	
1942	Miller, Robert S.	pjt	res	Fremont, OH
1942	Pittsfield Def. Plant	pjt	fcty	Pittsfield, MA
1942	Schwartz, B., bthse	pjt	res	Two Rivers, WI
1942	Sturges, G., adds	pjt	res	Los Angeles, CA
1942	Wall, Carl, Farm Unit	pjt	farm	Plymouth, MI
1942	Wall, Carl, gatehse	pjt	gatehse	Plymouth, MI
1942	Wall, C., mural scrn	pjt	mural	Plymouth, MI
1943	FSC Music Building #1	pjt	educ	Lakeland, FL
1943	Guggenheim Museum	EXE	mus	New York, NY
1943	Hein, M. N.	pjt	res	Chippewa Falls, WI
1943	Jacobs, Herbert (H.)	pjt	res	Middleton, WI
1943	Lewis, Lloyd, Farm Unit	EXE	farm	Libertyville, IL
1943	Richardson Rest. Sta.	pjt	srvst	Spring Green, WI
1944	FSC Whitney Memorial	pjt	educ	Lakeland, FL
1944	Harlan, P. K.	pjt	res	Omaha, NE
1944	Hillside Thtre Foyer	EXE	schl	Spring Green, WI
1944	Jacobs Solar Hemicyc.	EXE	res	Middleton, WI
1944	Johnson Resrch Twr	EXE	offc	Racine, WI
1944	LHJ Glass Hse Op. 497	pjt	res	
1944	Loeb, Gerald M.	pjt	res	Redding, CT
1944	Midway Barns/Cott.	EXE	farm	Spring Green, WI
1945	Adelman Laundry	pjt	lndry	Milwaukee, WI
1945	Arden Spa	pjt	rsrt	Phoenix, AZ
1945	Berdan, George	pjt	res	Ludington, MI
1945	Dana, Malcolm	pjt	res	Olivet, MI
1945	Daphne Funrl Chpls	pjt	fnrl	San Francisco, CA
1945	FSC Admin Bldg	EXE	educ	Lakeland, FL
1945	Friedman, Arnold	EXE	res	Pecos, NM
1945	Grieco, Vito	pjt	res	Andover, MA
1945	Haldorn, Stuart	pjt	res	Carmel, CA
1945	Hillside Gardn Cntr	EXE	schl	Spring Green, WI
1945	McDonald, T. L.	pjt	res	Washington, DC
1945	Morris, V. C., #1	pjt	res	San Francisco, CA
1945	Prout, George	pjt	res	Columbus, IN
1945	Stamm, John David	pjt	res	Lake Delavan, WI
1945	Taliesin Dams	EXE	res	Spring Green, WI
1945	Walter, Lowell	EXE	res	Quasqueton, IA
1945	Wells, Stuart	pjt	res	Minneapolis, MN
1945	Wheeler, Frank	pjt	res	Hinsdale, IL
1946	Adelman, A., #1	pjt	res	Fox Point, WI
1946	Adelman, A., #2	EXE	res	Fox Point, WI
1946	Alpaugh, Amy	EXE	res	Northport, MI
1946	Dayer, Walter, Pav.	pjt	stdo	Bloomfield Hills, MI
1946	Feenbert, Ben	pjt	res	Fox Point, WI
1946	FSC Esplanades	EXE	educ	Lakeland, FL
1946	FSC Music Bldg #2	pjt	educ	Lakeland, FL
1946	FSC Water Dome	EXE	educ	Lakeland, FL
1946	Grant, Douglas	EXE	res	Cedar Rapids, IA
1946	Griggs, Chauncey	EXE	res	Tacoma, WA
1946	Hanna House adds	EXE	res	Stanford, CA
1946	Hillside Gate Lodge	pjt	schl	Spring Green, WI
1946	Hillside Home Bldg rev	EXE	schl	Spring Green, WI
1946	Miller, Dr. Alvin	EXE	res	Charles City, IA
1946	Miller, Drs. A & C, clnc	pjt	medi	Charles City, IA
1946	Mossberg, Herman T.	EXE	res	South Bend, IN
1946	Munroe, Joe	pjt	res	Knox County, OH
1946	Oboler, A., studio	pjt	stdo	Los Angeles, CA
1946	Pinkerton, W. M.	pjt	res	Fairfax Cty, VA
1946	Rand, Ayn	pjt	res	Hollywood, CA
1946	Recent Furniture	EXE	furn	
1946	Rogers Lacy Hotel	pjt	htl	Dallas, TX
1946	Rosenbaum, Stan., add	EXE	res	Florence, AL
1946	San Antonio Transit	pjt	trns	San Antonio, TX
1946	Sarabhai Calico Mlls	pjt	dept	Ahmedabad
1946	Slater, William	pjt	res	Warwick, RI
1946	Smith, Melvin M.	EXE	res	Bloomfield Hills, MI
1947	Alsop, Carroll	EXE	res	Oskaloosa, IA
1947	Bell, Dr. Charles	pjt	res	East St. Louis, IL
1947	Black, Dr. B. Marden	pjt	res	Rochester, MN
1947	Bulbulian, Dr. A. H.	EXE	res	Rochester, MN
1947	Butterfly Bridge	pjt	brdg	Spring Green, WI
1947	Dairy & Machine Shed	EXE	farm	Spring Green, WI
1947	FSC Swimming Pool	pjt	educ	Lakeland, FL
1947	Galesburg Ctry Hms	EXE	hsng	Galesburg, MI
1947	Guggenheim Annex	pjt	mus	New York, NY
1947	Hamilton, Berta	pjt	res	Brookline, VT
1947	HH Cottage Group #1	pjt	rsrt	Hollywood, CA
1947	HH Residence	pjt	res	Hollywood, CA
1947	HH Sports Clbhse	pjt	clbhs	Hollywood, CA
1947	HH Stables	pjt	stbls	Hollywood, CA
1947	Kaufmann adds	EXE	res	Mill Run, PA
1947	Keith, Ruth, #1	pjt	res	Oakland County, PA
1947	Keith, Ruth, #2	pjt	res	Oakland County, PA
1947	Keys, Thomas, #1	pjt	res	Rochester, MN
1947	Marting, E. L.	pjt	res	North Hampton, OH
1947	Muelhberger, C. W.	pjt	res	East Lansing, MI
1947	Palmer, Dr. Paul V.	pjt	res	Phoenix, AZ
1947	Parkwyn Vill. Cm. Ctr	pjt	cmctr	Kalamazoo, MI
1947	Parkwyn Vill. homes	EXE	hsng	Kalamazoo, MI
1947	Pike, John J.	pjt	res	Los Angeles, CA
1947	PPP #1 Civic Center	pjt	cvctr	Pittsburgh, PA
1947	Unitarian Church	EXE	relig	Shorewood Hills, WI
1947	Usonia II New York	EXE	hsng	Pleasantville, NY
1947	VNB Daylight Bank	pjt	bnk	Tucson, AZ
1947	Wetmore	pjt	srvst	Detroit, MI
1947	Wilkie, Donald	pjt	res	Hennepin Cty, MN
1948	Adelman, B.	pjt	res	Fox Point, WI
1948	Adler, Arnold (S.)	EXE	res	Kansas City, MO
1948	Barney, Maginel	pjt	res	Spring Green, WI
1948	Bergman, Dr. Alfred	pjt	res	St. Petersburg, FL
1948	Bimson, Mrs. Walter	pjt	pthse	Phoenix, AZ
1948	Boomer-Pauson	pjt	res	Phoenix, AZ
1948	Brauner, Erling, #2	EXE	res	Okemos, MI
1948	Buehler, Maynard	EXE	res	Orinda, CA
1948	Daphne, Nicholas	pjt	res	San Francisco, CA
1948	Ellison, Harry	pjt	res	Bridgewater Twp, NJ
1948	Eppstein, Samuel	EXE	res	Galesburg, MI
1948	Friedman, S. (Usonia II)	EXE	res	Pleasantville, NY
1948	Greiner, Ward	pjt	res	Kalamazoo, MI
1948	Hageman, Arthur	pjt	res	Peoria, IL
1948	Hawkins Apartments	pjt	apts	Auburn, CA
1948	Hawkins Studio-Res.	pjt	stdo	Auburn, CA
1948	HH Cottage Group #2	pjt	rsrt	Hollywood, CA
1948	Lamberson, Jack	EXE	res	Oskaloosa, IA
1948	Levin, Robert	EXE	res	Kalamazoo, MI

1948 Lewis, Lloyd, guest	pjt	res	Libertyville, IL
1948 Margolis, Dr. Fred.	pjt	res	Kalamazoo, MI
1948 McCord, Glen	pjt	res	North Arlington, NJ
1948 Meteor Crater Inn	pjt	rsrt	Meteor Crater, AZ
1948 Meyer, Curtis	EXE	res	Galesburg, MI
1948 Morris Gift Shop	EXE	shop	San Francisco, CA
1948 PPP #2 Twin Bridges	pjt	brdg	Pittsburgh, PA
1948 Pratt, Eric	EXE	res	Galesburg, MI
1948 Scully, Vincent	pjt	res	Woodbridge, CT
1948 Smith, Talbot	pjt	res	Ann Arbor, MI
1948 VNB Sunnyslope	pjt	bnk	Sunnyslope, AZ
1948 Walter River Pavi.	EXE	boathse	Quasqueton, IA
1948 Weisblatt, David	EXE	res	Galesburg, MI
1948 Weltzheimer, C. R.	EXE	res	Oberlin, OH
1948 FLLW Sun Cottage	EXE	res	Scottsdale, AZ
1949 Achuff-Carroll	pjt	res	Wauwatosa, WI
1949 Anthony, Howard	EXE	res	Benton Harbor, MI
1949 Auerback, I., Usonia II	pjt	res	Pleasantville, NY
1949 Bloomfield, Louis	pjt	res	Tucson, AZ
1949 Bloomfield Theatre	pjt	thtr	Tucson, AZ
1949 Brown, Eric	EXE	res	Kalamazoo, MI
1949 Cabaret Thtre 3803	EXE	thtr	Scottsdale, AZ
1949 Dabney, Charles	pjt	res	Chicago, IL
1949 Drummond, Alan	pjt	res	Santa Fe, NM
1949 Edwards, James	EXE	res	Okemos, MI
1949 FSC Craft/Child Cnt.	pjt	educ	Lakeland, FL
1949 Goetsch-Winckler #2	pjt	res	Okemos, MI
1949 Griswold, Sen. Geo.	pjt	res	Greenwich, CT
1949 Hillside Hme Bldg rev	EXE	schl	Spring Green, WI
1949 Hughes, J. Willis	EXE	res	Jackson, MS
1949 Jacobsen, George, #1	pjt	res	Montreal, CN
1949 Kiva, Lloyd, Shops	pjt	res	Oconomowoc, WI
1949 Laurent, Kenneth	EXE	res	Rockford, IL
1949 Lea, Thomas	pjt	res	Asheville, NC
1949 McCartney, Ward	EXE	res	Kalamazoo, MI
1949 Miller, Syd., Usonia II	pjt	res	Pleasantville, NY
1949 Neils, Henry J.	EXE	res	Minneapolis, MN
1949 New Theatre	pjt	thtr	Hartford, CT
1949 San Francisco Bridge	pjt	brdg	San Francisco, CA
1949 Self Service Garage	pjt	garage	Pittsburgh, PA
1949 Serlin, Ed, Usonia II	EXE	res	Pleasantville, NY
1949 Usonian Automatic	EXE	res	developed later
1949 Walker, Mrs. Clinton	EXE	res	Carmel, CA
1949 Windfohr, Robert	pjt	res	Fort Worth, TX
1949 YWCA #1	pjt	clbhs	Racine, WI
1949 YWCA #2	pjt	clbhs	Racine, WI
1950 Berger, Robert	EXE	res	San Anselmo, CA
1950 Bush, Robert	pjt	res	Palo Alto, CA
1950 Carlson, Raymond	EXE	res	Phoenix, AZ
1950 Carr, John O.	EXE	res	Glenview, IL
1950 Chahroudi, A. K.	pjt	res	Lake Mahopac, NY
1950 Conklin, Tom	pjt	res	New Ulm, MN
1950 Davis, Dr. Richard	EXE	res	Marion, IN
1950 Elam, S. P.	EXE	res	Austin, MN
1950 Exhibition 60 Yrs Liv.	EXE	exhibn	Switz, Germany
1950 Gillin, John A.	EXE	res	Dallas, TX
1950 Grover, Donald	pjt	res	Syracuse, NY
1950 Hall, Louis B.	pjt	res	Ann Arbor, MI
1950 Hanson, Richard	pjt	res	Corvallis, OR
1950 Hargrove, Dr. Kenneth	pjt	res	Berkeley, CA
1950 Harper, Dr. Ina	EXE	res	St. Joseph, MI
1950 Haynes, John	EXE	res	Fort Wayne, IN
1950 Houston, Walter	pjt	res	Schuyler Cty, IL
1950 How to Live in the SW	EXE	res	Phoenix, AZ
1950 Jackson, Dr. Arnold	pjt	res	Madison, WI
1950 Jacobsen, Geo., #2	pjt	res	Montreal, CN
1950 Keys, Thomas, #2	EXE	res	Rochester, MN
1950 Mathews, Arthur	EXE	res	Atherton, CA
1950 Montooth, George	pjt	res	Rushville, IL
1950 Muirhead, Robert	EXE	res	Plato Center, IL
1950 O'Donnell, Dale	pjt	res	Lansing, MI
1950 Palmer, William	EXE	res	Ann Arbor, MI
1950 Pearce, Wilbur	EXE	res	Bradbury, CA
1950 Sabin, Brainerd	pjt	res	Battle Creek, MI
1950 Schaberg, Don	EXE	res	Okemos, MI
1950 Shavin, Seymour	EXE	res	Chattanooga, TN
1950 Sixty Yrs. Living Arch.	dmd	expo	Florence
1950 Small, Dr. L., clinic	pjt	res	West Orange, NJ
1950 Smith, Richard	EXE	res	Jefferson, WI
1950 Southwest Ch. Sem.	pjt	relig	Phoenix, AZ
1950 SW Ch. Sem. (1st Ch.)	EXE	relig	Phoenix, AZ
1950 Staley, Karl A.	EXE	res	N. Madison, OH
1950 Stevens, Arthur	pjt	res	Park Ridge, IL
1950 Strong, Laurence	pjt	res	Kalamazoo, MI
1950 Swan, Lawrence	pjt	res	Detroit, MI
1950 Sweeton, J. A.	EXE	res	Cherry Hill, NJ
1950 Wassell, William	pjt	res	Philadelphia, PA
1950 Winn, Robert	EXE	res	Kalamazoo, MI
1950 Wright, David	EXE	res	Phoenix, AZ
1950 Zimmerman, Isadore	EXE	res	Manchester, NH
1951 Adelman, B., Uson. Aut.	EXE	res	Phoenix, AZ
1951 Austin, Gabrielle	EXE	res	Greenville, SC
1951 Chahroudi Cottage	EXE	res	Lake Mahopac, NY
1951 Clark, George	pjt	res	Carmel, CA
1951 Fuller, W. L.	dmd	res	Pass Christian, MS
1951 Gifford Con. Blck Plt	pjt	fcty	Middleton, WI
1951 Glore, Charles F.	EXE	res	Lake Forest, IL
1951 House for GI Couple	pjt	hsng	
1951 Johnson Wax adds	EXE	bldg	Racine, WI
1951 Kaufmann Bldr Hse	pjt	res	Palm Springs, CA
1951 Kinney, Patrick	EXE	res	Lancaster, WI
1951 Kraus, Russell	EXE	res	Kirkwood, MO
1951 Publicker, Robert	pjt	res	Haverford, PA
1951 Reisley, R., Usonia II	EXE	res	Pleasantville, NY
1951 Rubin, Nathan	EXE	res	Canton, OH
1951 Stracke, Victor, #1	pjt	res	Appleton, WI
1951 Vallarino, J. J., #2	pjt	res	Panama City
1951 Vallarino, J. J., #3	pjt	res	Panama City
1951 Wetmore Shwrm rem	pjt	srvst	Detroit, MI
1951 Wright, D., rug design	EXE	crpt	Phoenix, AZ
1952 Affleck, George, #2	pjt	res	Bloomfield Hills, MI
1952 Anderton Ct. Shops	EXE	shop	Beverly Hills, CA
1952 Bailleres, Raul	pjt	res	Acapulco
1952 Blair, Quentin	EXE	res	Cody, WY
1952 Brandes, Ray	EXE	res	Issaquah, WA
1952 Clifton, William	pjt	res	Oakland, NJ
1952 Floating Grdns Rsrt	pjt	rsrt	Leesburg, FL
1952 Friedman, A., gatehse	EXE	res	Pecos, NM
1952 Goodard, Lewis, #1	pjt	res	Plymouth, MI
1952 Hillside Kitchen	EXE	schl	Spring Green, WI
1952 Hillside Playhse #2	EXE	schl	Spring Green, WI
1952 Hillside Th. Curtn #2	EXE	texti	Spring Green, WI
1952 Lee, Edgar	pjt	res	Midland, MI
1952 Lewis, George	EXE	res	Tallahassee, FL
1952 Lindholm, R. W.	EXE	res	Cloquet, MN
1952 Paradise on Wheels	pjt	hsng	Phoenix, AZ
1952 Penfield, Louis, #1	EXE	res	Willoughby, OH
1952 Pieper, A., Usoni. Aut.	EXE	res	Paradise Valley, AZ
1952 Point View Res. 1	pjt	apt	Pittsburgh, PA
1952 Price Tower	EXE	offc	Bartlesville, OK
1952 Rebhuhn, Ben	pjt	res	Fort Myers, FL
1952 Rhododendron Chpl	pjt	chpl	Mill Run, PA
1952 Sander, Frank	EXE	res	Stamford, CT
1952 Sturtevant, Horace	pjt	res	Oakland, CA

Year	Name	Type	Cat	Location
1952	Teater, Archie	EXE	res	Bliss, ID
1952	Wainer, Alexis	pjt	res	Valdosta, GA
1952	Zeta Beta Tau Frat.	pjt	frat	Gainesville, FL
1953	Boomer, Jorgine	EXE	res	Phoenix, AZ
1953	Brewer, Joseph	pjt	res	East Fishkill, NY
1953	Cooke, Andrew B., #1	EXE	res	Virginia Beach, VA
1953	Exhibition Hse. Uson.	dmd	res	New York, NY
1953	Exhibition Pav. NY	dmd	exhibn	New York, NY
1953	FM Radio Station	pjt	bldg	Jefferson, WI
1953	FSC Science & Csmg	EXE	educ	Lakeland, FL
1953	Goddard, Lewis, #2	EXE	res	Plymouth, MI
1953	Green, Aaron, off.	dmd	offc	San Francisco, CA
1953	Hillside Godown (VLT)	pjt	schl	Spring Green, WI
1953	Marden, Luis	EXE	res	McLean, VA
1953	Masieri Memorial	pjt	frat	Venice
1953	Morehead, Elizabeth	pjt	res	Marin Cty, CA
1953	Pieper-Montooth Off.	pjt	bldg	Scottsdale, AZ
1953	Point View Res. 2	pjt	apt	Pittsburgh, PA
1953	Price, Harold (B.)	EXE	res	Bartlesville, OK
1953	Riverview Terr. Rest.	EXE	rest	Spring Green, WI
1953	Taliesin Viaduct	pjt	rdway	Spring Green, WI
1953	Taliesin West Sign	EXE	sign	Scottsdale, AZ
1953	Thaxton, William	EXE	res	Bunker Hill, TX
1953	Wright, R. L., #1	pjt	res	Bethesda, MD
1954	Adelman, Benjamin	pjt	res	Whitefish Bay, WI
1954	Arnold, E. Clarke	EXE	res	Columbus, WI
1954	Bachman-Wilson	EXE	res	Millstone, NY
1954	Beth Sholom Syn.	EXE	relig	Elkins Park, PA
1954	Boulter, Cedric	EXE	res	Cincinnati, OH
1954	Christian, John E.	EXE	res	West Lafayette, IN
1954	Christian Sc. Rd. Rm #1	pjt	relig	Riverside, IL
1954	Christian Sc. Rd. Rm #2	pjt	relig	Riverside, IL
1954	Cornwell, Gibbons #1	pjt	res	West Goshen, PA
1954	Exhibition Pav.	dmd	exhibn	Los Angeles, CA
1954	Feiman, Ellis	EXE	res	Canton, OH
1954	FSC Danforth Chpl	EXE	chpl	Lakeland, FL
1954	Frederick, Louis B.	EXE	res	Barrington Hill, IL
1954	Greenberg, Dr. M.	EXE	res	Dousman, WI
1954	Hagan, I. N.	EXE	res	Chalkhill, PA
1954	Hagan Ice Cream Co.	pjt	bldg	Uniontown, PA
1954	Hoffman, G. M.	pjt	res	Winnetka, IL
1954	Hoffman, Max, #1	pjt	res	Rye, NY
1954	Hoffman, Max, #2	pjt	res	Rye, NY
1954	Hoffman, Jag. Shwrm	EXE	bldg	New York, NY
1954	Keland, Willard	EXE	res	Racine, WI
1954	Korricks Dept. Store	pjt	dept	Phoenix, AZ
1954	Monona Terr. C. C. #2	pjt	cvctr	Madison, WI
1954	Oboler "Contin"	pjt	res	Malibu, CA
1954	Price, Harold	EXE	res	Paradise Valley, AZ
1954	Price, Harold, Jr.	EXE	crpt	Bartlesville, OK
1954	Schwenn, Roger	pjt	res	Verona, WI
1954	Smith, J. L.	pjt	res	Kane County, IL
1954	Terne Metal Grphs	pjt	grph	
1954	Tipshus Med. Clinic	pjt	medi	Stockton, CA
1954	Tonkens, Gerald	EXE	res	Amberley Villge, OH
1954	Tracy, W. B.	EXE	res	Normandy Park, WA
1954	Wright, David, guest	EXE	res	Phoenix, AZ
1954	FLLW Plaza Apt.	dmd	stdo	New York, NY
1954	Yosemite Ntl Pk Rest	pjt	rest	Yosemite, CA
1955	Air Force Academy	pjt	educ	Boulder, CO
1955	Barton, A. D.	pjt	res	Downer's Grove, IL
1955	Blumberg, Mel	pjt	res	Des Moines, IA
1955	Boswell, William #1	pjt	res	Cincinnati, OH
1955	Coats, Robert	pjt	res	Hillsborough, CA
1955	Cornwell, Gibbons #2	pjt	res	West Goshen, PA
1955	Dallas Theater Ctr.	EXE	thtr	Dallas, TX
1955	Dlesk, George, #1	pjt	res	Manistee, MI
1955	Fawcett, Randall	EXE	res	Los Banos, CA
1955	Freund y Cia.	pjt	dept	San Salvador
1955	Hartman, Stanley	pjt	res	Lansing, MI
1955	Herberger, Robt, #1	pjt	res	Maricopa Cty, AZ
1955	Herberger, Robt, #2	pjt	res	Maricopa Cty, AZ
1955	Heritage-Henredon	EXE	furn	"Four Square"
1955	Heritage-Henredon	pjt	furn	"Honeycomb"
1955	Heritage-Henredon	pjt	furn	"Burberry"
1955	Hoffman, Max, #3	EXE	res	Rye, NY
1955	Jankowski, L., #1	pjt	res	Oakland City, MI
1955	Jankowski, L., #2	pjt	res	Oakland City, MI
1955	Kalil, Dr. Toufic	EXE	res	Manchester, NH
1955	Kinney, Sterling, #1	pjt	res	Amarillo, TX
1955	Kundert Med. Clinic	EXE	medi	San Luis Obispo, CA
1955	Kundert-Fogo Clnc 1	pjt	medi	San Luis Obispo, CA
1955	Lenkurt Electric #1	pjt	fcty	San Carlos, CA
1955	Lovness, Don	EXE	res	Stillwater, MN
1955	Miller, Oscar	pjt	res	Milford, MN
1955	Morris, V. C., #2	pjt	res	San Francisco, CA
1955	Morris, V. C., guest	pjt	res	San Francisco, CA
1955	Neuroseum Hospital	pjt	hspl	Madison, WI
1955	Pappas, T. A.	EXE	res	St. Louis, MO
1955	Pieper, C. R.	pjt	res	Paradise Valley, AZ
1955	Rayward, John	EXE	res	New Canaan, CT
1955	Road Machine	pjt	auto	
1955	Roberts, Jay	pjt	res	Seattle, WA
1955	Schumacher Fabrics	EXE	texti	New York, NY
1955	Scott, Warren alts	EXE	res	River Forest, IL
1955	Sunday, Robert, #1	pjt	res	Marshalltown, IA
1955	Sunday, Robert, #2	EXE	res	Marshalltown, IA
1955	Sussman, Gerald	pjt	res	Rye, NY
1955	Trowbridge, Dr. C.	pjt	res	Oak Park, IL
1955	Turkel, Dr. Dorothy	EXE	res	Detroit, MI
1955	Vallarino, J. J., #2	pjt	res	Panama City
1955	Wright, R. L., #2	EXE	res	Bethesda, MD
1956	Adams, Lee	pjt	res	St. Paul, MN
1956	Annunciation Greek	EXE	relig	Wauwatosa, WI
1956	Boebel, Robert	pjt	res	Boscobel, WI
1956	Boswell, William, #2	EXE	res	Cincinnati, OH
1956	Bott, Frank	EXE	res	Kansas City, MO
1956	Bramlett Mtr Hotel	pjt	mtel	Memphis, TN
1956	Christian Sc. Ch. #1	pjt	relig	Bolinas, CA
1956	Christian Sc. Ch. #2	pjt	relig	Bolinas, CA
1956	City by the Sea	dmd	mural	Scottsdale, AZ
1956	Cooke, Andrew B., #2	pjt	res	Virginia Beach, VA
1956	Erdman Prefab #1	EXE	hsng	Madison, WI
1956	Fiberthin Village	pjt	hsng	Mishawaka, IN
1956	Friedman, Allen	EXE	res	Bannockburn, IL
1956	Gillin, John (Alladin)	pjt	res	Hollywood, CA
1956	Golden Beach Twr	pjt	apt	Chicago, IL
1956	Gordon, C. E.	EXE	res	Aurora, OR
1956	Gross, Nelson	pjt	res	Hackensack, NJ
1956	Hanna, Paul & Jean	EXE	res	Stanford, CA
1956	Hennessy, Jack, #1	pjt	res	Smoke Rise, NJ
1956	Hotel Sherman Ex.	dmd	exhibn	Chicago, IL
1956	House Beautiful, The	pjt	grph	
1956	Hunt, David	pjt	res	Scottsdale, AZ
1956	Kaufmann Uson. Aut	pjt	res	Mill Run, PA
1956	Lenkurt Electric #2	pjt	fcty	San Carlos, CA
1956	Levin, Arthur	pjt	res	Palo Alto, CA
1956	Lindholm Service Sta	EXE	srvst	Cloquet, MN
1956	Meyers, Dr. Ken. Clin	EXE	medi	Dayton, OH
1956	Mile High Illinois	pjt	offc	Chicago, IL
1956	Mills, Bradford, #1	pjt	res	Princeton, NJ
1956	Moreland, Ralph	pjt	res	Austin, TX
1956	Morris, Lillian	pjt	res	Stinson Beach, CA
1956	Music Pavilion	EXE	schl	Scottsdale, AZ

1956 New Sports Pavilion	pjt	clbhs	Belmont Park, NY
1956 Nooker, C., FLLW	EXE	res	Oak Park, IL
1956 O'Keeffe, Dr. Arthur	pjt	res	Santa Barbara, CA
1956 Post Office	pjt	p.o.	Spring Green, WI
1956 Schuck, Victoria	pjt	res	South Hadley, MA
1956 Sottil, Helen	pjt	res	Cuernavaca
1956 Spencer, Dudley, #1	pjt	res	Brandywine Hd, DE
1956 Spencer, Dudley, #2	EXE	res	Brandywine Hd, DE
1956 Stracke, Victor, #2	pjt	res	Appleton, WI
1956 Taliesin Parkway Sign	pjt	sign	Spring Green, WI
1956 Trier, Dr. Apul	EXE	res	Des Moines, IA
1956 Usonian Auto Details	EXE	auto	
1956 Wieland Motor Hotel	pjt	motel	Hagerstown, MD
1956 Wilson, T. Henry	pjt	res	Morganton, NC
1956 Wright, Duey, #1	pjt	res	Wausau, WI
1956 Wyoming Valley Schl	EXE	schl	Wyoming Valley, WI
1956 Zieger, Dr. Allen	pjt	res	Grosse Pointe, MI
1957 Amery, Nezam	pjt	res	Teheran
1957 Arizona State Capitol	pjt	gvt	Phoenix, AZ
1957 Baghdad Art Museum	pjt	mus	Baghdad
1957 Baghdad Casino	pjt	casino	Baghdad
1957 Baghdad Cres. Opera	pjt	opera	Baghdad
1957 Baghdad Grter Pln	pjt	plan	Baghdad
1957 Baghdad Kiosks	pjt	shop	Baghdad
1957 Baghdad Monument	pjt	mnmt	Baghdad
1957 Baghdad Mus/Sculpt.	pjt	mus	Baghdad
1957 Baghdad Post Tel.	pjt	p.o.	Baghdad
1957 Baghdad University	pjt	educ	Baghdad
1957 Barnsdall Pk Gallery	pjt	mus	Los Angeles, CA
1957 Bimson Housing	pjt	hsng	Phoenix, AZ
1957 Brooks, Robert	pjt	res	Middleton, WI
1957 Dlesk, George, #2	pjt	res	Manistee, MI
1957 Erdman Prefab #1	EXE	hsng	Barrington, IL
1957 Erdman Prefab #1	EXE	hsng	Bayside, WI
1957 Erdman Prefab #1	EXE	hsng	Richmond, NY
1957 Erdman Prefab #1	EXE	hsng	Stevens Pt, WI
1957 Erdman Prefab #2	EXE	hsng	Madison, WI
1957 Erdman Prefab #2	EXE	hsng	Rochester, MN
1957 Fasbender Clinic	EXE	medi	Hastings, MN
1957 FSC Music Bldg. #3	pjt	educ	Lakeland, FL
1957 Hillside Grounds Pln	EXE	schl	Spring Green, WI
1957 Hofmann Rug Design	EXE	crpt	Spring Green, WI
1957 Housing for Negro Fam.	pjt	quhse	Whiteville, NC
1957 Hoyer, Carl	pjt	res	Maricopa Cty, AZ
1957 Kinney, Sterling, #2	EXE	res	Amarillo, TX
1957 Marin Co. Amphi.	pjt	fair	San Raphael, CA
1957 Marin Co. Chld Pk	pjt	fair	San Raphael, CA
1957 Marin Co. Civ. Ctr	EXE	cvctr	San Raphael, CA
1957 Marin Co. Fair Pav.	pjt	fair	San Raphael, CA
1957 Marin Co. Health	pjt	bldg	San Raphael, CA
1957 Marin Co. Post Off.	EXE	p.o.	San Raphael, CA
1957 McKinney, Darryl	pjt	res	Cloquet, MN
1957 Miller, Arthur	pjt	res	Roxbury, CT
1957 Mills, Bradford, #2	pjt	res	Princeton, NJ
1957 Motel for Erdman	pjt	motel	Madison, WI
1957 Motel for Zeckendorf	pjt	motel	New York, NY
1957 Rayward, J., playhse	EXE	res	New Canaan, CT
1957 Schanbackers Stre	pjt	shop	Springfield, IL
1957 Schultz, Carl	EXE	res	St. Joseph, MI
1957 Shelton, Wilson, #1	pjt	res	Long Island, NY
1957 Shelton, Wilson, #2	pjt	res	Long Island, NY
1957 Spring Green Sign	pjt	sign	Spring Green, WI
1957 Stillman, Calvin, #1	pjt	res	Cornwall-on-H., NY
1957 Stillman, Calvin, #2	pjt	res	Cornwall-on-H., NY
1957 Tonkens Loan Off.	pjt	bldg	Cincinnati, OH
1957 Valley of the Sun	pjt	sign	Pasadena, CA
1957 Walton, Dr. Robert	EXE	res	Modesto, CA
1957 Wedding Chapel #1	pjt	chpl	Berkeley, CA
1957 Wedding Chapel #2	pjt	chpl	Berkeley, CA
1957 Wright, Duey, #2	EXE	res	Wausau, WI
1958 Ablin, Dr. George	EXE	res	Bakersfield, CA
1958 Colegrove, Ralph	pjt	res	Hamilton, OH
1958 Crosby-Lambert, L.	pjt	res	Colbert Cty, AL
1958 Franklin, Jesse	pjt	res	Louisville, KY
1958 Gutierrez, Dr. James	pjt	res	Albuquerque, NM
1958 Helicopter	pjt	hel	
1958 Hennessy, Jack, #2	pjt	res	Smoke Rise, NJ
1958 Juvenile Cult. Ctr. A	pjt	educ	Wichita, KS
1958 Juvenile Cult. Ctr. A	EXE	educ	Wichita, KS
1958 Libbey, Wesley	pjt	res	Grand Rapids, MI
1958 Living City	pjt	city	
1958 Lockridge Med. Clnc	EXE	medi	Whitefish, MT
1958 Logomarsino, Frank	pjt	res	San Jose, CA
1958 Lovness, Don, 3 cott.	pjt	res	Stillwater, MN
1958 Olfelt, Paul	EXE	res	St. Louis Park, MN
1958 Petersen, Seth	EXE	res	Lake Delton, WI
1958 Petersen, Seth (L.)	EXE	res	Stillwater, MN
1958 Pilgrim Cong. Church	EXE	relig	Redding, CA
1958 Rayward, John adds	EXE	res	New Canaan, CT
1958 Road Machine	pjt	auto	
1958 Spring Grn Civic Ctr	pjt	cvctr	Spring Green, WI
1958 Spring Grn Med. Clnc	pjt	medi	Spring Green, WI
1958 Stromquist, Don	EXE	res	Bountiful, UT
1958 Todd A-O Scheme A	pjt	cnma	
1958 Todd A-O Scheme B	pjt	cnma	
1958 Train	pjt	train	
1958 Trinity Chapel—Jones	pjt	chpl	Norman, OK
1958 Unity Temple, Taliesin	pjt	chpl	Spring Green, WI
1959 ASU Fine Arts Cntr	pjt	educ	Tempe, AZ
1959 ASU Fine Arts Gall	pjt	mus	Tempe, AZ
1959 ASU Fine Arts Music	pjt	educ	Tempe, AZ
1959 ASU Fine Arts Recital	pjt	thtr	Tempe, AZ
1959 Dobkins, John	EXE	res	Canton, OH
1959 Donahoe, Mrs. H.	pjt	res	Paradise Valley, AZ
1959 Furgatch, Harvey	pjt	res	San Diego, CA
1959 Grady Gammage Aud.	EXE	audi	Tempe, AZ
1959 Hanley, Pat, hangar	pjt	srvst	Benton Harbor, MI
1959 Holy Trinity Greek	pjt	relig	San Francisco, CA
1959 Key Project	pjt	civic	Ellis Island, NY
1959 Leuchauer, Dr. J., clinic	pjt	medi	Fresno, CA
1959 Lykes, Norman	EXE	res	Phoenix, AZ
1959 Mann, Dr. John D.	pjt	res	Putnam Cty, NY
1959 Penfield, Louis, #2	pjt	res	Willoughby, OH
1959 Prefab #3 Erdman	pjt	hsng	Madison, WI
1959 Wieland, Daniel	pjt	res	Hagerstown, MD
1959 Wieland, Gilbert	pjt	res	Hagerstown, MD
1959 OLLW Enclosed Grdn	EXE	grdn	Spring Green, WI
1967 Southwest Ch. Semin.	EXE	relig	Phoenix, AZ
1974 Jester, Ralph (P.)	EXE*	res	Scottsdale, AZ
1997 Monona Terrace	EXE	cvctr	Madison, WI

*by Bruce Pfeiffer

Geometric Archetypes

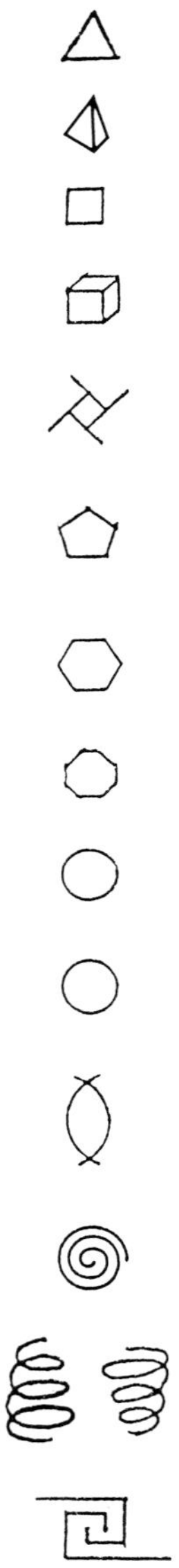

Elements

Symbol	Elements	Description
△	3	Triangle: Trinity. San Marcos in the Desert, etc.
◁		Pyramid: Tripod. Cathedral for a Million People, etc.
□	4	Square: Earth. Integrity. Unity Temple, etc.
⬠		Cube: Larkin Building, Imperial Hotel, etc.
⊠	4	Pinwheel and swastika: based on the ancient form of the sun wheel. Plan of St. Mark's Tower, Johnson residence, etc.
⬠	5	Pentagram: Occult symbol of humankind, in the Middle Ages. Daphne Mortuary five chapels.
⬡	6	Hexagon: Hanna House Plan, Beth Sholom Synagogue, etc.
⯃	8	Octagon: Romeo & Juliet, Wright's studio, early houses, etc.
○		Circle: Completeness. Infinity. Sun. Stonehenge, 2000 B.C., was oriented to the sun. Jacobs Solar Hemicycle, Jester, etc.
○		Sphere: Huntington Hartford Residence, Music Building, etc.
⬮		Vesica of Pisces: Celtic fertility symbol. Wright's "seed form." Pottery House, Guggenheim pool, shallow disk domes of Huntington Hartford Complex, Greek Orthodox Church, etc.
⦿		Spiral: Ancient symbol for growth.
⬚		Ziggurat: Ancient Sumer, Babylon, 3000 B.C. Strong Planetarium, Morris Shop, David Wright House, Guggenheim Museum, etc.
⊐		Labyrinth: Knossos. Wright's logo. It appears as a Navajo petroglyph on the boulder at the entry to Taliesin.

182

Index

Continuous Creation:
The Seven Ages of
Frank Lloyd Wright

". . . what we call genius is the response of a creative mind to a new challenge."
Frank Lloyd Wright

"Only a rare genius has the capacity for true three-dimensional imagination."
C. P. Snow

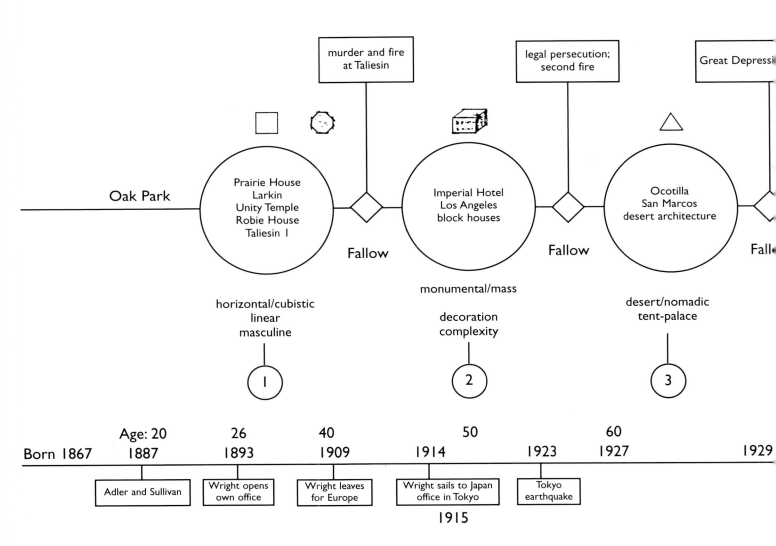

The Metamorphosis of an Architecture

I was surprised by Wright's lack of bitterness after a turbulent lifetime that included more than a normal share of tragedy. Like the phoenix, he seemed to be led to yet another metamorphosis of his work by each disaster. Other architects were content to develop a well-known style, but he preferred to experiment endlessly with new forms and concepts. His roots ran deep into the archetypal sources of architecture. Square, cube, triangle, pyramid, circle, sphere, spiral, ziggurat—the archetypal forms were the elements of his work.

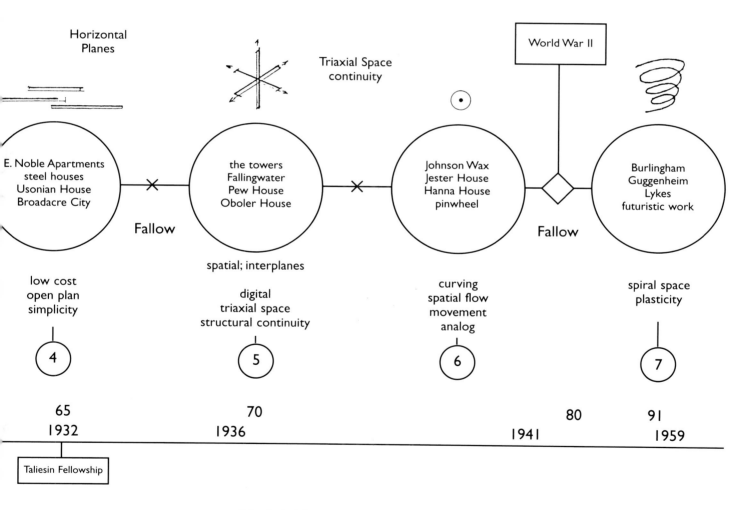

Wright's life demonstrates his enormous capacity for renewal. Forty years after his death, construction of his work continues. The Monona Terrace Civic Center project, Madison, Wisconsin, was completed in 1997.

Sam Dabney

DONALD HOPPEN, born in London, studied engineering and architecture in England and the United States. He received a scholarship from Frank Lloyd Wright to study under him at Taliesin East and West. Hoppen also worked in Wright's San Francisco office on the Marin County Civic Center project.

Hoppen has been a visiting professor of architecture at the Ecole Polytechnique (France's most prestigious university) and has lectured throughout the world on the architecture of Frank Lloyd Wright. His work and writings have appeared in *Architectural Review, Architectural Design* and *International Architect.* He maintains an active architectural practice and divides his time between the United States and France.